SELLOUT

SELLOUT

The Inside Story of
President Clinton's Impeachment

David P. Schippers
with Alan P. Henry

Since 1947
REGNERY
PUBLISHING, INC.
An Eagle Publishing Company • Washington, DC

Library of Congress Cataloging-in-Publication Data

Schippers, David.
     Sellout : the inside story of President Clinton's impeachment / David P. Schippers, with Alan P. Henry.
       p.   cm.
     Includes index.
     ISBN 0-89526-243-6
     1. Clinton, Bill, 1946– —Impeachment. I. Title: Sellout. II. Henry, Alan P. III. Title.

E886.2.S36 2000
973.929'092—dc21

                              00-055324

Published in the United States by
Regnery Publishing, Inc.
An Eagle Publishing Company
One Massachusetts Avenue, NW
Washington, DC 20001

Visit us at <www.regnery.com>.

Distributed to the trade by
National Book Network
4720-A Boston Way
Lanham, MD 20706

Printed on acid-free paper
Manufactured in the United States of America

BOOK DESIGN BY MARJA WALKER

10 9 8 7 6 5 4 3

Books are available in quantity for promotional or premium use. Write to Director of Special Sales, Regnery Publishing, Inc., One Massachusetts Avenue, NW, Washington, DC 20001, for information on discounts and terms or call (202) 216-0600.

To the thirteen House Managers

CONTENTS

Author's Note

This book is a factual account of the impeachment of President Bill Clinton. As Chief Investigative Counsel for the House Judiciary Committee, I was responsible for compiling the case against the President, and the information contained in this book comes from the evidentiary material assembled by the Office of the Independent Counsel as well as from certain material that my staff and I gathered independently.

The book is also an insider's account based on my own personal observations as well as those of members of my staff. Quotation marks are sometimes used where discussions have been reconstructed from memory. In these instances, I have relied on my own recollections as well as those of other witnesses present during the conversations. In many cases, contemporaneous notes taken by me or by members of my staff confirm the substance of the conversations recounted.

Quotations from transcripts, depositions, and other printed material, as well as from interviews, have received editing to a very limited degree. However, any editing that has been done has not caused a material change in meaning, and I have generally included brackets to indicate changes.

—*David P. Schippers*
July 2000

CHAPTER 1
The Sellout

I f you ever plan to eat another sausage, you'd be well advised not to visit a sausage factory. It ain't a pretty sight.

If you ever plan to vote again, you might not want to know what went on behind the scenes in the Capitol Hill meat grinder leading up to and during the impeachment proceedings against President William Jefferson Clinton.

What I saw, as Chief Investigative Counsel for the House Judiciary Committee and therefore the man in charge of compiling the case against the President, was not a pretty sight, either.

Lies, cowardice, hypocrisy, cynicism, amorality, butt-covering—these were the squalid political body parts that, squeezed through the political processor, combined to make a mockery of the impeachment process. By comparison, sausage never looked so good.

Plenty of "outsiders" have told the impeachment story. Almost by definition, their accounts are secondhand reports of public events that for the most part are already well documented. There haven't been extensive "insider" accounts for obvious reasons. The Democratic players in the impeachment drama certainly aren't going to thump their chests. After all, what would they say? "Yeah, we knew the President was a serial felon who made Richard Nixon look like a Boy Scout, but we don't care." And the Republicans couldn't do much better. "Yeah, we knew he was subverting the Constitution, too, but some of us were too scared to tie our own shoes."

When you get down to it, with the exception of the Republican Judiciary Committee members, nearly every insider politician would have something to lose by going public with the details of what really happened behind closed doors on Capitol Hill in the last half of 1998 and early 1999. I don't suffer from the same qualms. Fortunately, I need not run for reelection. I am not hostile to the Democrats, nor do I feel beholden to the Republicans. But so far, the truth has been dominated by political spin, leaving much of the public purposely misinformed.

Indeed, the scheme to rewrite history and to downplay the seriousness of President Clinton's malfeasance in office is well under way. The President's supporters attack the nebulous "vast right-wing conspiracy" and blame its members for daring, in their words, to "undo the verdict of the electorate." Further, in the wake of impeachment, the White House spin machine has attempted to convince Americans that the House impeachment managers were enemies of due process and the Constitution, while President Clinton was a long-suffering victim—a role he is only too willing to assume.

In April 2000, sixteen months after William Jefferson Clinton attained the dubious distinction of being only the second American president in more than two hundred years to be impeached, he had the unmitigated nerve to blame the House of Representatives for his adversity. He said: "On the impeachment, let me tell you, I am proud of what we did there because I think we saved the Constitution of the United States. I am not ashamed of the fact that they impeached me. That was their decision, not mine. And it was wrong. As a matter of law, the Constitution, and history, it was wrong. And I am glad I didn't quit, and I'm glad we fought it."

Well, as I hope you will realize after reading this book, it was not wrong. Impeachment was not only the proper remedy, it was the only constitutional remedy available to correct some of the most outrageous conduct ever engaged in by a president of the United States. Mr. Clinton was impeached for obstruction of justice and for perjury, both federal criminal offenses, yet he is not ashamed. To the contrary, he is proud of his actions. Nobody knows what the verdict of history will be, but if the truth is known, the reputation of the House Managers should soar, and that of Mr. Clinton and the United States Senate should suffer.

Repeatedly, we hear that the whole case was about sex and that everybody lies about sex. If that were true, there might be some merit to the argument that the country was put through wholly unnecessary hell for such a venial fault. Once the truth is known, though, it becomes apparent that the President's transgressions were neither defensible nor only about sex. Evidence showed a far-reaching conspiracy to obstruct justice and to deprive Paula Jones of her constitutional right as an American citizen to have her day in court to redress wrongs committed against her by Mr. Clinton. Those wrongs, in themselves, are not impeachable offenses. Likewise, the President's conduct toward Monica Lewinsky and other women is not an impeachable offense. No reasonable person ever suggested otherwise. If sexual misconduct were all that could be shown, there would have been no inquiry or impeachment. No, the impeachable offenses were committed much later: perjury, lies, witness tampering, suborning perjury—all to achieve a personal and political result, whatever the cost. What's more, my staff was preparing to document other potentially impeachable offenses completely unrelated to Paula Jones or Monica Lewinsky when the politicians lost their nerve and severely limited the scope of the inquiry.

A great deal of evidentiary material remains under seal or in the executive protection of the House Judiciary Committee. While I cannot discuss that evidence, except in general terms, I am free to reveal other evidence and testimony that my staff developed independently, both during the oversight investigation of the Justice Department and while engaged in the impeachment inquiry. Some of that material is discussed in this book. In the telling, neither political party will be happy. But so be it.

What I have tried to do is recount my firsthand knowledge of the impeachment process as viewed by an outsider—a life-long Chicago Democrat, I might add—who became intimately involved. The account encompasses our investigation of the Department of Justice during the spring and summer of 1998, prior to the receipt of Independent Counsel Kenneth Starr's referral. Also, events in the House Judiciary Committee once the material was received will be discussed, as will the impeachment inquiry itself, the proceedings in the House of Representatives, and the "trial" in the Senate.

The Founders of our nation established the impeachment process as part of the checks and balances that are so vital to the operation of the United States government. Impeachment of the President, according to our constitutional system, requires that the House of Representatives charge the nation's chief executive with high crimes and misdemeanors. That charge must be proved by the House Managers with clear and convincing evidence in a trial that is to be held exclusively by the Senate. You will see that, despite all road-blocks and obstacles, the system worked in the House but utterly collapsed in the Senate.

When the time came to name this book, one word came immediately to mind: "Sellout." The Republican leadership in the Senate and House sold out the House Managers and our investigation. Democrats in both Houses sold out basic principles of law and decency for the sake of protecting one of their own. But most distressingly, the President of the United States of America and his White House water boys sold out the American people—not just in a one-time spasm of political expedience, but in a deliberate snarl of sophistry and cynical manipulation of public opinion, the singular aim of which was political self-preservation. In the process, he soiled not just himself, but the Constitution, the public trust, and the Presidency itself.

Democracy in. Sausage out. Not a pretty sight at all.

CHAPTER 2

Three Strikes, We're Out

W hen people ask me what's the one thing Americans should know that they don't already know about the impeachment process, it's that before we ever appeared on the floor of the United States Senate, the House impeachment managers and I knew we didn't have a shot to win.

It was a flat-out rigged ball game, what we in Chicago would refer to as a First Ward election. No shot. No way.

The bottom line was this: In the U.S. Senate, politics trumped principles, and polls trumped honor. It wasn't all the Senators. But it was the ones that counted—the leadership. And not just the Democratic leadership. The Republican leaders—they're really the ones we couldn't believe. Our own guys, selling us down the river!

The sellout came in three closed-door meetings between various groups of House Managers, Senate leaders, and me in the first and second weeks of January 1999. Three high hard ones. Right between the eyes.

Strike One! "You're Not Going to Dump This Garbage on Us"

Everything was going according to Hoyle, or so I thought. "They," and by that I mean the so-called pundits, had told us we couldn't win in the House Judiciary Committee. The members of that committee saw all the evidence and voted four articles of impeachment. Then they had said we couldn't prevail in the full House of Representatives. The doubtful members came over, read the evidence, and voted to impeach. Now, we were about to present that same evidence and more to the Senate and the American people. We felt that when people saw for the first time all the deceitful, poisonous little details of what their President had done, the polls would change, Clinton's standing with the public would plummet, the Senate would follow the public's lead, and he would be convicted.

Against that backdrop, I got a call to go to the House Judiciary Committee in the Rayburn Building because Senate Majority Leader Trent Lott of Mississippi, contrary to common practice, wanted to come to the House side of the Hill to meet with the Managers to discuss procedures. Right away we were pumped up, not yet knowing we were living in a fool's paradise. We figured, okay, here's our chance to tell the Senate Republican leader what we need to conduct the impeachment trial and make all the evidence available, not just to the Senate, but to the American people as a whole.

It was 7 or 8 PM when we got there. Naturally, the newspaper people had heard about it, so they were in the corridor doing what they do best—getting in the way.

We were in a big reception area near the committee hearing room: the thirteen Managers, myself, and a few others—a total of maybe twenty people. Politicians love to make entrances, and Senator Lott, no exception to the rule, had not yet arrived. Finally Senator Lott and Republican Senator Rick Santorum of Pennsylvania entered and sat at the head of a big rectangular table.

Lott leaned back in his chair with a power lean that said, "I'm in charge." I'll never forget the very first words out of his mouth: "Henry, you're not going to dump this garbage on us."

"Huh?" came the bewildered reply from House Judiciary Committee Chairman Henry Hyde, Republican of Illinois.

"You're not going to dump this garbage on us."

I immediately thought of Jay McMullen, who once covered City Hall for the *Chicago Sun-Times*. When McMullen saw a do-gooder get upset, he'd point at the guy, laugh, and say: "Look at him. He thinks it's all on the legit!"

Stupid me, I guess I thought everything was on the legit, too. But no, it was clear right off the bat that things were not at all legit. Rather, the Senate Republican leadership wanted to sink us.

"You know," Lott said, "we've been discussing this with the Democrats, and everybody wants a fair hearing, but we don't want to spend weeks on this. We can't just shut down the Senate. We have important matters to address."

"Important?" I thought. "Like the impeachment of a president isn't important?"

Lott mentioned the importance of "bipartisanship." He had an idea he thought "could fly." We'd be given one day to present our case, the President would get one day to present his case, and then the Senate would vote.

I didn't always think this way, but I learned that every time I heard the word "bipartisan" on Capitol Hill we were about to be sold out, because bipartisan meant doing the will of the Democrats. Bipartisan meant two articles of impeachment instead of four. It meant emasculating the inquiry by limiting the witnesses. It meant limiting the impeachment inquiry to Monica Lewinsky. When Lott talked about bipartisanship, we knew he was waving the white flag.

Congressman Chris Cannon of Utah was the first to explode. He's one tough cookie, and his face just started getting redder and redder. Then he leaned forward, screaming and pointing his finger: "What in the hell are you talking about? One day? We've got two articles of impeachment. We're supposed to be doing the people's business. Who the hell are you to tell us we have one day?"

Then Congressman Charles Canady of Florida said, "You know, Senator, if this is the way you're going to operate in the Senate, maybe we'll just appear on the floor of the

Senate and say we won't participate in this kangaroo court or this travesty."

There were shouts of: "We've got boxes of evidence here. We've got witnesses. One day? That's insane."

Congressman Jim Rogan of California added the exclamation point to the whole exchange: "We're entitled to a trial. Why are we being sold out? You're double-crossing us. We've done our duty; it's up to you to do your duty. We are all Republicans. You're going to let them make fools out of us."

Lott was obviously shocked.

My friend Congressman Hyde said nothing, but I sensed that he was deeply angry and thinking, "There goes my committee."

We had held together through the Judiciary Committee hearings and the House debate. Now he could foresee a wild, divisive fight between House and Senate Republicans, especially in the leadership. Despite an uphill battle in the House, we'd won anyhow: We'd achieved the impeachment of the President. Now we were going to get sold out by the Republicans in the Senate.

Lott, of course, started trying to make peace by throwing out bromides: "Please understand, we're not trying to sell you out. We want to give you your day in court. We figured this was the best way to do it. We only have so many votes. We are the majority, but we can't look partisan." Every time he did that, somebody jumped on him. The meeting lasted about thirty minutes. I'd say it was two minutes of him talking and twenty minutes of him getting jumped. Finally, he and Santorum tossed a few bones. You know, the kind of stuff you say when you want to get out of a fight in one piece: "Maybe we'll set up some kind of a meeting. We'll get back to you." Bones—that's all it was. They got out quickly, with a revolution on their hands. The fury continued after they left.

I would say that the most angry were Congressmen Bob Barr of Georgia, Cannon, Rogan, Canady, Asa Hutchinson of Arkansas, James Sensenbrenner of Wisconsin, and Bill McCollum of Florida. The cooler heads were Lindsey Graham of South Carolina, Stephen Buyer of Indiana, Steve Chabot of Ohio, Ed Bryant of Tennessee, and George Gekas of Pennsylvania—and they weren't that cool. Hyde was the referee.

Sensenbrenner was particularly upset. He spoke for everyone when he said: "Look, the Senate's got rules. If we're supposed to get a trial, we're supposed to be allowed to put on witnesses. They're flying in the face of their own rules." Mind you, these were rules set up by the Senate in 1986 to cover impeachments.

Someone warned against breaking with their own party in the Senate. Bob Barr snapped back: "Hey, they're the ones that are breaking with us. We've got to put their feet to the fire. We can't take this."

McCollum was fuming. He is usually a quiet, unassuming, gentlemanly individual. But he was pounding the table, saying: "We are another House of the Congress. They're treating us like we're an embarrassment. They don't even want to see us in there. I suggest that we walk on the floor of the Senate and refuse to participate in this charade."

At one point, Lindsey Graham—who had the finest political sense of anyone I met in Congress—sat back and said: "Well, let's think of this politically. What happens if we go in there and take on the Republicans in the Senate by refusing to participate?" That caused the others to reconsider. Graham was right. We couldn't just take our ball and go home.

Lott was only floating a proposal. Henry Hyde would give him the committee's answer: "No way are we going to accept this."

Strike Two! "We Make Our Own Rules"

The next day, a meeting was arranged between the House Managers and a six-man bipartisan committee of Senators. Theoretically, the purpose was to negotiate procedures for the trial. In truth, it was for the Senate to jam a totally untenable procedure down the House Managers' throats.

What we didn't know yet, but were to find out later, was that, essentially, the Senate leadership had come up with a game plan. The leaders were going to give the President twenty-four hours, give us twenty-four hours—or three eight-hour days apiece—and then the Senators would have sixteen hours to ask questions. The Senators asking questions: now *there* was a joke. They were *afraid* to ask questions because they were *afraid* to look at the evidence.

Then the Senate would decide whether to allow witnesses. We could ask for them if we could make a strong case for why they were necessary. Once a witness was identified, and before he was allowed to appear, the President's attorneys could depose him, which was a backdoor way of keeping live testimony off the Senate floor. The Senate set up rules for motions, legal memoranda, pleadings—the entire process—without input from the House Managers.

The procedural meeting took place in the Senate Majority Leader's office, with three Democrats—Senators Joseph Biden of Delaware, Joseph Lieberman of Connecticut, and Carl Levin of Michigan—and three Republicans: Fred Thompson of Tennessee, Ted Stevens of Alaska, and Pete Domenici of New Mexico. Representing the House, we had Managers Bryant, Rogan, Hutchinson—the three who would be presenting evidence—and Henry Hyde. I was there with a number of committee staffers. As usual, there were also a lot of people I didn't know, but they all looked important and no doubt felt important.

Right away we started hearing the same old song: "We're here to work this out. We here in the Senate want to give you guys a real opportunity." When I hear lines like that, I'm already looking for the grease.

Senator Domenici was the first to let us know the score, Senate-style: "We don't want you to think we are whitewashing or shortchanging the process. However, I assure you that you will never get sixty-seven votes to remove the President from office. You don't want to hear this, but it's true."

How to get out of this mess: that seemed to be the main thing Domenici cared about. The attitude was: "We are the judges who set the rules, and we are the triers of fact. We are putting together a program that will get us out of here as quickly as possible."

Now, to me, that showed incredible disrespect for the House of Representatives, no different from what Biden said a few minutes later: "We want to work with you, even though, technically, you don't have a say in the matter." He was reminding us, not so gently, who makes the rules.

That did not sit well with Hyde, and he let them know it: "We are here because of the Constitution. No one wants to be here. It is nothing but a political loser for all of us concerned."

Then Hyde got off a good shot. After having just been told by the Senate leadership that in effect the trial was over before it began, he said, "I doubt if you would want to get the Senators on record, before a trial, stating they would never vote for impeachment."

Senator Stevens interrupted, "We could get them for you tonight."

"Then do that and let America see who has prejudged this case before trial."

That shut Stevens up, at least temporarily.

One of the red herrings the Senators tried to throw at us was the specter of testimony on the subject of extramarital sex, as though no one in the Senate would know what that is.

"Look," said Biden, "we don't want tawdry sex on the floor of the Senate. We don't want you bringing in Monica Lewinsky, having her sitting down in the well of the Senate seducing the world."

Rogan said, "You know, Senator, we have no intention of going into sexual stuff. The sexual stuff is the mere background. Our evidence is going to involve perjury and ongoing obstruction of justice—the real criminal activity."

One of the Senators asked how long we'd need. The answer: about five weeks.

"What do you mean, five weeks?" sputtered Stevens. "You're going to bring the Senate of the United States to a screeching halt for five weeks? While we are trying this, bombs are falling on Iraq."

Asa Hutchinson reminded him, "Senator, you don't normally do anything until March anyhow."

Rogan then reminded the gathering that the Senate hadn't seemed worried about time when it let the impeachment of Florida Judge Alcee Hastings drag out in committee for four hundred days.

Hyde tried to be the peacemaker. "Perhaps we could cut it down. But we do need time to put on witnesses and bring in evidence." He added: "I would like to make a request of the Senate at this time. You know, some of our Congressmen have been prosecutors. They're fine trial lawyers, but it's been years since they have done any work like this. We're asking the Senate to permit Mr. Schippers here to put the witnesses on and perhaps even argue the case."

You'd have thought Henry had told Biden that Delaware had just been reduced to protectorate status. Biden turned the color of a tomato, pointing at me. "No way! No way is that guy going to open his mouth on the floor of the Senate." Then he got a smile on his face—I learned later that when Biden smiles, you've got trouble.

Hyde asked, "Why not, what's the problem?"

"Because it's not in the rules," Biden blurted back. "The rules don't provide for it. The rules require that only Congressmen can speak."

Wrong! I had read the Senate rules on impeachment procedure, and I knew that they specifically provided that counsel for the parties be admitted to appear and to be heard in an impeachment trial. Nevertheless, I kept my mouth shut.

"But, perhaps...." That's all Hyde could get out. Biden would not be silenced. "No! No way! That's off the table. Now what?"

Henry said, "We'd like to put live witnesses on, and we have ten to fifteen witnesses that we would like to put on the stand."

Biden freaked out again. "Oh, come on, Henry, come on, you've got to be.... I mean live witnesses.... You put on live witnesses, then the President brings a hundred witnesses, then you want to put more witnesses on—we'll still be trying this case in June."

Hyde responded, "Senator, your rules provide for a trial—for witnesses and evidence to be taken."

That's when Biden gave it to us in plain English. He leaned back and said, "We make our own rules."

Let me see if I've got this straight, I was thinking to myself. If something is not in the rules, there is nothing the House Managers can do to get it addressed. On the other hand, if something else is not in the rules, but a Senator suddenly wants it to be, then they can make the rule and do what they want. Really, this committee of Senators, with Biden taking the lead, was saying, in effect: "We're going to tell you how we're operating, you're going to tell us nothing. This is the Senate, we run the show." It was almost an ultimatum, and obviously humiliating to the Managers—appointed representatives of the House. The fact of the matter is that if the Senators had honestly wanted to shorten the process, they could have admitted witnesses' testimonies that were corroborated and leave it to the White House to challenge.

Meanwhile, through all of this, Fred Thompson was sitting in the corner with his head down. To my recollection, he didn't open his mouth. Stevens wasn't much better. He thought the Senate had better things to do. The reality was that we had no Republican friends in that room. The Democrats ran the whole show. In fact, it was a Democrat, Senator Lieberman, who asked the reasonable questions. "What are you hoping to prove in the Senate that you haven't already proved?" and "Why didn't you present those witnesses in the House?"

We had wanted to use witnesses in the committee, I said, but we ran out of time. Anyway, the House only had to find probable cause. The real evidence would be decided in the Senate.

"Approximately how many witnesses would you be putting on and how long do you think it would take?" Senator Lieberman asked.

I told him we could do it in three weeks. I also told him we didn't expect that the President would put on any witnesses. The President might threaten to produce hundreds of witnesses, but that was only to intimidate the Senate into curtailing the trial. He had tried the same bluff in the House and called no witnesses at all.

That was it. Walking out with Hyde and Rogan, I said, "Would you believe it, the best friend we had in the room was Senator Lieberman?"

They agreed. With friends like these Republicans, we didn't need enemies.

Strike Three! "I Don't Care If You Prove He Raped a Woman and Then Stood Up and Shot Her Dead"

Now things happened quickly, as Hyde and some of the Managers worked to get concessions from the Senate.

At one point, Hyde told us we would have three or four days for the entire Senate trial, so we worked to shorten the number and testimony of the witnesses. I started preparing Offers of Proof for each witness (that is, the answers that each witness would give at a trial). I wanted to give the offers to Lott so we could win the fifty-one votes the Senate required to call any witnesses. I also wanted to present the Offers of Proof to the Senate in open session. That would make the evidence public, even if we weren't allowed to put these witnesses on the stand.

In one conversation, Hyde told us that Lott doubted he could get fifty-one votes for all the witnesses.

Rogan threw up his hands. "Henry, they've got fifty-five votes."

"Yeah, I mentioned that to Lott, but he said that some of the Republicans might defect and vote against *all* witnesses. They're mad because we asked for too many."

In another flare-up, Barr said: "Let those Republican Senators stand up in front of the public and God and tell the world that they don't think we should be allowed to prove our case. Then let them go back to their states and try to explain why."

Despite all the horse-trading, the trial officially began on January 7, 1999. The Chief Justice of the United States entered the Senate, and each Senator took a solemn oath to do equal and impartial justice.

As I watched the ceremony on TV with my staff, I had tears in my eyes, and I think everybody else did, too. One by one, the Senators walked down to the well of the Senate and signed the oath.

When I left our office, a journalist asked me, "What do you think the Senate will do?"

"Come on—I just watched each one of them take a solemn oath to do equal and impartial justice. I hope they'll do it."

The reporters rolled their eyes.

I suppose, being from Chicago, I should have known better, but I believed those Senators were sincere in that oath and their commitment to the Constitution. Sure, I felt that there were probably fifteen Republicans in the Senate who would vote guilty even without evidence and fifteen Democrats who would vote not guilty even if we had videotape of Clinton killing somebody. But I trusted the other seventy Senators to vote their consciences.

When the Senate voted 100-0 on a procedure for impeachment, reality began to take hold. When I heard the vote, I turned to Hyde and said, "When that gang votes 100-0 for anything, we're in trouble." He responded, "Yeah, I think you're right."

The next day, we were called to a meeting in Lott's conference room. We went over there flat-out, hat-in-hand begging to get the leadership's backing to put on the case, because up until then we had been clobbered. And not just by Democrats. The Republicans had simply been holding the Democrats' coats, just standing by, not doing shortcake. On our side were Rogan, Hutchinson, Bryant, and Hyde. On their side: Domenici, Stevens, Thompson, Rod Grams of Minnesota, James Inhofe of Oklahoma, and Robert Bennett of Utah.

Hyde said: "Senator, we really are begging you to go to bat for us. We'd like to put some evidence on and live witnesses. The American people have not seen what we've got. All you've seen is the public documents."

Domenici replied: "Henry, you know if we ask for too much, we'll get nothing. We have to be bipartisan on this." There was that word again. Bipartisan. As in, appeasement.

Then Stevens chimed in: "You know we need fifty-one votes for each and every witness, and if you don't get the fifty-one votes, we are going to look silly. The Democrats will beat us; we'll lose on a preliminary matter. That will set the stage for everything. We'll look goofy."

I kept wondering where these men had gone to school. Or maybe they just missed math class the day it was explained that fifty-five is greater than fifty-one. Rogan exploded again: "You've got fifty-five Senators! Put it to the floor or put it to a vote. Or better yet, caucus your Senators and find out if we can get fifty-one of them to vote for live witnesses. If there is any witness that you can't pick up fifty-one votes for, we won't ask for that witness."

The conversation turned to Monica Lewinsky. We volunteered to put our material into Executive Session so that it wouldn't be public, but at least then the Senators could make an informed judgment about what to do with it.

One of the Senators asked, "You want the Senators to spend their time going over documents that you've already gone over?"

Rogan replied: "Absolutely. We did—why don't you? How else can you reach a rational decision on guilt or innocence?"

The argument went on, with Senator Stevens getting mad. He said, "Henry, we're just trying to prevent you from embarrassing yourself."

"Senator," Hyde responded, "remember, we'd like to bring over all the evidence."

Stevens cut Hyde off. "Henry, come on. You want to put all this stuff in, you want to spend all this time, you want to go through this dog and pony show—there's no way you're going to get sixty-seven votes no matter what you do."

Hyde didn't give up. He told the Senators the committee had evidence to indicate that the President had actually committed a brutal assault on another woman. Though he didn't identify her, he was referring to a woman in Arkansas named Juanita Broaddrick. We had no intention of bringing that evidence before the Senate. But this was Hyde's way of saying, "Look, you don't know everything we have." That's when Stevens said, "Henry, I don't care if you prove he raped a woman and then stood up and shot her dead—you are not going to get sixty-seven votes."

Silence. I raised my hand. "Senator, can I ask a question? I just watched one hundred Senators raise their right hand to God and swear to do equal and impartial justice. I'm only a Democrat from Chicago, but are you telling me that the Senators are going to ignore that oath also?"

Without hesitation he said, "You're damn right they are."

Then I said, "The system doesn't work." Not too loudly, but I'm sure they heard me.

I sat down, and they kept talking about how they would not tolerate the word "sex" on the Senate floor. Again our people promised that the word would not be used in the well of the Senate. They had no answer to that.

When the meeting was over, we went back to Hyde's office and just shook our heads. A little later we learned that the Senate would allow us only to use evidence that had already been made public. Another deal gave us three witnesses, but it didn't look like we would ever get live testimony in the Senate.

Three meetings. Three strikes. We were out.

When I think about it now, I keep going back to the guys on my staff who sat there with me, all of us with tears in our eyes, watching the Senators take the oath, thinking that this is the way it should be, that this epitomizes the honor and dignity of the Congress. By the time these three meetings were over, it seemed the oath had meant nothing to them, absolutely nothing.

I'm sure that a number of them did do what they felt was equal and impartial justice. But I'm talking about the ones who were setting this up—the leadership on both sides. Politicians, they say, care only about getting reelected. I found that that didn't apply in the House. It didn't apply to the House Managers. It didn't apply to the Republicans on the House Judiciary Committee. They did what justice demanded without thinking about reelection.

Then I came into the U.S. Senate. It was pathetic and sickening. They would break each other's backs to get in front of a camera and announce how they'd vote—before they'd even looked at a word of our evidence. I was disenchanted, disgusted, and frankly ashamed. I told my staff at the time that the public has to know what the Senate did, that I don't know how the American people could see this and not be outraged.

As I said: a First Ward election. Rigged all the way.

A year earlier, almost to the day, I'd have never guessed I would soon become so disillusioned by my government.

The Call

I t was the morning of January 14, 1998. I remember
I'd just slopped coffee all over my tie and eaten a jelly
doughnut, and as I walked into my law office in
Chicago I was wondering who would be madder at me: my
wife, about the tie, or my doctor, about the doughnut.

Then I saw a message on my desk to call Henry Hyde. I
was used to getting political fund-raising calls, but when I
saw his name, I thought to myself, "Oh, no, don't tell me
they're going to use Henry now to raise money."

I called thinking I was going to get the same spiel, but
Ann Kelly, his secretary, answered the phone, so I immediately knew something else was up. He called me back an
hour or two later and said that he, as the Chairman of the
Judiciary Committee, was interested in beginning an oversight investigation of the Justice Department. He told me

the Justice Department hadn't had any oversight for something like twenty years and asked me if I knew anybody who might be interested in heading up a group of investigators and lawyers to do this. Then he started talking about the type of person he wanted. He said he wanted a Democrat, someone who'd been around for a while, someone with a lot of experience in court but who had no preconceived ideas about who's right and who's wrong. When he finished with "Do you know anybody?" I replied, "Well, Henry, I'm not trying to be a wise guy, but, frankly, you've just been describing me."

Laughing, he told me I was right. He gave me some broad background of what he wanted to do, and over the course of several days we agreed that he'd come out and see me to talk it over.

Then the story broke about the President, the intern, a possible cover-up, and a likelihood that Independent Counsel Kenneth Starr—whose people were already investigating Bill Clinton's alleged sexual assault on Paula Jones, not to mention Whitewater, former Associate Attorney General Webb Hubbell, and campaign fund-raising irregularities involving China, Indonesia, and the Riady group—might be involved.

So, the next time I talked to Henry, in the last week of January, he said to me, "Dave, I think there is a possibility that we may have the 'I' problem."

"The 'I' problem?"

"God forbid we may have to go into an impeachment inquiry."

I reminded Henry that not only was I a Democrat, but my cousin Tom Lyons was the Cook County Chairman of the Democratic Party, and that I wasn't interested in destroying my family by getting into an ugly, partisan impeachment process.

"Well, it's highly unlikely it will come to that, but if you're doing oversight and Starr brings over material, you need to be prepared to change horses immediately and analyze it."

I had known Henry since 1968. At that time I was a Democratic appointee to the Illinois Crime Commission, and he was a state representative. One of the first things he said to me was, "Just remember, don't let anybody interfere with your ideas of what you think is right and wrong; just do what you have to do and everything will be fine." I always respected him, even if I disagreed with him politically.

I had worked for U.S. Attorney General Robert Kennedy and was extremely active in Democratic politics—as my entire family had been for generations. I didn't realize until I was ten that it was "Republican," not "damn Republican," and I grew up believing that the lowest thing you could do was to be a registered Democrat and vote Republican. I voted for Bill Clinton. Twice. I did it because he was the Democratic candidate for President of the United States. It was that simple.

Despite all that, I was also interested in doing what sounded like a necessary and important job, and my family supported that decision. So I took the next step and was interviewed by Henry's Chief of Staff and Majority Counsel on the House Judiciary Committee, Tom Mooney.

Mooney had a stack of papers in front of him. "You know, Dave, if we ever go beyond the oversight role, you're going to be under a microscope. There are a few things I have to ask you about."

For instance, in 1986 I represented a man accused of committing multiple murders. I defended him in one case by showing that the evidence was obtained in an illegal search. Several months later the same defendant was charged with killing a sixteen-year-old boy, placing his mutilated body in garbage bags, and throwing the bags in a dumpster behind his apartment. I defended him again because he adamantly professed his innocence. He was found guilty. Later, he obtained a new lawyer and accused me of doing all sorts of illegal things. Mooney questioned me about this case, and I assured him that there had been a full hearing before the original trial judge, who found that all the charges were false. I knew it would help if I told Mooney about any complaints to the Bar Association in which I was involved. I assured him that this sort of thing happened to all trial lawyers, and that all complaints were dismissed without even an investigation. I added that I knew of nothing in my background that might embarrass the committee or the Chairman.

It seemed as if we went through my entire life history. But I got the job, full authority to hire my own staff, and the promise—which was kept—of no political interference.

My first call was to Peter Wacks, who had just retired from the FBI. He had been involved in the investigation of the Teamsters during the 1980s and 1990s and later was very active in the investigation of alleged corruption involving the Laborers International Union. He was used to handling national cases, and he had just begun working for a private investigating firm when I called him.

The next person I contacted was Al Tracy. Al was a criminal investigator for the IRS whom I'd known for twenty to twenty-five years. I asked him if he would be willing to go to Washington. He was at retirement age and accepted the chance to take on a new challenge.

Peter Wacks and Al Tracy were excellent federal law enforcement agents with extensive experience in developing, handling, interrogating, and assessing potential witnesses. I knew no one who did it better.

Tracy recommended another recently retired IRS agent, Berle Littman. Whereas Al was a street agent, Berle was a razor-sharp researcher who could analyze the numbers in account books, financial records, and computers.

Another recruit was Diana Woznicki. She had been my secretary and legal assistant before she joined the Chicago Police Department, where she was now a sergeant. She had worked in some of the toughest districts in the city, was streetwise, and had a terrific memory. As it turned out, it was her experience in rape counseling that would make her especially valuable.

I told Mooney and Hyde that I thought the staff should

be kept small. When the Judiciary Committee handled the Watergate investigation, they had more than one hundred staffers, of which forty-three were lawyers and only four were investigators. The actual work was performed by five or six people. That was ridiculous. I wanted to start with four investigators—which I now had—and four lawyers, counting myself.

First, I talked to my son Tom, who at the time was working for a law firm in northern Illinois. He wasn't interested but referred me to Jeff Pavletic, who was First Assistant State Attorney in Lake County. Jeff had tried and won a case almost identical to the Paula Jones case. He was also a great administrator. I offered him a job.

Then I called Susan Bogart, a former student of mine at Loyola University in Chicago. She had been a federal prosecutor and a law clerk to a federal judge, and was now teaching at Loyola's law school. She was excellent at organizing evidence and taking it to trial.

I also brought into the group my paralegal, Nancy Ruggero, who had worked with me for twenty-five years and who knows more about the law than most lawyers.

Henry met my people and approved them.

Three more lawyers would join us between the summer and the end of the year—my son Tom; John Kocoras, a brilliant young attorney; and the diligent Bob Hoover. I also asked Hyde to hire Jerry O'Sullivan and, later, his brother Patrick as clerks.

Hyde's decision to hire me wasn't popular, as I discovered when he introduced me to the Republican members of the Judiciary Committee. It was no secret that I lacked experience in Washington politics. I often heard people say, "He's not a K Street lawyer." By that they meant I wasn't one of those fancy-suit, $500-an-hour, Ivy League guys from an influential Washington firm. They said, "You put this guy up on K Street and someone will start putting money in his cup."

Congressman Jim Rogan of California, who later recounted the story to me, was only half-joking when he questioned Hyde's sanity: "I don't know where Henry came up with this Schippers, but he just doesn't seem like the kind of person we need for this job. You don't think that maybe Henry has gone a little around the bend? You know, he is over seventy."

Because so many Republicans regarded me either with political suspicion or as "a lost sheep in Washington," Hyde eventually asked Washington lawyer Charlie Marino to consult with me. I knew Charlie, and I was happy to have his counsel.

Of course, not all Republicans were suspicious. I was standing next to the coffeepot after the introductory meeting when a young woman came up, stuck out her hand, and said, "Hi, I'm Mary. I don't know what I'm doing here."

I replied, "I'm Dave, and I don't know what the hell I'm doing here either."

It turned out she was Republican Congresswoman Mary Bono of California. She was just a delightful person with no pretensions about herself and, as it turned out, a very hard worker.

A couple of days later, Hyde told me the Democrats on the committee had "checked me out" and wouldn't make an issue of my appointment.

Our oversight investigation began by analyzing more than a dozen separate allegations concerning the Department of Justice and its subagencies. We knew our time was limited and that once Judge Starr's referral on impeachable offenses was received, we would have to abandon our efforts in other areas. So we quickly narrowed our scope.

It was narrowed further because the Justice Department flat-out wouldn't cooperate with our investigation. We asked to talk to some people in the Immigration and Naturalization Service (INS). They said, "No."

We asked to talk to some Assistant U.S. Attorneys. They said, "No."

And so on.

Henry Hyde arranged a meeting between me and Attorney General Janet Reno and members of her staff so that I could talk this through with her. She promised to cooperate fully but then added that we would have to clear any interviews with the department. I reminded her: "We have people who are claiming that their own bosses are doing illegal activities. We're not going to go through you. We're going to talk to these people."

"They're not allowed to talk to you."

"If we have people who are Justice Department employees who have information about illegal activity in the Justice Department, I'm not going to go to the Justice Department and tell them who we're talking to and what they're telling us."

"They're not supposed to talk to you."

"I really don't care. We're going to do it."

After that meeting, a Justice Department staffer told me: "Dave, you're not from Washington. You don't know how we operate out here."

"You're right, I'm not from Washington—but you don't know how *I* operate. We're going to get this stuff and we're going to do it. If you try to stop us, you may find yourself involved in obstruction of Congress."

I did this without approval from anybody; I didn't think I needed it. When I told the Judiciary Committee staff, they were appalled.

All they could say was, "You can't do that!"

And all I could say was, "I just did."

CHAPTER 4

Injustice for All

My staff and I agreed that we needed to focus on the Immigration and Naturalization Service (INS), which appeared to be running out of control.

By the time we came to the subject, investigations by the General Accounting Office (GAO) and congressional committees had already indicated that the White House used the INS to further its political agenda. A blatant politicization of the agency took place during the 1996 presidential campaign when the White House pressured the INS into expediting its "Citizenship USA" (CUSA) program to grant citizenship to thousands of aliens that the White House counted as likely Democratic voters. To ensure maximum impact, the INS concentrated on aliens in key states—California, Florida, Illinois, New York, New Jersey, and

Texas—that hold a combined 181 electoral votes, just 89 short of the total needed to win the election.

The program was placed under the direction of Vice President Al Gore. We received from the GAO a few e-mails indicating Vice President Gore's role in the plan (which are included in Appendix A at the back of this book). He was responsible for keeping the pressure on, to make sure the aliens were pushed through by September 1, the last day to register for the presidential election.

In our investigation we uncovered a case study evidencing what is pejoratively known in political science circles as "Chicago Politics."

Back in the early years of the twentieth century, "Hinky Dink" Kenna and "Bathouse" John Coughlin were recognized as the very models of the unsavory Chicago politician. The two once fixed an aldermanic election in Chicago's First Ward. To do so, they imported thousands of ward heelers, friends, associates, and city workers and had them registered to vote from every building in the ward—from homes (of which there were few) to taverns and cribs (of which there were many). On Election Day the recent arrivals stopped at Hinky Dink's tavern, picked up fifty cents, ate a free lunch, and went out to vote their consciences. Guess who won that election?

Essentially, the same tactics were used during President Clinton's reelection in 1996. Only this time the Democrats weren't handing out sandwiches. Instead, through CUSA, they were circumventing normal procedures for naturalizing aliens—procedures that check backgrounds and weed out criminals—and consequently they were handing out citizenship papers to questionable characters.

The possibility of using CUSA apparently occurred to the White House in February 1996, when Henry Cisneros, then Secretary of Housing and Urban Development, forwarded a memo to President Clinton. The memo, from the California Active Citizenship Campaign (ACC), complained of a backlog of alien applications for naturalization in Los Angeles. It contained the magic words: "INS inaction [on the backlog] will deny 300,000 Latinos the right to vote in the 1996 presidential elections [sic] in California."

The memo outlined the services that the Industrial Areas Foundation (IAF) in Los Angeles could provide. The IAF offered thousands of volunteers to help process voter applications, register thousands of new voters, conduct 5,000 house meetings, encourage voting by mail, and get more than 50,000 occasional voters out to vote in the presidential election. Most interesting were the promises that the IAF would "create voter interest around issues of Affirmative Action and Minimum Wage,... influence 300,000 voters in the preparation for Nov. 1996,... produce 5,000 precinct leaders and turn out 96,000 voters for the 1996 presidential election."

The White House discovered a problem, however: INS Commissioner Doris Meissner didn't want to speed up the naturalization process and warned President Clinton's people that such a push might be viewed as politically motivated.

Documents show that President Clinton asked Doug Farbrother of the National Performance Review (NPR) staff to look into removing barriers to citizenship not only in Los Angeles but also in San Francisco, Chicago, New York, and Miami—major cities in four swing states. In a memo to the President, Farbrother noted Commissioner Meissner's concern and suggested two options. Farbrother stated that "we can reduce—but not eliminate—the risk of controversy over our motives by appointing one of our proven NPR reinventors as Deputy INS Commissioner.... As part of the official INS management team, our reinventor would have more direct influence and the INS staff would be less likely to go public with complaints than they would over the interference of an outsider." The memo observed that "reinventors" should be put in many other agencies, as well, to replace leaders who "don't 'get it.'"

The second option was to let the INS do the best it could and to hope for success—though, Farbrother added, "a lot of people will still be waiting for their citizenship papers for a long time."

It appears the second option was never seriously considered. In his memo, Farbrother recommended option one to the President because, "[t]o get anywhere near a million applicants naturalized" by summer's end, the administration would have "to force some serious 'reinvention' on INS."

Farbrother and the NPR won the assignment of getting the INS to process more than a million applicants by the end of the summer. As early as March 1996, GAO documents reveal, he was reporting his efforts, recommendations, and results to Vice President Gore. Farbrother reported how he had told the INS and the Justice Department to waive "stupid rules," and he told Gore that unless reforms were implemented, the backlog wouldn't be "processed in time."

As Farbrother noted in a March 22 e-mail to Gore, he had told INS Deputy Commissioner Chris Sale and Deputy Attorney General Jamie Gorelick "to delegate broad authority to the managers in" New York, Chicago, Miami, San Francisco, and Los Angeles. But the INS and the Justice Department were not immediately complying with his demands, he said. Keeping the pressure on, Farbrother sent Sale a fax reiterating how important this delegation was in order "to get the results the Vice President wants." In the fax he also commented, "I need you or Doris [Meissner] to sign something like the attached," referring to a memo giving those INS district directors "full authority to waive, suspend, or deviate from DOJ and INS nonstatutory policies, regulations, and procedures provided you operate within the confines of the law."

The White House wanted any applicant for citizenship to be naturalized in time to register for the November election, so the pressure on the INS was constant. On March 21 Elaine Kamarck in the Vice President's office sent an e-mail to Farbrother saying: "THE PRESIDENT IS SICK OF THIS

AND WANTS ACTION. IF NOTHING MOVES TODAY WE'LL HAVE TO TAKE SOME PRETTY DRASTIC MEASURES." Farbrother responded, "I favor drastic measures." If he couldn't get what he wanted from the INS, he wrote, he would "call for heavy artillery."

In a March 26 e-mail to the Vice President, Farbrother reported that Chris Sale had indeed "delegated hiring authority to the five cities and increased their budgets by 20%." But, he wrote, "I still don't think the city directors have enough freedom to do the job." Two days later Farbrother told the Vice President by e-mail, "[U]nless we blast INS headquarters loose from their grip on the frontline managers, we are going to have way too many people still waiting for citizenship in November." He added, "I can't make Doris Meissner delegate broad authority to her field managers. Can you?"

Gore answered, "We'll explore it. Thanks." By the end of March, Doris Meissner capitulated. On April 4, 1996, Elaine Kamarck, to prepare the Vice President for a lunch with Clinton, drafted a memo to Gore briefing him on the INS progress. In time, Newark, New Jersey, and Houston, Texas, would be added to the list of targeted cities, and in all, more than a million aliens would be naturalized in time to vote in the 1996 election.

Because of time constraints, we focused our own investigation on the INS district office in Chicago, which Gore had visited in 1996 to check on the registration progress. We quickly discovered that the most flagrant and critical breakdown occurred in fingerprint checks.

Federal regulations require that, for an alien to obtain citizenship, his application for naturalization (citizenship) *must* be accompanied by a complete set of the alien's fingerprints. The fingerprint cards are then sent to the FBI to determine if the applicant has a criminal or arrest record. The law provides that an application may be denied if the alien has a serious criminal record or if he falsely denies ever having been arrested, even if he was never convicted.

In the INS district offices, the alien applicant for naturalization cannot be scheduled for a personal interview until at least sixty days after the application is submitted. This delay is specifically intended to allow sufficient time for an FBI fingerprint check. If the check reveals an arrest record identification, the arrest report is inserted in the alien's file prior to the interview. An arrest record does not automatically result in a denial of citizenship, but it alerts an examiner to spend additional time questioning the applicant and to request that he furnish further information.

If there is no criminal arrest record in the file prior to the interview, the examiner will assume that none exists. For that reason, the INS has always considered the FBI fingerprint check to be the only practical way of preventing violent felons, dope peddlers, and the like from obtaining citizenship. Any breakdown in the collecting, checking, and reporting of the fingerprints can cause a breakdown of the entire process.

In our investigation we developed sources inside the INS with specific knowledge of the facts who revealed that FBI arrest records that were being sent to the Chicago INS office simply were not being inserted into the aliens' files. As a result, aliens with criminal records were being granted citizenship.

Our sources also disclosed that, just prior to the 1996 voter registration deadline, a box was discovered in the Chicago INS office containing nearly five thousand FBI arrest reports—reports that had arrived in time but had been ignored.

Later, when the office discovered that those reports had never been processed, the INS initially tried to blame the FBI, claiming that the Bureau had not provided the arrest records within the sixty-day window. But the FBI had done its job in a timely manner. Then the INS tried to convince the public that the foul-up really hadn't harmed the process much. The agency cited statistics showing that the rejection rate of 17 percent was just about what it had always been, so no harm, no foul. But the INS neglected to take into account the thousands of aliens with criminal arrest records who were not rejected, even though they would have been under the normal procedures. If the traditional process had been followed, the rejection rate in the summer of 1996 would have easily exceeded 30 percent and perhaps have been even higher.

The White House, the INS, and the Justice Department publicly denied any political motive in the CUSA program to expedite the citizenship procedure. What the United States got is undeniable:

1) More than 75,000 new citizens who had arrest records when they applied;

2) An additional 115,000 citizens whose fingerprints were unclassifiable for various technical reasons and were never resubmitted; and

3) Another 61,000 people who were given citizenship with no fingerprints submitted at all.

Those numbers were developed by the accounting firm of KPMG Peat Marwick as a result of an audit of the 1996 CUSA program.

What we had here was a perfect example of the Clinton-Gore administration's overarching political philosophy: "The ends justify the means," coupled with "win at any cost." It was a philosophy of governance that, as our investigations into other areas proceeded, we would find repeated again and again.

When the results of the KPMG Peat Marwick audit were made public, the INS and Justice vowed to remedy the situation, root out the felons, and revoke erroneously awarded citizenship. Everyone congratulated the administration for acting so quickly—and then promptly forgot about it.

In June 1998, as part of our oversight investigation of the Justice Department, we continued the investigation of CUSA. Our interest intensified when we heard unconfirmed reports that a similar plan was in the works for the next presidential election.

One of the first things we learned from our INS sources

was that the INS had refused to employ the quickest and most effective method for revoking improperly granted citizenship—there is a federal statute that can be used in such cases. Instead the INS chose to conduct administrative revocations. But the agency acted under the authority of an INS regulation whose enforcement a District Court judge enjoined on July 7, 1998, citing the regulation's dubious constitutionality. In other words, the agency had willingly maneuvered itself into a do-nothing position.

In the course of our investigation, we discovered that FBI arrest records were still missing from the proper files; many were still in boxes. We unearthed that several individuals who had been naturalized illegally were now trying to sponsor their relatives for citizenship. We found sponsors who were unable to speak a word of English, a condition that should have prevented naturalization. Similarly, we uncovered arrest records or other information that should have been disqualifiers for naturalization. But, according to interviews my staff conducted with sources inside INS offices, INS agents who had found these irregularities were ordered to ignore them and to revoke citizenship only in cases ordered by the auditors.

Our sources inside the INS revealed that, in preparation for the 2000 elections, INS agents in the district offices were directed to relax the testing for English, complete every interview within twenty minutes, and ensure that all applicants pass the Civics test by continuing to ask questions until an applicant got a sufficient number right. Sometimes it was necessary to ask twenty or twenty-five questions before four or five were answered correctly.

We received no cooperation from either the Justice Department or the INS. Instead we received nothing but complaints about not going through proper channels, investigating old news, being partisan—if not racist—and so on. But we reasoned that if criminals were given citizenship in 1996, at least some of them had probably continued their criminal activity in the two years since. We asked the GAO—an investigative agency that works for Congress and is therefore not subject to White House or Justice Department pressures—to give us FBI arrest records related to the CUSA program. We were given unquestioned cooperation and boxes of FBI reports.

We reviewed every document in those boxes, pulling out about a hundred of the most violent or serious crimes committed by aliens prior to naturalization and documented by arrest records. I specifically excluded minor immigration crimes, tax offenses, or white-collar crimes such as driving under the influence. I asked the staff to search for drug trafficking and violent crimes such as rape and child abuse. Those are the types of crimes that are most often repeated. A child abuser tends to abuse again, and a rapist tends to rape again.

After a few days—and going through only a few of the twenty or so boxes—we had our basic one hundred heinous crimes, including one criminal who was actually in jail at the time he was naturalized.

We asked the FBI if it had arrest records for crimes committed by the same aliens in this country since 1996 and sent them our one hundred profiles.

Less than a week later, the FBI sent the updated arrest records to the Justice Department. (Per an agreement between the FBI and the Justice Department, all materials requested from the Bureau must go through Justice.) But when we inquired about them, the department claimed that it hadn't yet received the records. An hour later, however, Justice called back to say that the "misplaced" reports had been located.

Of those one hundred arrest records updated by the Bureau, some 20 percent showed arrests for serious crimes after the subject was given citizenship. Based on these random results, we asked for updates on every arrest record in our twenty boxes. Our plan was to update every report, using only FBI numbers and with the FBI redacting all identifying information to address the issue of privacy concerns. If, as we anticipated, anywhere near 20 percent came back with subsequent crimes, we would then confront the Justice Department, demand the identity and address of these known criminals, and point out that they had been given citizenship illegally and were still engaged in criminal activity. Unfortunately, before we could go further, the referral from Independent Counsel Kenneth Starr arrived. Had we been given sufficient time to develop evidence and witnesses, the CUSA matter might have been included in the abuse of power impeachment article.

The 1996 arrest records are still available, and I am sure the FBI is still willing to update all of them. In the meantime, thousands of criminals are now citizens of the United States because it was assumed they would vote for Bill Clinton and Al Gore.

That was just one of the things we were doing during the summer months of 1998. We had investigations opened on the Drug Enforcement Administration and the Bureau of Prisons, where allegedly a prison employee had killed an inmate in jail and officials there had covered it up.

We were also looking into the many referrals to the Justice Department that had been ignored. There were accusations that lies had been told about who was on Hillary Clinton's health care task force. A judge had recommended that the Justice Department investigate, but nothing had been done. Allegations of serious campaign abuses in New York had been brought to the Justice Department, but again no action resulted.

I was also researching everything I could find on impeachment. I reviewed the Constitution, the Federalist Papers, the notes on the Constitutional Convention, and other historical documents. I was reading about every impeachment case in Great Britain and the United States.

On procedures, if it came to impeachment, all the House committee chairmen eventually agreed that we should follow the Watergate procedure as much as possible. We also consulted with Peter Rodino, who had been the Democratic Chairman of the Judiciary Committee during Watergate.

Under our plan, all material received from the Independent Counsel would be placed into a totally secure room. The documents in the room would be locked in safes with access limited to those who were authorized. This room would be under guard at all times, and everyone would be required to sign in and out. It was an elaborate plan, but it was necessary to protect the Starr material. We knew that if every member of the House were given access, there would be no security from leaks, no method to trace such leaks, and no end of partisan name-calling.

We didn't know what would be in the referral, but we nevertheless had many discussions about what sort of material should be made public.

At this time, the President was enjoying a 65 to 70 percent approval rating. Most of us felt that once it was known what the President had done, he'd lose 40 points overnight.

I thought we should take up to two weeks to prepare a full and fair analysis of the referral before releasing it—or a summary of it—to the press and public.

Congressman Bob Barr and Speaker of the House Newt Gingrich wanted everything to be made public. We felt that would be insanity because it would cause press-driven chaos. There would be people rummaging through our evidence before we had a chance to analyze it ourselves.

Henry Hyde and most Republicans on the Judiciary Committee sided with us and the counsel of prudence.

Throughout this period, the permanent Judiciary staffers were careful to avoid any indication that we were getting ready for an impeachment inquiry. I don't know why. For example, one day one of our staff members brought in a chart from the *Wall Street Journal* that showed the players and how impeachment would work legally. Well, Jon Dudas, the Deputy Chief of Staff on the Judiciary Committee, happened to see it and got upset. He told us he didn't want to give any indication that we were getting ready for impeachment.

I kept saying, "Jon, we *are* getting ready for impeachment. Why are we hiding anything? Everybody in the world knows that sooner or later the referral is going to come over and we are going to have to do something with it. We can't just put everything in a hallway for two weeks. We should be getting ready."

Finally, everybody agreed to begin preparing to receive the Starr report. We asked the House leaders for a room where we could set up the special security. After a couple of weeks, they came up with a room directly across from ours in the Ford Building, which was absolutely perfect. Then they redid the whole thing, locks and all. That stirred more speculation that the referral was imminent.

The strongest rumor was that Kenneth Starr's referral would arrive on July 9, before Congress's summer recess. On July 9, I went to the noon Mass at St. Peter's Catholic Church across the street from the Rayburn Building. Some of the Capitol press corps noticed me coming out of the church. One said, "I hear you go to church during the week."

I acknowledged that I did whenever possible.

"Are you one of those religious fanatics like Ken Starr?" (It had been reported that Starr sang hymns when he went jogging.)

My first reaction was anger. I was about to lecture the young man when I suddenly thought better of it and decided to treat the question lightly. I smiled and said, "Why of course I'm a religious fanatic. Don't you have to be a religious fanatic to be allowed into the vast right-wing conspiracy?" Everyone laughed, and the moment passed. Although nothing appeared in print, I still think the question was serious, and they were trying to bait me.

The referral didn't arrive, and Congress went home for the summer while my staff and I continued our oversight investigation of the Justice Department and the INS.

On September 9, I received a call from a reporter who said, "It's coming over today, and it's only about Monica." Because I had received many other false alarms, I kept this one to myself.

But this one was true, as we learned from watching the TV and seeing boxes of materials arriving for the House Sergeant-at-Arms.

Now our work would begin in earnest.

CHAPTER 5
The 800-Pound Gorilla

H ow do you handle an 800-pound gorilla? Well, for starters, you lock him up in a secure room and put some guys with guns outside the doors.

That's what we did with the two identical seventeen-box sets of evidence that Starr delivered to us on the morning of Friday, September 9. The room was about thirty-five feet long and twenty feet wide. There was only a single entrance, which had a keypad combination lock. Immediately outside the door was a table containing sign-in sheets in the custody of a uniformed member of the Capitol Hill Police. Nobody was allowed to enter or to leave, even for a minute or two, without signing the log, together with the time in and the time out. Nobody was permitted to take anything into or out of the room, including cameras, phones, tape recorders, or even purses. Every once in a while that rule caused a stir. Two female Democratic members of the committee, Maxine Waters and Sheila Jackson Lee, tried to get into the room with their purses. They were indignant that the police officer made them leave their bags outside.

Both our office and the secure room were at the very end of a long corridor. The other offices in that hall were occupied by the Capitol Police. Halfway down the hall, about a hundred feet or so, another officer was stationed to limit access. Only authorized personnel were allowed past that point, which kept the press from wandering by. If anyone who was not a member of the committee wanted to see us, one of my staff would have to go down to the security checkpoint and personally escort him or her. The officers came to know the regulars, so there was little inconvenience.

In the secure room, there was a common area with tables and chairs to be shared by both investigative staffs while examining the material. At each end of the room was a small private office. One room was reserved for Republicans, one for Democrats. These rooms were equipped with a cassette player and earphones to listen to audiotapes.

There were also two large file cabinets with combination locks. These held the Starr material—one set aside for the Republicans, one for the Democrats. Each had its own combination and was not available to anyone but the investigators.

In addition to making every person sign in and out of the room, we arranged that anyone who obtained material from the locked cabinets signed for it when he or she took it out and signed for it when it was returned. That way we were able to maintain a running record of who saw what, and when. We also agreed to make copies of documents that the Congressmen could leave in their own file in the room.

But right away, within hours of the boxes' being delivered, I noticed that there was a telephone in the room. I said to the police, "What in the hell is a telephone doing in there?" and had Nancy Ruggero yank it out while Minority Special Counsel Abbe Lowell, who had wandered in, was using it. Lowell came up to me and said, "What the hell are you doing to me? You sent her in there. I'm in the middle of a conversation."

"I'm sorry, no phones."

In Washington, "the Leak" is the most popular of indoor sports, engaged in by the White House, the Justice Department, Representatives, Senators, and, above all, their staffers. The entire Executive and Legislative Branches of government are like a sieve.

Still, in our case it was essential that there be no leaks. If all members of the House were given access, there would be no hope of stemming leaks. That is why, early on, Hyde and other Republican members decided that access to the room would be strictly limited to those with a "need to know." Only members of the Judiciary Committee, the Republican and Democratic investigative staffs, and a very limited number of Judiciary Committee staffers would have access. A list of names, together with identifying pictures, was given to Capitol Police guards. Even the top staffers of Judiciary Committee members were denied access to the information.

Among those denied access was Newt Gingrich, because the Democrats had so successfully demonized him. We didn't want the Democrats using him to discredit our work. So Hyde had to talk Gingrich into accepting that he would be kept in the dark, as would Majority Leader Dick Armey.

Members of the committee were told we needed the weekend to unload and file the boxes. They honored that, and we spent about forty hours that weekend getting things organized. The Democrats were in there, too, doing the same thing with their boxes.

Almost immediately, we got a call from Gingrich's office saying that House Minority Leader Richard Gephardt of Missouri wanted to release everything to the public. Some Republican members of the committee agreed. I thought that they were all crazy, but my opinion carried about as much weight as toothpicks in a tornado. Gingrich and Gephardt decided that they were going to release some of the material and that we would open the doors to a number of other staffers on the Judiciary Committee to figure out what to release. As it turned out, the staffers spent at least a full week, almost twenty-four hours a day, pulling material, taking words out, fighting over what they were going to leave in and take out. It was just a mess. They'd go through it, and then they would argue with each other and say: Well, all right, we'll let you release this, but you can't release that. There must have been ten of them in the room going over this stuff, fighting like dogs.

The final decision about what to release came from Chairman Hyde and ranking Democrat John Conyers of Michigan, after the staffers had come to a consensus, which they did on 99 percent of the documents. It amounted to roughly one-and-a-half boxes worth of material out of the seventeen boxes Starr had sent over.

That is also when the decision was made to release the videotape of the President's four hours of testimony from his August 17, 1998, appearance before the grand jury in the Paula Jones case. It was a terrible mistake, as the spin doctors easily deflated its evidence by leaking wildly exaggerated stories about the tapes. Using a tactic that proved successful throughout the impeachment process—lessening the impact of adverse information by anticipating it and making it sound worse than it was—Clinton's people made everyone believe that the President had lost his temper, stalked out, and generally made a fool of himself. What the American people actually saw didn't come close to their expectations. More importantly, because people had been primed to look for him acting up, they missed the most important part of his testimony—the obvious lies.

In hindsight, I would not have released the grand jury testimony. Given my druthers, if something had to be released, I would have released the videotape of Clinton's sworn deposition in the Jones case because it was much more damning. It set the stage for everything because,

almost immediately after he gave his name, it was one ver-
ifiable lie after another. The grand jury testimony contained a lot of Mickey Mouse stuff, whereas the deposition
included dead-bang denials of things we had substantial
evidence showing were true.

But the problem with the deposition was that it was still
under seal in the Jones case in Arkansas. When a document
is under seal, it cannot be made public without the court's
approval. By the time we received approval, it was too late
to influence public opinion and, therefore, the House.

I am an old prosecutor, and it drove me nuts that Clinton
wasn't pressed harder in the questioning before the grand jury.
Starr's people were interrogating the President of the United
States. He was appearing "voluntarily"—even though he had
been subpoenaed—and, like gentlemen, they deferred to him.
Clinton was even allowed to give a statement at the opening
of his testimony. Whenever questions cut too close for com-
fort, he'd say, "I stand on my statement." The statement itself
was false, but they never forced him to defend it. Starr's people would ask, "Did she perform oral sex on you?"

"I stand on my statement."

Starr's team let him get away with that. Clinton would
not have gotten away with it on the stand, on trial, in the
Senate. A witness has three choices: tell the truth, lie, or
take the Fifth Amendment. There is no "stand on my statement" in cross-examination.

Most of the rest of the material that was released was
about sex because it was about Monica. The media picked

up on the sex—like the infamous cigar episode—to the exclusion of everything else. The White House immediately dismissed the entire investigation as being merely about sex, and the public largely agreed. So Gephardt got everything he wanted in his selective releases, and the Republicans got hurt badly.

The Republicans wrongly assumed that Clinton would emerge from the sex revelations as a distrusted figure, without public support. I remember asking Congressman Asa Hutchinson, "How are things back home in Arkansas?"

"I walked into a hornet's nest down there," he said. "Every minister, priest, everybody I ran into asked how we could put this filth out in public. They're blaming us." So the myth was created that "it's all about sex" and that it was the Republicans' fault for airing it. The whole Watergate model fell apart. The rest of the story never got out, and unfortunately it still hasn't. It is under lock and key in the National Archives now, and it can be held there, unavailable to the press or to the public, for fifty years. The House Judiciary Committee could decide to take it out of Executive Session, which would make it public, but don't hold your breath.

Once the ground rules had been laid, the Republicans started coming to the secure room in droves. Mary Bono, the only female Republican on the committee, came to see me. "Look," she said, "I'm not a lawyer, I don't know anything about the legality of this thing. I'm kind of ambivalent if it's just sex. Would you be willing to guide me through it?"

"Mary, anytime, anywhere, anything you need, ask me."

She spent hours and hours studying the case. In fact, all of the Republican committee members spent a great deal of time examining evidence.

I didn't watch the Democrats, but my staff reported to me that one Democratic committee member came over to hear the phone sex tapes. When told there were no tapes, the Democrat said, "What the hell am I wasting my time for?" and left.

I did notice that Democratic staffers weren't going through the material with a fine-tooth comb as we were. They cared only about what Monica or Linda Tripp said. They didn't realize—or didn't care—that we were focusing on many more issues.

Five Democrats on the committee never signed into the secure room at all, according to the sign-in sheets. One of them was Barney Frank of Massachusetts, who kept saying, "There's no evidence, there's no evidence." The others were Howard Berman of California, Rick Boucher of Virginia, Jerrold Nadler of New York, and Melvin Watt of North Carolina.

That told me that, long before any vote—indeed, from the very beginning—the Democrats had decided to hold the line. In hindsight, the Democrats' plan seems obvious: "We don't want to know what's in there because it may be too much for us to pass the red face test. On the other hand, we want to hold the line so that there is no way a Democrat will break ranks. By doing so, we can say that this is a partisan impeachment." In other words, they manufactured the partisanship by being partisan themselves.

Of course, what the politicians wanted to do with the material was their business. My mandate was simple: go through the material and decide if the President of the United States had committed impeachable offenses. If he had, he would be punished. If he hadn't, that was the end of it.

The day the material was delivered, I had a meeting with all of my investigators and lawyers—Susan Bogart, John Kocoras, Berle Littman, Jeff Pavletic, Nancy Ruggero, Tom Schippers, Al Tracy, Pete Wacks, and Diana Woznicki.

"Before we begin, is there anyone who has a preconceived idea concerning the President's guilt or innocence?"

Nobody did. "One thing that I *do* want you to assume is that everything Monica Lewinsky said—under oath or not—is not true. Only credit what she said if it is corroborated. Don't just take her word. We are not prosecuting; we are looking only for the truth." I also told them to take copious notes and look for anything that would be helpful to the President. On every issue, I said, "I want you to look for exculpatory evidence first." I wanted no bias. If we didn't have a case, better to end it now than later. I wanted only facts.

Before we began to examine the evidence, I had the secure room and our offices swept for possible electronic surveillance instruments, commonly called "bugs." In addition, not one sensitive conversation was held in a room with windows facing the street, since a parabolic micro-phone outside could pick up the discussion.

With security concerns out of the way, we read every single piece of evidence. The review took approximately two weeks. This was the most intense part of our work. It was seven days a week, fourteen to sixteen hours a day. One day I was told that a Democratic Congressman went into the Democrats' private room with Minority Special Counsel Abbe Lowell. At one point the Congressman blurted out: "My God, this is indefensible. The man is a perjurer, a liar, he's obstructing justice. How can we defend him?" That Democratic Congressman, like all the rest, voted against impeachment.

Starr's referral listed ten specific offenses that were possibly impeachable. I personally researched the law on each of these crimes. I also personally investigated the testimony of Monica Lewinsky, the President, and Clinton's friend Vernon Jordan, as well as related documents. The referral had two hundred to three hundred footnotes. We went over every single one. My staff researched and verified everything, and double-checked it. We found nothing that cast doubt on the evidence or the charges in the referral.

Hyde wanted a report on the referral by the first week in October. He told me that if there were felonies, they should go in the report, but I should avoid esoteric issues.

That's when I took Starr's tenth article regarding abuse of power off the table. Frankly, Starr made an extremely good argument, and normally I would have accepted it. Abuse of power *is* an impeachable offense—and it later became what I thought was one of the strongest articles of impeachment—but it's not a felony.

I was constantly giving Hyde verbal reports on our progress. I told him: "When I do my report to the Judiciary Committee, I'm going to limit the evidence that I announce publicly to the evidence contained in the referral. I'm not going to talk about his deposition testimony because it's not public. But if we move beyond this point, there is a lot of other evidence to pursue."

One thing that was obvious to me was the strength of the evidence that the President had orchestrated a conspiracy to obstruct justice in the Jones case. In my report, I also concluded that there was strong evidence of a conspiracy to obstruct justice between the President, Monica Lewinsky, and others "known and unknown"—a reference both to Lewinsky's false affidavit and to the other material in the secure room boxes that had not been made public. If we had gone to a real trial on the floor of the Senate, we would have brought forward other evidence and other individuals.

The President encouraged Lewinsky to lie, which is a felony. Moreover, we had substantial evidence of witness tampering, in particular with Betty Currie, Clinton's personal secretary.

The President was deposed in the Paula Jones case on Saturday, January 17, 1998. Monica Lewinsky had signed the false affidavit on January 7, and after a major scurry it was filed that Saturday morning, just before the President gave his deposition. If she hadn't filed the affidavit saying that nothing had happened, Clinton probably would have Mickey Moused around in his deposition. But now that Lewinsky was on record denying the relationship, he could assume she was on board.

But in the deposition, Clinton was suddenly being asked about Lewinsky. The questions must have indicated that somebody had been talking to Jones's people. One of the questions, in fact, was, "What would you say if Monica told someone that you had this relationship?" He played around it, but he must have thought that Monica had talked to someone, even though she had denied the relationship all along. As it turns out, of course, it was Linda Tripp. In any case, when he came out of the deposition, he had to find out what was going on.

So the very next day, a Sunday, he had Betty Currie come down to the White House to meet with him. That's when he told her, "I was never alone with her [Lewinsky], right?" He then instigated a flurry of telephone calls trying to get Lewinsky on her beeper. Currie left messages along the lines of "Family emergency, please call" and "Good news, please call." What Clinton didn't know was that Lewinsky had been grabbed by the Independent Counsel; she was not calling back except to tell Currie that she couldn't talk. We had a chart showing this round robin of calls that occurred over a period of two days and involved Betty Currie, the President, Vernon Jordan, and Monica Lewinsky. There were dozens of calls.

Before I had written my report, Lindsey Graham told a newsman that I was prepared to list a bunch of felonies. That was something I didn't want anyone to know. The next day we had a meeting with all the Republican members, and Henry made it abundantly clear that we should keep this stuff to ourselves, that he didn't want leaks because whatever was leaked would lose its impact. At the same time, I was getting calls from Abbe Lowell and the Democrats asking what I was going to say. But I wasn't talking. With my staff I prepared a draft outlining the report but minus the guts—the fifteen felonies I intended to incorporate. I gave the draft to Hyde, and he shared it with other Republicans, who came back with suggestions and questions. There were so many meetings hashing out what we would say that I went through eight drafts.

It was extremely frustrating, but I had twenty Republican Congressmen who were lawyers, most of whom had been prosecutors, and they all had great ideas. And plenty of others had ideas, too. But every day we had a leak to the newspaper. We were drowning in leaks.

Once I even received a message from Republican Congressman Dan Burton's Government Reform and Oversight Committee telling me that the latest draft had turned up on their computer, which meant it could be blasted all over the world! Thank God, it turned out not to be the latest draft, but a very early one with only a vague reference to felonies. But even some of the charts we were making to highlight certain testimony were leaked. Pretty soon the fact that we were looking at conspiracy was leaked. The fact that I had identified several felonies leaked. The fact that we'd taken the abuse of power off the table leaked. When I went back to my office after the seventh draft I threw it at the wall. "We've got to start over. We'll never get this son of a bitch done."

I started the eighth draft on October 3. Hyde wanted it the next day. I finished writing at about 3 PM, and we spent the rest of the day poring over every word, rechecking our references, and editing it.

The next morning, we had the text put in large type. I grabbed my copy and headed over to the committee room in the Rayburn Building to meet with twenty-one Republican members and various staff to brief them on the report.

After I finished, they started in on me, picking the whole thing apart. Again.

I was saved by Bill Jenkins, an old prosecutor from Tennessee: "Wait a minute, folks. Why don't you let this man alone? He has to go before the committee tomorrow, and he has to do what he does best. Why don't you let him do it?"

I think it was Steve Buyer who concurred first, and then they all backed off.

Hyde wrapped up by pleading with everyone not to leak anything, especially the information we had about the President's phone calls.

I said: "I'll make it easy. If I hear anything or see anything about those calls, I won't use them." This time, nothing leaked.

Hyde asked me to end the report with these words: "Whatever you decide, I will be prepared to work with you and under your jurisdiction or under your guidance if you decide to go forward." I didn't like it. Old trial lawyers like me always want to end with something that will grab the jury. A couple of weeks earlier my wife, Jackie, and I had been down at Fredericksburg, Virginia, and I had been wandering around in the military cemetery up on Mayre's Heights. There I came up with an idea to quote St. Thomas More. But I kept it out of my draft.

The next morning—October 5, 1998—just before my official presentation, I asked Hyde, "Would you mind terribly if I made a personal observation at the end?" and got his okay without telling him what it was.

As I walked to my seat, I was nervous. My hands were shaking. Here is what I said:

Mr. Chairman, Mr. Conyers, Members of the Committee, as Chief Investigative Counsel for the Majority, I have been called upon to advise the Judiciary Committee of the results of our analysis and review of the September 9, 1998, Referral from the Office of the Independent Counsel, in which it concluded that there is substantial and credible information that President William Jefferson Clinton committed acts that may constitute grounds for an impeachment.

In executing the task assigned to us, my staff and I have made a deliberate effort to discount the political aspects of our examination and to ignore any partisan tactics and strategy. The standard of review was set by me in our very first meeting following the delivery of the material. I reminded the staff that we are not advocates, but professionals asked to perform a professional, albeit distasteful duty. Therefore, I asked them to review the Referral and supporting data in the light most favorable to the President.

Throughout this effort we have been determined to avoid even the *suggestion* of preference. We view our responsibility as requiring an unbiased, full, and expeditious review, untrammeled by any preconceived notions or opinions. Our approach has been solely in keeping with constitutional and legal standards of fairness and impartiality.

Before moving on to the substantive areas of the report, I would like to address two elementary, but basic, concepts of our constitutional government. They will serve to put our conclusions in the proper perspective.

FIRST: The President of the United States enjoys a singular and appropriately lofty position in our system of government. But that position by its very nature involves equally unique and onerous responsibilities, among which are included affirmative obligations that apply to no other citizen.

Specifically, the Constitution of the United States imposes upon the President the *explicit* and affirmative duty to "take care that the laws be faithfully executed."

Moreover, before entering upon the duties of his office, the President is constitutionally commanded to take the following oath: "I do solemnly swear (or affirm) that I will faithfully execute the Office of President of the United States, and will to the best of my ability, preserve, protect, and defend the Constitution of the United States."

The President, then, is the chief law enforcement officer of the United States. Although he is neither above nor below the laws, he is, by virtue of his office, held to a higher standard than any other American. Furthermore, as Chief Executive Officer and Commander in Chief, he is the repository of a special trust.

SECOND: *Many* defendants who face legal action, whether it be civil or criminal, may honestly believe that the case against them is unwarranted and factually deficient. It is not, however, in the discretion of the litigant to decide that any tactics are justified to defeat the lawsuit in that situation. Rather, it is incumbent upon that individual to testify fully and truthfully during the truth-seeking phase. It is then the function of the system of law to expose the frivolous cases. The litigant may not with impunity mislead, deceive, or lie under oath in order to prevail in the lawsuit or for other personal gain. Any other result would be subversive of the American rule of law.

The principle that every witness in every case must tell the truth, the whole truth, and nothing *but* the truth, is the foundation of the American system of justice, which is the envy of every civilized nation. The sanctity of the oath taken by a witness is the most essential bulwark of the truth-seeking function of a trial, the American method of ascertaining the facts. If lying under oath is tolerated and, when exposed, is not visited with immediate and substantial adverse consequences, the integrity of this country's entire judicial process is fatally compromised and that process will inevitably collapse. The subject matter of the underlying case, whether civil or criminal, and the circumstances under which the testimony is given are of no significance whatever. It is the oath itself that is sacred and must be enforced.

The Independent Counsel Act provides in relevant part that: "An independent counsel shall advise the House of Representatives of any substantial and credible information that may constitute grounds for an impeachment."

In compliance with the statutory mandate, the Office of Independent Counsel Kenneth Starr informed the House of Representatives on September 9, 1998, that it was prepared to submit a referral under the statute. On that day, the Independent Counsel's Office delivered to the House the following material:

A Referral consisting of an Introduction, a Narrative of Relevant Events, and an Identification and Analysis of the Substantial and Credible Information that may support grounds for impeachment of William Jefferson Clinton;

An Appendix in six three-ring binders totaling in excess of 2,500 pages of the most relevant testimony and other material cited in the Referral;

Seventeen transmittal boxes containing grand jury transcripts, deposition transcripts, FBI reports, reports of interviews, and thousands of pages of incidental back-up documents.

Pursuant to House Resolution 525, all of this material was turned over to the Committee on the Judiciary to be held in Executive Session until September 28, 1998. At that time the House ordered that all materials be released to the public, except those which were withheld by action of the Committee.

My staff and the Minority staff were instructed by the Committee to review the Referral, together with all of the other evidence and testimony that was submitted, for the purpose of determining whether there actually existed "substantial and credible" evidence that President William Jefferson Clinton may have committed acts that constitute grounds to proceed to a resolution for an impeachment inquiry.

Because of the narrow scope of our directive, the investigation and the analysis were necessarily circumscribed by the information delivered with the Referral together with some information and analysis furnished by the counsel for the President. For that reason, we did not seek to procure any additional evidence or testimony from any other source. Particularly, we did not seek to obtain or review the material that remained in the possession of the OIC [Office of the Independent Counsel]. In two telephone conversations with Mr. [Bob] Bittman [of the OIC], Mr. Lowell and I were assured that the retained material was deemed unnecessary to comply with the statutory requirement under Section 595(c). Though Mr. Bittman offered to make available to both counsel all of that material, my staff and I did not deem it necessary or even proper to go beyond the submission itself.

At the suggestion of the Minority Counsel, the retained material was reviewed by members of both staffs. The material was, as anticipated, irrelevant.

To support the Referral, the House has been furnished with grand jury transcripts, FBI interview memoranda, transcripts of depositions, other interview memoranda, statements, audio recordings, and, where available, video recordings of all persons named in the Referral. In addition, the House was provided with a copy of every document cited and a mass of documentary and other evidence produced by witnesses, the White House, the President, the Secret Service, and the Department of Defense.

This report is confined solely to that Referral and supporting evidence and testimony supplied to the House and then to this Committee, supplemented only by the information provided by the

President's counsel. Although the original submission contained a transcript of the President's deposition testimony, no videotape was included. Pursuant to a request by Chairman Hyde, a videotape of the entire deposition was later provided to the Committee by the District Judge. Both that video and the video of the President's testimony before the grand jury have been thoroughly reviewed by all members of my staff and by me personally. Apart from the thorough review of President Clinton's deposition and grand jury testimony, the following functions were performed in preparation for this report:

• All grand jury transcripts and memoranda of interviews of Ms. Currie, Mr. Jordan, Ms. Lewinsky, the Secret Service agents, and Ms. Tripp were independently reviewed, compared, and analyzed by at least three members of the staff; and those of Ms. Currie, Mr. Jordan, Ms. Lewinsky, Ms. Tripp, and both appearances of the President by me personally.

• All of the remaining grand jury transcripts, deposition transcripts, and memoranda of the others interviewed were likewise reviewed, compared, and analyzed. This involved more than 250 separate documents, some consisting of hundreds of pages. In this regard, my staff was instructed to seek any information that might cast doubt upon the legal or factual conclusions of the Independent Counsel.

• The entire Appendix, consisting of in excess of two thousand pages, was systematically reviewed and analyzed against the statements contained in the Referral. I personally read the entire Evidence Reference and Legal Reference that accompanied the Referral. I analyzed the legal precepts and theories and read at least portions of each case cited.

• In addition to other members of the staff, I personally read and analyzed the eleven specific allegations made by the Independent Counsel and reviewed the evidentiary basis for those allegations. Each footnote supporting the charges was checked to insure that it did, in fact, support the underlying evidentiary proposition. In cases where relevant inferences were drawn in the body of the Referral, the validity of those inferences was tested under acceptable principles of federal trial practice.

• Each of the literally thousands of back-up documents was reviewed in order to insure that no relevant evidence had been overlooked.

• Meetings of the entire staff were conducted on virtually a daily basis for the purpose of coordinating efforts and synthesizing the divergent material into a coherent report.

Having completed all of the tasks assigned to us, we are now prepared to report our findings to you, the Members of this Committee. We are fully aware that the purpose of this Hearing is solely for the Committee to decide whether there is sufficient credible and substantial evidence to proceed to an impeachment inquiry. This and nothing more.

Of course, as Members of this Committee, you and only you are authorized and encouraged eventually to make your own independent judgment on what constitutes impeachable offenses and the standards of proof that might be applicable. My report, then, represents only a distillation and consensus of the staff's efforts and conclusions for your guidance and consideration.

At the outset, one point needs to be made. The witness Monica Lewinsky's credibility may be subject to some skepticism. At an appropriate stage of the proceedings, that credibility will, of necessity, be assessed together with the credibility of all witnesses in the light of all other evidence. Ms. Lewinsky admitted to having lied on occasion to Linda Tripp and to having executed and caused to be filed a false affidavit in the Paula Jones case.

On the other hand, Ms. Lewinsky obtained a grant of immunity for her testimony before the grand jury and, therefore, had no reason to lie thereafter. Furthermore, the witness's account of the relevant events could well have been much more damaging. For the most part, though, the record reflects that she was an embarrassed and reluctant witness who actually downplayed her White House encounters. In testifying, Ms. Lewinsky demonstrated a remarkable memory, supported by her personal diary, concerning dates and events. Finally, the record includes ample corroboration of her testimony by independent and disinterested witnesses, by documentary evidence, and, in part, by the grand jury testimony of the President himself. Consequently, for the limited purpose of this report, we suggest that Monica Lewinsky's testimony is both substantial and credible.

It has been the considered judgment of my staff and myself that our main focus should be on those alleged acts and omissions by the President which affect the rule of law and the structure and integrity of our court system. Deplorable as the numerous sexual encounters related in the evidence may be, we chose to emphasize the consequences of those acts as they affect the administration of justice and the unique role the President occupies in carrying out his oath faithfully to execute the laws of the nation.

The prurient aspect of the Referral is, at best, merely peripheral to the central issues. The assertions of presidential misconduct cited in the Referral, though arising initially out of sexual indiscretions, are completely distinct and involve allegations of an ongoing series of deliberate and direct assaults by Mr. Clinton upon the justice system of the United States and upon the Judicial Branch of our government, which holds a place in the constitutional framework of checks and balances equal to that of the Executive and the Legislative Branches.

As a result of our research and review of the Referral and supporting documentation, we respectfully submit that there exists substantial and credible evidence of fifteen separate events directly involving President William Jefferson Clinton that could constitute felonies which, in turn, may constitute grounds to proceed with an impeachment inquiry. I will now present the catalog of those charges, together with a brief statement of the evidence supporting each.

Please understand that nothing contained in this report is intended to constitute an accusation against the President or anyone else; nor should it be construed as such. What follows is nothing more than a litany of the crimes that *might have* been committed based upon the substantial and credible evidence provided by the Independent Counsel and reviewed, tested, and analyzed by the staff.

With that caution in mind, I will proceed:

I. There is substantial and credible evidence that the President may have been part of a conspiracy with Monica Lewinsky and others to obstruct justice and the due administration of justice by:

1) Providing false and misleading testimony under oath in a civil deposition and before the grand jury;

2) Withholding evidence and causing evidence to be withheld and concealed; and

3) Tampering with prospective witnesses in a civil lawsuit and before a federal grand jury.

The President and Ms. Lewinsky had developed a "cover story" to conceal their activities. On December 6, 1997, the President learned that Ms. Lewinsky's name had appeared on the *Jones* v. *Clinton* witness list. He informed Ms. Lewinsky of that fact on December 17, 1997, and the two agreed that they would employ the same cover story in the Jones case. The President at that time suggested that an affidavit might be enough to prevent Ms. Lewinsky from testifying. On December 19, 1997, Ms. Lewinsky was subpoenaed to give a deposition in the Jones case. Thereafter, the record tends to establish that the following events took place:

1) Ms. Lewinsky told Ms. Tripp that she would lie if called to testify and tried to convince Ms. Tripp to do the same.

2) Ms. Lewinsky attempted on several occasions to get Ms. Tripp to contact the White House before giving testimony in the Jones case.

3) Ms. Lewinsky participated in preparing a false and intentionally misleading affidavit to be filed in the Jones case.

4) Ms. Lewinsky provided a copy of the draft affidavit to a third party for approval and discussed changes calculated to mislead.

5) Ms. Lewinsky and the President talked by phone on January 6, 1998, and agreed that she would give false and misleading answers to questions about her job at the Pentagon.

6) On January 7, 1998, Ms. Lewinsky signed the false and misleading affidavit. Conspirators intended to use the affidavit to avoid Ms. Lewinsky's giving a deposition.

7) After Ms. Lewinsky's name surfaced, the conspirators began to employ code names in their contacts.

8) On December 28, 1997, Ms. Lewinsky and the President met at the White House and discussed the subpoena she had received. Ms. Lewinsky suggested that she conceal the gifts received from the President.

9) Shortly thereafter, the President's personal secretary, Betty Currie, picked up a box of the gifts from Ms. Lewinsky.

10) Betty Currie hid the box of gifts under her bed at home.

11) The President gave false answers to questions contained in interrogatories in the Jones case.

12) On December 31, 1997, Ms. Lewinsky, at the suggestion of a third party, deleted fifty draft notes to the President. She had already been subpoenaed in the Jones case.

13) On January 17, 1998, the President's attorney produced Ms. Lewinsky's false affidavit at the President's deposition and the President adopted it as true.

14) On January 17, 1998, in his deposition, the President gave false and misleading testimony under oath concerning his relationship with Ms. Lewinsky about the gifts she had given him and several other matters.

15) The President, on January 18, 1998, and thereafter, coached his personal secretary, Betty Currie, to give a false and misleading account of the Lewinsky relationship if called to testify.

16) The President narrated elaborate detailed false accounts of his relationship with Monica Lewinsky to prospective witnesses with the intention that those false accounts would be repeated in testimony.

17) On August 17, 1998, the President gave false and misleading testimony under oath to a federal grand jury on the following points: his relationship with Ms. Lewinsky, his testimony in the January 17, 1998, deposition, his conversations with various individuals, and his knowledge of Ms. Lewinsky's affidavit and its falsity.

At this point, I would like to illustrate some of the details concerning the events immediately before and after the President's deposition on January 17, 1998.

These facts appear in the record:

On January 7, 1998, Ms. Lewinsky signed the false affidavit, and it was furnished to Mr. Clinton's civil lawyer. The President reviewed it, so he knew that she had denied their relationship when the deposition began.

During the questioning, however, it became more and more apparent to the President that Ms. Jones's attorneys possessed a lot more specific detail than the President anticipated.

When the President returned to the White House, the calls began:

After completing his deposition testimony on Saturday, January 17, 1998, in the Jones case, the President and Vernon Jordan exchange three telephone calls. The President also calls Betty Currie and asks her to meet with him in the Oval Office the following day.

On Sunday, January 18, at a little after 6:00 in the morning, the President learns of the existence of the Linda Tripp tapes through the *Drudge Report*. At 11:49 AM, Vernon Jordan telephones the White House and, within forty minutes, meets Deputy White House Counsel Bruce Lindsey for lunch.

At approximately 1 PM, the President calls both Vernon Jordan and Betty Currie at their homes. Between 2:15 and 2:55 PM, records show that Vernon Jordan places one call to the White House and one call to the President. At 5 PM, the President meets with Betty Currie. In that meeting, the President informs Ms. Currie that he had been questioned at his deposition about Monica Lewinsky.

During the next three hours and sixteen minutes, Betty Currie places four pages to Monica Lewinsky requesting that Monica call "Kay," a previously agreed-upon code name used by Ms. Currie and Ms. Lewinsky. At 10:09 PM, Monica Lewinsky telephones Betty Currie at home. At 11:02 PM, the President telephones Betty Currie at home as well. That evening, Vernon Jordan calls Deputy White House Counsel Cheryl Mills.

Although the following day, Monday, January 19, 1998, was a national holiday honoring Martin Luther King, the flurry of activity continues. Between 7:02 and 8:33 AM, Betty Currie places three pages to Monica Lewinsky instructing her to "Please call Kay." When Ms. Currie receives no response, she places another page four minutes later stating, "Please call Kay at home. It's a social call. Thank you." Four minutes after that page, Ms. Currie pages Monica again with the message "Kay is at home. Please call." Ms. Currie receives no response to either of those pages.

Two minutes later, Betty Currie telephones the President from her home. Immediately following her phone call to the President, Ms. Currie places another page to Ms. Lewinsky telling her to "Please call Kay, Re: Family Emergency." At 8:50 AM, six minutes later, the President calls Ms. Currie at home. Immediately after the phone call from the President, Ms. Currie once again pages Monica and states, "Msg. from Kay. Please call, have good news."

Six minutes after the President calls Ms. Currie at her home, he places a call to Vernon Jordan at his home. During a twenty-four–minute time span, from 10:29 to 10:53 AM, Vernon Jordan places five calls.

Three of those calls are placed to the White House, one of which is to Deputy Assistant to the President Nancy Hernreich and one to White House Chief of Staff Erskine Bowles. Mr. Jordan also pages Monica Lewinsky, instructing her to call him at his office. Mr. Jordan's final call in this time period is to Ms. Lewinsky's attorney, Frank Carter. After Mr. Jordan concludes his call to Carter, he receives a phone call from the President.

Between 11:04 and 11:17 AM, Vernon Jordan places two calls to Deputy White House Counsel Bruce Lindsey. Mr. Jordan again pages Monica Lewinsky with the message, "Please call Mr. Jordan." At 12:31 PM, Mr. Jordan uses his cellular phone to, once again, contact the White House.

At 1:45 PM, the President telephones Betty Currie at home. At 2:29 PM, Vernon Jordan again telephones the White House from a cellular phone and then enters the White House fifteen minutes later. Once at the White House, Mr. Jordan meets with President Clinton, Erskine Bowles, Bruce Lindsey, Cheryl Mills, White House Counsel [Charles] Ruff, Rahm Emanuel, and others. At 2:46 PM, Frank Carter pages Monica and requests her to "Please call Frank Carter."

Beginning at 4:51 PM, the next one hour and four minutes show Vernon Jordan placing fourteen calls. Six of those calls are to Bruce Lindsey, three are to Frank Carter, two are to Cheryl Mills, one is to Charles Ruff, and two are to Betty Currie. At 5:56 PM, the President telephones Jordan at his office. Eight minutes later, Mr.

Jordan telephones Betty Currie at her home. Finally, at 6:26 PM, Vernon telephones presidential aide Stephen Goodin.

II. There is substantial and credible evidence that the President may have aided, abetted, counseled, and procured Monica Lewinsky to file and caused to be filed a false affidavit in the case of *Jones* v. *Clinton, et al.*

The record tends to establish the following:

In a telephone conversation with Ms. Lewinsky on December 17, 1997, the President told her that her name was on the witness list in the Jones case. The President then suggested that she might submit an affidavit to avoid testimony. Both the President and Ms. Lewinsky knew that the affidavit would *need to be* false in order to accomplish that result. In that conversation, the President also suggested, "You know, you can always say you were coming to see Betty or that you were bringing me letters." Ms. Lewinsky knew exactly what he meant because it was the same "cover story" that they had agreed upon earlier.

Thereafter, Ms. Lewinsky discussed the affidavit with and furnished a copy to a confidant of the President for approval. Ms. Lewinsky signed the false affidavit and caused her attorney to provide it to the President's lawyer for use in the Jones case.

III. There is substantial and credible evidence that the President may have aided, abetted, counseled, and procured Monica Lewinsky in obstruction of justice when she executed and caused to be filed a false affidavit in the case of *Jones* v. *Clinton, et al.*, with knowledge of the pending proceedings and with the intent to influence, obstruct, or impede that proceeding in the due administration of justice.

The record tends to establish that the President not only aided and abetted Monica Lewinsky in preparing, signing, and causing to be filed a false affidavit, he also aided and abetted her in using that false affidavit to obstruct justice.

Both Ms. Lewinsky and the President knew that her false affidavit would be used to mislead the Plaintiff's attorneys and the court. Specifically, they intended that the affidavit would be sufficient to avoid Ms. Lewinsky being required to give a deposition in the Jones case. Moreover, it was the natural and probable effect of the false statement that it would interfere with the due administration of justice. If the court and the Jones attorneys were convinced by the affidavit, there would be no deposition of Ms. Lewinsky, and the Plaintiff's attorneys would be denied the ability to learn about material facts and to decide whether to introduce evidence of those facts.

Mr. Clinton caused his attorney to employ the knowingly false affidavit not only to avoid Ms. Lewinsky's deposition, but to preclude the attorneys from interrogating the President about the same subject.

IV. There is substantial and credible evidence that the President may have engaged in misprision of Monica Lewinsky's felonies of submitting a false affidavit and of obstructing the due administration of justice both by taking affirmative steps to conceal those felonies, and by failing to disclose the felonies though under a constitutional and statutory duty to do so.

The record tends to establish the following:

Monica Lewinsky admitted to the commission of two felonies:

Signing a false affidavit under oath, and endeavoring to obstruct justice by using the false affidavit to mislead the court and the lawyers in the Jones case so that she would not be deposed and be required to give evidence concerning her activities with the President. In addition, the President was fully aware that those felonies had been committed when he gave his deposition testimony on January 1998.

Nonetheless, Mr. Clinton took affirmative steps to conceal these felonies, including allowing his attorney, in his presence, to use the affidavit and to suggest that it was true. More importantly, the President himself, while being questioned by his own counsel referring to one of the clearly false paragraphs in Ms. Lewinsky's affidavit, stated, "That is absolutely true."

More importantly, the President is the chief law enforcement officer of the United States. He is under a constitutional duty to take care that the laws be faithfully executed. When confronted with direct knowledge of the commission of a felony, he is required by his office, as is every other law enforcement officer, agent, or attorney, to bring to the attention of the appropriate authorities the fact of the felony and the identity of the perpetrator. If he did not do so, the President could be guilty of misprision of felony.

V. There is substantial and credible evidence that the President may have testified falsely under oath in his deposition in *Jones* v. *Clinton, et al.*, January 17, 1998, regarding his relationship with Monica Lewinsky.

The record tends to establish the following:

There are three instances where credible evidence exists that the President may have testified falsely about this relationship:

1) When he denied a "sexual relationship" in sworn answers to interrogatories;

2) When he denied having an "extramarital sexual affair" in his deposition; and

3) When he denied having "sexual relations" or "an affair" with Monica Lewinsky in his deposition.

When the President denied a sexual relationship he was not bound by the definition the court had provided. There is substantial evidence obtained from Ms. Lewinsky, the President's grand jury testimony, and DNA test results that Ms. Lewinsky performed sexual acts with the President on numerous occasions. Those terms, given their common meaning, could reasonably be construed to include oral sex. The President also denied having sexual relations with Ms. Lewinsky, as the court defined the term. In the context of the lawsuit and the wording of that definition, there is substantial evidence that the President's explanation given to the grand jury is an afterthought and is unreasonably narrow under the circumstances. Consequently, there is substantial evidence that the President's denial under oath in his deposition of a "sexual relationship," a "sexual affair," or "sexual relations" with Ms. Lewinsky was not true.

VI. There is substantial and credible evidence that the President may have given false testimony under oath before the federal grand jury on August 17, 1998, concerning his relationship with Monica Lewinsky.

The record tends to establish the following:

During his grand jury testimony, the President admitted only to "inappropriate intimate contact" with Monica Lewinsky. He did not admit to any specific acts.

He categorically denied ever touching Ms. Lewinsky on the breasts or genitalia for the purpose of giving her sexual gratification. There is, however, substantial contradictory evidence from Ms. Lewinsky. She testified at length and with specificity that the President kissed and fondled her breasts on numerous occasions during their encounters, and at times there was also direct genital contact. Moreover, testimony is corroborated by friends. The President described himself as a non-reciprocating recipient of Ms. Lewinsky's services. Therefore, he suggested that he did not engage in "sexual relations" within the definition given him at the Jones case deposition.

He also testified that his interpretation of the word "cause" in the definition meant the use of force or contact with the intent to arouse or gratify. The inference drawn by the Independent Counsel that the President's explanation was merely an afterthought, calculated to explain away testimony that had been proved false by Ms. Lewinsky's evidence, appears credible under the circumstances.

VII. There is substantial and credible evidence that the President may have given false testimony under oath in his deposition given in *Jones* v. *Clinton, et al.*, on January 17, 1998, regarding his statement that he could not recall being alone with Monica Lewinsky and regarding his minimizing the number of gifts that they had exchanged.

The record tends to establish the following:

President Clinton testified at his deposition that he had "no specific recollection" of being alone with Ms. Lewinsky in any room at the White House.

There is ample evidence from other sources to the contrary. They include: Betty Currie; Monica Lewinsky; several Secret Service agents; and White House logs. Moreover, the President testified in the grand jury that he was "alone" with Ms. Lewinsky in 1996 and 1997 and that he had a "specific recollection" of certain instances when he was alone with her. He admitted to the grand jury that he was alone with her on December 28, 1997, only three weeks prior to his deposition testimony.

The President was also asked at this deposition whether he had ever given gifts to Ms. Lewinsky. He responded, "I don't recall." He then asked the Jones attorney if he knew what they were. After the attorney named specific gifts, the President finally remembered giving Ms. Lewinsky something from the Black Dog. That testimony was given less than three weeks after Ms. Currie had picked up a box of the President's gifts and hidden them under her bed.

In his grand jury testimony nearly seven months later, he admitted giving Ms. Lewinsky Christmas gifts on December 28, 1997, and "on other occasions." When confronted with his lack of memory at his deposition, the President responded that his statement "I don't recall" referred to the identity of specific gifts, not whether or not he actually gave her gifts.

The President also testified at his deposition that Ms. Lewinsky gave him gifts "once or twice." Ms. Lewinsky says that she gave a substantial number of gifts to the President. This is corroborated by gifts turned over by Ms. Lewinsky to the Independent Counsel and by a letter to the Independent Counsel from the President's attorney acknowledging that certain gifts given by Monica Lewinsky to the President could not be located.

Thus, there is substantial and credible evidence that the President may have testified falsely about being alone with Monica Lewinsky and the gifts he gave to her.

VIII. There is substantial and credible evidence that the President may have testified falsely under oath in his deposition given in *Jones* v. *Clinton, et al.*, on January 17, 1998, concerning conversations with Monica Lewinsky about her involvement in the Jones case.

The record tends to reflect the following:

The President was asked at his deposition if he ever talked to Ms. Lewinsky about the possibility that she would testify in the Jones case.

He answered, "I'm not sure." He then related a conversation with Ms. Lewinsky where he joked about how the Jones attorneys would probably subpoena every female witness with whom he has ever spoken. He was also asked whether Ms. Lewinsky told him that she had been subpoenaed. The answer was, "No, I don't know if she had been."

There is substantial evidence—much from the President's own grand jury testimony—that those statements are false. The President testified before the grand jury that he spoke with Ms. Lewinsky at the White House on December 28, 1997, about the "prospect that she might have to give testimony." He also later testified that Vernon Jordan told him on December 19, 1997 that Ms. Lewinsky had been subpoenaed. Mr. Jordan also recalled telling the same thing to the President twice on December 19, 1997, once over the telephone and once in person. Despite his deposition testimony, the President admitted that he knew Ms. Lewinsky had been subpoenaed when he met her on December 28, 1997. There is substantial and credible evidence that his statement that he was "not sure" if he spoke with Ms. Lewinsky about her testimony is false.

IX. There is substantial and credible evidence that the President may have endeavored to obstruct justice by engaging in a pattern of activity calculated to conceal evidence from the judicial proceedings in *Jones* v. *Clinton, et al.*, regarding his relationship with Monica Lewinsky.

The record tends to establish that on Sunday, December 28, 1997, the President gave Ms. Lewinsky Christmas gifts in the Oval Office during a visit arranged by Ms. Currie. According to Ms. Lewinsky, when she suggested that the gifts he had given her should be concealed because they were the subject of a subpoena, the President stated, "I don't know" or "Let me think about that."

Ms. Lewinsky testified that Ms. Currie contacted her at home several hours later and stated, "I understand you have something to give me," or "the President said you have something to give me." Later that same day, Ms. Currie picked up a box of gifts from Ms. Lewinsky's home.

The evidence indicates that the President may have instructed Ms. Currie to conceal evidence. The President has denied giving that instruction, and he contended under oath that he advised Ms. Lewinsky to provide all of the gifts to the Jones attorneys pursuant to the subpoena. In contrast, Ms. Lewinsky testified that the

President never challenged her suggestion that the gifts should be concealed.

X. There is substantial and credible evidence that the President may have endeavored to obstruct justice in the case of *Jones* v. *Clinton, et al.*, by agreeing with Monica Lewinsky on a cover story about their relationship, by causing a false affidavit to be filed by Ms. Lewinsky, and by giving false and misleading testimony in the deposition given on January 17, 1998.

The record tends to establish that the President and Ms. Lewinsky agreed on false explanations for her private visits to the Oval Office. Ms. Lewinsky testified that when the President contacted her and told her that she was on the Jones witness list, he advised her that she could always repeat these cover stories, and he suggested that she file an affidavit. After this conversation, Ms. Lewinsky filed a false affidavit. The President learned of Ms. Lewinsky's affidavit prior to his deposition in the Jones case.

Subsequently, during his deposition, the President stated that he never had a sexual relationship or affair with Ms. Lewinsky. He further stated that the paragraph in Ms. Lewinsky's affidavit denying a sexual relationship with the President was "absolutely true," even though his attorney had argued that the affidavit covered "sex of any kind in any manner, shape, or form."

XI. There is substantial and credible evidence that the President may have endeavored to obstruct justice by helping Monica Lewinsky to obtain a job in New York City at a time when she would have given evidence adverse to Mr. Clinton if she told the truth in the case of *Jones* v. *Clinton*.

The record tends to establish the following:

In October 1997, the President and Ms. Lewinsky discussed the possibility of Vernon Jordan assisting Ms. Lewinsky in finding a job in New York. On November 5, 1997, Mr. Jordan and Ms. Lewinsky discussed employment possibilities, and Mr. Jordan told her that she came "highly recommended."

However, no significant action was taken on Ms. Lewinsky's behalf until December, when the Jones attorneys identified Ms. Lewinsky as a witness. Within days after Mr. Jordan again met with Ms. Lewinsky, he contacted a number of people in the private sector who could help Ms. Lewinsky find work in New York.

Additional evidence indicates that on the day Ms. Lewinsky signed a false affidavit denying a sexual relationship with the President, Mr. Jordan contacted the President and discussed the affidavit.

The next day, Ms. Lewinsky interviewed with MacAndrews & Forbes, an interview arranged with Mr. Jordan's assistance. When Ms. Lewinsky told Mr. Jordan that the interview went poorly, Mr. Jordan contacted the CEO of MacAndrews & Forbes. The following day, Ms. Lewinsky was offered the job, and Mr. Jordan contacted the White House with the message "mission accomplished." In sum, Mr. Jordan secured a job for Ms. Lewinsky with a phone call placed on the day after Ms. Lewinsky signed a false affidavit protecting the President. Evidence indicates that this timing was not coincidental.

XII. There is substantial and credible evidence that the President may have testified falsely under oath in his deposition given in

Jones v. *Clinton, et al.* on January 17, 1998, concerning his conversations with Vernon Jordan about Ms. Lewinsky.

The record tends to establish that Mr. Jordan and the President discussed Ms. Lewinsky on various occasions from the time she was served [the subpoena] until she fired Mr. [Frank] Carter [as her lawyer] and hired Mr. [William] Ginsburg. This is contrary to the President's deposition testimony. The President was asked in his deposition whether anyone besides his attorney told him that Ms. Lewinsky had been served.

"I don't think so," he responded. He then said that Bruce Lindsey was the first person who told him. In the grand jury, the President was specifically asked if Mr. Jordan informed him that Ms. Lewinsky was under subpoena. "No sir," he answered. Later in the testimony, when confronted with the date [the evening of December 19, 1997], the President admitted that he spoke with Mr. Jordan about the subpoena.

Both the President and Mr. Jordan testified in the grand jury that Mr. Jordan informed the President on January 7 that Ms. Lewinsky had signed the affidavit. Ms. Lewinsky said she too informed the President of the subpoena.

The President was also asked during his deposition if anyone [had] reported to him within the past two weeks [from January 17, 1998] that they had a conversation with Monica Lewinsky concerning the lawsuit. The President said, "I don't think so." As noted, Mr. Jordan told the President on January 7, 1998, that Ms. Lewinsky signed the affidavit. In addition, the President was asked if he [had] had a conversation with Mr. Jordan where Ms. Lewinsky's name was mentioned. He said, yes, that Mr. Jordan mentioned that she asked for advice about moving to New York. Actually, the President had conversations with Mr. Jordan concerning three general subjects: choosing an attorney to represent Ms. Lewinsky after she had been subpoenaed; Ms. Lewinsky's subpoena and the contents of her executed affidavit; and Vernon Jordan's success in procuring a New York job for Ms. Lewinsky.

XIII. There is substantial and credible evidence that the President may have endeavored to obstruct justice and engage in witness tampering in attempting to coach and influence the testimony of Betty Currie before the grand jury.

The record tends to establish the following:

According to Ms. Currie, the President contacted her on the day he was deposed in the Jones case and asked her to meet him the following day. The next day, Ms. Currie met with the President, and he asked her whether she agreed with a series of possibly false statements, including, "We were never really alone," "You could always see and hear everything," and "Monica came on to me, and I never touched her, right?" Ms. Currie stated that the President's tone and demeanor indicated that he wanted her to agree with these statements. According to Ms. Currie, the President called her into the Oval Office several days later and reiterated his previous statements using the same tone and demeanor. Ms. Currie later stated that she felt she was free to disagree with the President.

The President testified concerning those statements before the grand jury, and he did not deny that he made them. Rather, the President testified that in some of the statements he was referring only to meetings with Ms. Lewinsky in 1997, and that he intended the word "alone" to mean the entire Oval Office complex.

XIV. There is substantial and credible evidence that the President may have engaged in witness tampering by coaching prospective witnesses and by narrating elaborate detailed false accounts of his relationship with Ms. Lewinsky as if those stories were true, intending that the witnesses believe the story and testify to it before a grand jury.

John Podesta, the President's Deputy Chief of Staff, testified that the President told him that he did not have sex with Ms. Lewinsky "in any way whatsoever" and "that they had not had oral sex." Mr. Podesta repeated these statements to the grand jury.

Sidney Blumenthal, an Assistant to the President, said the President told him more detailed stories. He testified that the President told him that Ms. Lewinsky, who the President claimed had a reputation as a stalker, came at him, made sexual demands of him, and threatened him, but he rebuffed her. Mr. Blumenthal further testified that the President told him that he could recall placing only one call to Ms. Lewinsky. Mr. Blumenthal mentioned to the President that there were press reports that he, the President, had made telephone calls to Ms. Lewinsky, and also left voice mail messages. The President then told Mr. Blumenthal that he remembered calling Ms. Lewinsky after Betty Currie's brother died.

XV. There is substantial and credible evidence that the President may have given false testimony under oath before the federal grand jury on August 17, 1998, concerning his knowledge of the contents of Monica Lewinsky's affidavit and his knowledge of remarks made in his presence by his counsel.

The record tends to establish the following:

During the deposition, the President's attorney attempted to thwart questions pertaining to Ms. Lewinsky by citing her affidavit and asserting to the court that the affidavit represents that there "is absolutely no sex of any kind, in any manner, shape, or form, with President Clinton." At several points in his grand jury testimony, the President maintained that he cannot be held responsible for this representation made by his lawyer because he was not paying attention to the interchange between his lawyer and the court. The videotape of the deposition shows the President apparently listening intently to the interchange. In addition, Mr. Clinton's counsel represented to the court that the President was fully aware of the affidavit and its contents.

The President's own attorney asked him during the deposition whether Ms. Lewinsky's affidavit denying a sexual relationship was "true and accurate." The President was unequivocal; he said, "This is absolutely true." Ms. Lewinsky later said the affidavit contained false and misleading statements. The President explained to the grand jury that Ms. Lewinsky may have believed that her affidavit was true if she believed "sexual relationship" meant intercourse. However, counsel did not ask the President if Ms. Lewinsky thought it was true; he asked the President if it was, in fact, a true statement.

The President was bound by the court's definition at that point, and under his own interpretation of that definition, Ms. Lewinsky engaged in sexual relations. An affidavit denying this, by the President's own interpretation of the definition, is false.

That is my report to this Committee. The guiding object of our efforts over the past three weeks has been to search for the truth. We felt it our obligation to follow the facts and the law wherever they might lead, fairly and impartially. If this Committee sees fit to proceed to the next level of inquiry, we will continue to do so under your guidance.

When I finished, I looked at Henry Hyde and said, "Mr. Chairman, I wonder if I might be allowed to make a personal observation?"

"Certainly."

What I did not know was that I was reporting as an employee of the committee. As a consequence, I had no right whatsoever to make any personal statements without being subpoenaed. I saw the Republican staffers starting to choke. But the Democrats were reading, not even listening to me.

"I am speaking no longer as Chief Investigative Counsel, but rather as a citizen of the United States who happens to be a father and a grandfather. To paraphrase St. Thomas More in Robert Bolt's excellent play *A Man for All Seasons*, the laws of this country are the great barriers that protect the citizens from the winds of evil and tyranny. If we are to permit one of those laws to fall, who will be able to stand in the gusts that will follow?"

A few Democrats finally looked up.

"You are not being watched only by the individuals in this room or even by the immense television audience throughout the world; fifteen generations of our fellow Americans, many of whom are reposing in military cemeteries throughout the world, are looking down upon and judging what you do today. Thank you, Mr. Chairman."

I got up and walked out.

Without my knowledge, as I went back to the committee lounge, Congresswoman Maxine Waters angrily hissed at Chairman Hyde, "Why didn't you stop him?"

Hyde calmed her down with the assurance that my final remark would be stricken.

Later, Bob Barr read my statement into the committee record.

I realized after giving my report the advantages of going last, because Abbe Lowell, who followed me, had the perfect opportunity to try to dismiss our report.

The debate now was whether there needed to be an inquiry in the full House of Representatives. Were there grounds for an impeachment trial? To my total shock, the Democrats on the Judiciary Committee voted right down the party line against even an inquiry. To my mind that was insanity given the existence of overwhelming evidence.

Even though some of them had not even bothered to look at the evidence, I still thought I saw signs that at least three, maybe five, committee Democrats would vote to hold an inquiry: Howard Berman of California, Tom Barrett of Wisconsin, Chuck Schumer of New York, maybe even Barney Frank of Massachusetts and Michigan's John Conyers, the ranking member and an honorable man who had been on the committee during the Watergate hearings.

During his closing statement following my address, Abbe Lowell said, "[T]his inquiry is not on whether [the President's] statements were or were not truthful, but what were their context, what were their impact, what were their subject matter?"

I reject that logic. I do not care what you are lying about. If you're the President of the United States and you lie under oath, you should be removed from office.

But my fellow Democrats voted unanimously to put the President above the law.

They affirmed that a Democratic president can get away with lying, obstructing justice, and doing anything necessary to stay in office, even if it means destroying the legal underpinning of our political system.

They treated the legal rights of a private citizen—Paula Jones—as a trifle to be brushed aside.

They treated Lady Justice as though she were a harlot.

And they should be held accountable where it hurts—at the ballot box—by Americans who believe that truth matters, that we live by the rule of law, and that justice should be done.

CHAPTER 6

Gut Check

The Republicans had enough votes on the Judiciary Committee to authorize an inquiry. The next step was to have the full House pass a similar resolution, which it did on October 8, 1998, by a vote of 258 to 176, including 31 Democrats who joined the Republican majority. We were authorized to pursue an open-ended inquiry into whether the House should impeach the President over a wide range of possible offenses going far beyond the Starr material. Although the resolution placed no time limits on the investigation, Hyde, at a news conference following the vote, suggested that we would try to complete our task by the end of the year. We knew that the time estimate was unrealistic if we were to do our job properly, but it was also an olive branch to bipartisanship. On the night of October 8, we went home assuming we had a wide-open mandate to investigate possible impeachable offenses and could always extend Hyde's time limit.

Almost immediately, our optimism was dampened. We were told to lie low until after the election. The Republican leadership had concluded that the Democrats couldn't win the midterm election in November. But the Republicans could lose it and wanted to avoid controversy. We were assured we'd have plenty of time after the election to do our job.

But in reality, we wasted almost a month of the short time we did have.

Before we were told to lie low until after the election, I had told Hyde we intended to expand the investigation into Filegate, the potentially unlawful procurement of raw FBI files on literally hundreds of people and the use of that material by the White House. In addition, we wanted to look into campaign finance issues and what later became known as "Chinagate"—that is, the allegedly illegal receipt of campaign funds from the Chinese military and high officials of the Communist Party in China. We also wanted to investigate some possible abuses of power by the President and White House personnel.

I told Hyde we should be done by about May or June of 1999, and that, according to our research, an impeachment inquiry could legally be carried over from one Congress to the next. It also seemed that we were gaining support in the Senate, where we felt some Democrats, such as Robert Byrd of West Virginia, Joseph Lieberman of Connecticut, Russell

Feingold of Wisconsin, and Mary Landrieu of Louisiana, might vote to remove the President on the basis of Starr's evidence. With the Republicans expected to pick up seats, and some Democrats moving in our direction, we thought we were developing a winning case.

Meanwhile, in what in hindsight was a brilliant move, the Democrats had decided to turn the President's sexual proclivities into a plus. They attacked the Republicans as sex- and impeachment-obsessed, and trumpeted the President's announcement the week before the election that there would be a federal government surplus for the first time in a generation.

The stock market was booming, unemployment was low, and the country simply didn't want to mess with a good thing. On Election Day, November 3, instead of picking up seats in the House, the Republicans lost five, leaving them with a razor-thin majority. In the Senate they held their own but lost big races in California and New York. Exit polls showed that two out of every three Americans opposed impeaching the President.

Now the primary question in the minds of my staff members was whether the whole impeachment inquiry would be scrapped.

Then lightning struck. Newt Gingrich resigned not only the Speakership but also the seat to which he had just been reelected.

Finally, the Republicans settled on Bob Livingston, who was in his eleventh term from Louisiana, to be the new

Speaker. Of course, he too would eventually fall, resigning before the final impeachment vote in the House. His resignation underlined the irony that the impeachment proceedings seemed to claim only Republican victims.

During the second week of November, the Republicans on the committee met in the Judiciary lounge for the first time since the election. All the committee members were there, several staffers, and most of my crew. The mood was somber. Hyde told us that the new leadership wanted to start fresh in the 106th Congress. "I have been told in no uncertain terms that we need to finish the inquiry, take it to the floor, and get it voted up or down before the Christmas recess."

If the Judiciary Committee didn't expedite the inquiry, Hyde would be replaced as chairman or the inquiry would be deep-sixed. The message was clear. The election results and the President's poll numbers had turned the House Republican leadership's backbone to mush. My staff now had only a little more than a month to wind up all investigations, prepare the witnesses and evidence for a full hearing, brief the members for the hearing, and prepare for a debate and vote in the full House. Our infant inquiries into Chinagate, Filegate, Travelgate (the firing of White House Travel Office staffers, possibly in an effort to give business to a Friend of Bill), and other possible offenses were abandoned. We would focus exclusively on the evidence of a conspiracy to obstruct justice, lie, suborn perjury, tamper with witnesses, bribe, threaten, falsify documents, and abuse the power of the Presidency to deny Paula Jones her constitutional right to her day in court. We agreed that we had more than enough evidence both from Starr and from our independent investigations to establish, in a hearing, probable cause to impeach the President.

Tom Schippers and Pete Wacks suggested that at least two of the open investigations should be pursued, both of which concerned what we called "the China Connection." Given enough time, we intended to delve deeper into money reportedly given to the Democratic National Committee and the Clinton Defense Fund from the Chinese military and high government offices. We then wanted to investigate what, if anything, the Chinese had gotten in return, and whether there had been any impact on the security of the United States. Now, under the gun, it would be impossible to do a fair and thorough job. Tom said that minimal due diligence required that we at least look at the Justice Department reports from FBI Director Louis Freeh and prosecutor Charles LaBella. Depending on what we found, we would perhaps then be able to convince even the poll-driven leadership to give us more time. It would only take a few hours to read and analyze both reports, if we could get full versions of them, and then to determine whether we should try to go further.

Another issue with possible security implications was the President's reported phone sex. Almost every phone line in the White House is totally secure. But if, as Lewinsky testified under oath, the President was engaging in tawdry phone sex, he was on an unsecure line, opening the question of whether a foreign power might have intercepted and recorded these calls, which was a chilling possibility given the potential for blackmail.

We were eager to pursue these leads because we were still under the naive belief that the Democrats would put principles above politics and that if we got a break on Filegate or Chinagate, they would want the truth. We had hope. As it turned out, that's all we had.

Not long after, I was summoned to a caucus of the Republican members in the majority lounge.

Shortly before the meeting, I'd gotten word that a schedule for the impeachment hearing had been developed and would be announced to the committee Republicans that afternoon. But when my staff tried to get the schedule faxed over to us, one of the Judiciary staffers said he had been told that we were not to be given a copy.

In all the time I had been in Washington, this was the first instance in which we had been denied access to any committee material or plans. Here was a schedule of events in which we were to take part, and we weren't permitted to see it. I told my staff that there must have been some mistake, because we certainly would have been asked for our input, and that I'd clear it up at the meeting.

Hyde began the meeting by reminding us again of the strict time constraints, then said, "If we get impeachment articles out of the committee, that's the best we will ever do with this President."

Most of the people in the room nodded in the affirmative, and Hyde went on, "You must have all been given a copy of the schedule...." At that point I raised my hand to speak. Hyde recognized me, and I told him that I did not have a copy of any schedule. I said we had asked for one that morning but had been informed that we were not to be given a copy.

Hyde looked puzzled. "Nobody is keeping anything from you, Dave," Majority Counsel Tom Mooney said. "I honestly thought that you already had seen this." With that, one of the staffers gave me his copy.

One look told me why I had not been given an opportunity to review the schedule prior to the meeting. There was to be no real hearing, just a short show for the media. The time given to complete everything was sliced to just a percentage of what we had thought we would have. It was obvious to me that, with this schedule, the Chairman was correct: We would be fortunate if any articles were voted out of the committee, and there would be little chance that impeachment would ever be voted on in the full House.

The Democrats will be very happy, I thought. The White House will be deliriously happy! The media and the President's supporters will vilify the Republicans and tell the world that it really was a "vast right-wing conspiracy."

As I seethed, the meeting continued. Hyde emphasized, "We are not going to put a bunch of witnesses on the stand

and go over the Lewinsky situation. We don't need any more sex material before the committee. They are already saying the Republicans are obsessed with sex. The Democrats will be all over us, and the White House spin-meisters will have a field day. So we will confine ourselves to hearing one witness, Ken Starr."

This was a dangerous move. Starr had been a judge, but he had never testified at a trial, and the White House, the Democrats, and the mainstream media had demonized him in the public mind. Hyde told us that Starr would appear before the committee in about a week. He would testify for one day.

"Then we can have final arguments by Dave and Abbe and the President's counsel, if he wants to be heard. We will debate any articles and have the committee vote on those articles before the Thanksgiving recess. The House vote will then be scheduled for December. No doubt we will lose in that vote. Then we can all go home for Christmas and come back to a new Congress."

Thanksgiving was only two weeks away. There was no way we could get our evidence together in that time. Worse, I had just been told that I would have no witnesses except Judge Starr, and that I could develop no other evidence. All of the work my staff had done for five months had been wasted.

Again I raised my hand to speak.

"Mr. Chairman, some months ago you asked me if I would be willing to put together a team that would be capable of conducting a thorough impeachment inquiry. I did that. I have the most dedicated and competent group of professionals over at the Ford Building. They have worked day and night to put together a full investigation and to develop witnesses and evidence. You will never know the sacrifices that they have made. They have suffered seriously in their finances and they are exhausted. Now you are going to put on a half-assed show and turn your back on these people. What the hell am I going to say to them? My God, are the polls going to call all the shots? We are on the brink of finding dynamite, but now we won't have a chance."

Hyde said that he'd consider changing the schedule, if necessary.

But Lindsey Graham—speaking as a political realist— was pessimistic. There was simply no time to get more evidence, and nothing, he said, could change the polls that were dead-set against us.

But the next day, at another meeting of Republican committee members, Jim Rogan of California was the voice of courage:

"You know, my race [for reelection] was probably one of the ones in which the whole question of what we are doing here was a major issue. No, it was actually the *only* issue. I was attacked by my opponent constantly for being involved in the impeachment. I won with a 50.2 percent vote, but I won! The people of my district sent me here to do my duty and by God, I'm going to do it. We are not surrogates; we are Representatives. We have to be worthy of our office.

We have to be prepared to lose our seats if that results from doing our duty. A man who once sat in the Senate told me that one must put honor above politics and principle above incumbency. I have to believe him!"

Rogan was talking my language. One by one other Republicans stood up and agreed with him.

From that moment on there was no question that my staff and I were associated with twenty-one of the most courageous and decent people on the American political scene. When I told my staff about the meeting, Jeff Pavletic said, "Well, now it's up to us to be worthy of them."

We had a new life and a new goal.

CHAPTER 7

Contemptible Behavior

As our deadline approached, we still wanted to expand our inquiry beyond Monica Lewinsky. I asked Jeff Pavletic to find out what other information the Office of the Independent Counsel would be willing to release to us. We knew that much of it would be off-limits—if it might hinder or compromise an ongoing criminal investigation—but we were finding too many clues that suggested a much bigger conspiracy to obstruct justice.

We were right.

The Independent Counsel's Office sent over two large file boxes—one for the Democrats and an identical one for us. It was stuffed with transcripts of grand jury testimony, witness interviews, and FBI reports.

There was information about alleged hush money pay-offs to Webster Hubbell by John Huang and the Riady group, which tied into our investigation of Chinagate. But more shocking were the investigative reports about the alleged rape of a woman named Juanita Broaddrick. There was also information—more than we knew from previous *60 Minutes* coverage—of the President's alleged groping of Kathleen Willey.

Because of the nature of the alleged offenses, both the Willey case and the Broaddrick case were important—if the charges could be proven—in establishing a pattern of obstruction, perjury, and witness tampering. In the Willey case in particular, the President had given a deposition in which he emphatically denied the allegations. Julie Steele, a former friend of Willey's, had testified against her, saying that Willey had encouraged her to lie.

To avoid the media, Al Tracy, Nancy Ruggero, and I met with Willey and her lawyer, Daniel Gecker, at a restaurant in Fredericksburg, Virginia, midway between Washington and Willey's home in Richmond.

The story Willey told us is one I came to believe. If we had been able to call live witnesses in the Senate trial, I would have called her to the stand.

Willey first met Clinton at the Richmond airport during the 1992 campaign. He gave a short speech and shook hands. He also gave Willey a hug. A friend had this captured on videotape. A short time later Clinton had his aide Nancy Hernreich get Willey's telephone number.

Later that afternoon, Willey was surprised to receive a telephone call from Clinton. He told her he would be in

Williamsburg, Virginia, for the evening, without his wife, and that he could get rid of his Secret Service detail. Willey didn't respond. At about 6 PM Clinton called again with the same offer. Willey refused to meet him.

Two days later Willey and her mother attended a large rally on the grounds of the Virginia State Capitol in Richmond. Clinton was present, so Willey approached him and introduced her mother. Clinton talked to her mother while caressing Willey's neck and hair.

On Election Night, 1992, Willey, her husband, her two children, and a friend attended a victory celebration in Little Rock, where she met the President-elect and congratulated him.

About a week later, Clinton called her at home. He was attending a party in Washington and wondered, "Do you think you could come up here and see me?"

"Like how?"

"I mean could you come up and spend some time with me?"

Willey told him she was not sure, and he dropped the subject. Later, she worked as a volunteer on several inaugural events, in the White House Correspondence Office, and in the White House Social Office.

After her husband's death, she obtained a part-time job working for White House Counsel Bernard Nussbaum. There she met Linda Tripp, who, according to Willey, hated her as a possible rival who threatened her job security, though Tripp had extensive responsibilities and a good salary, while Willey had neither.

Just before she left the White House, Tripp verbally attacked Willey in the White House parking lot, saying she was a backbiter and responsible for Tripp's transfer to the Pentagon. Tripp also indicated she would get revenge on Willey one day.

According to Willey, that threat explains why Linda Tripp later said that Willey was happy and excited after the alleged encounter with the President. I have never talked to Linda Tripp, but I did talk for hours with Kathleen Willey, and, in my opinion, she was telling the truth. My associates felt the same way. She answered every question without hesitation and looked us right in the eye as she did so.

Discovering that her husband—who was slipping into depression—had put the family into deep financial straits, Willey desperately sought a better paying job. She asked for an appointment to see the President. On November 28, 1993, the day before she met with Clinton, her husband disappeared. She didn't yet know that he had committed suicide.

Kathleen Willey told us—in detail—everything that happened from the moment she met Clinton in the Oval Office until she met Linda Tripp and other White House staffers immediately after the encounter. There is no need at this point, when they are so well known, to go over the sordid details again.

Shortly after Willey went public, the White House—in an action one federal judge ruled was illegal—released several letters she had written to the President. The letters evinced no animosity. To the contrary, Willey seemed interested in supporting the President, and some of the letters were written after her encounter with the President in the Oval Office. The White House said the letters proved Willey was lying about the groping incident. Releasing the letters may have violated the Privacy Act and could have been an abuse of the Presidency. But before I could call Kathleen Willey as a witness in an impeachment inquiry or trial, I needed an explanation.

Willey told us that it wasn't until after her husband committed suicide that she learned how dire her financial straits were. She was an unemployed widow, deeply in debt, with two children.

The last time Kathleen had met with the President, she had stalked away angrily after having been groped by him. But in her desperation, she saw the President as the one powerful person who could quickly set her up in a well-paying job. Perhaps, she thought, if I write conciliatory letters to Clinton, giving the impression that all is forgiven and that I hold no grudge, I could reopen the dialogue, and he will help me find a good job. Willey had no intention of ever going public with the President's misbehavior.

Willey discussed what to do with her lawyer and friend Daniel Gecker. He knew about the groping incident and warned her that anything she wrote would need to be completely innocuous, without the remotest suggestion of blackmail, extortion, or veiled threat or suggestion that she wanted a job in exchange for keeping quiet. Kathleen understood. To ensure that nothing she wrote could be misconstrued as a threat, Willey had Gecker review and approve the letters.

In 1994 Kathleen was invited to attend a World Summit in Copenhagen, and in 1995 she represented the United States at a biodiversity summit in Jakarta, Indonesia. She was totally unqualified for either position.

But bad things happened after Willey was subpoenaed to give a deposition in the Paula Jones case. This story was even more shocking than the President's alleged assault on a married woman.

On July 31, 1997, Gecker received, without warning, a fax from the office of the President's attorney. Both Willey and her attorney, who was present during our interview, confirmed to us that it was a document entitled "Statement of Kathleen Willey" and that it came with the instruction that she was to read it as a public statement. It said: "The President of the United States never sexually harassed me in any way, and I have always considered myself to be on excellent terms with him." She ignored the request.

In August 1997 the groping incident was reported in the *Drudge Report* and *Newsweek*. Around this time she received a phone call from an acquaintance who was a major financial donor to President Clinton. He told her to avoid giving a deposition if she was subpoenaed in the Jones case and to deny that anything had ever happened because only two people knew and "all you have to do is deny it, too." He called several other times, encouraging her to say, "I can't remember; it's none of your business."

Willey was subpoenaed in the fall of 1997 but wasn't actually called to testify until January 10, 1998. Shortly after she received the subpoena, Gecker was visited by one of the President's lawyers. Gecker told Kathleen the gist of the meeting: Clinton's lawyer was suggesting she avoid testifying by taking the Fifth Amendment privilege against self-incrimination. Gecker told Clinton's attorney that his client wouldn't take the Fifth because she had done nothing wrong.

A short time after that initial meeting, Gecker told us, he received an unsolicited package from the President's lawyers. It contained a form affidavit, a form motion to quash the deposition subpoena, and a memorandum of law in support of the motion to quash.

A short while before Willey was scheduled to testify, Gecker received another visit from the same lawyer. This time Gecker was told that he was only "a real estate lawyer" and that Kathleen Willey should really be represented by a top criminal attorney. Gecker responded that he was perfectly capable of handling a deposition and that he could not see any possible reason that Kathleen needed a criminal lawyer. Gecker added that even if she wanted such a lawyer, Willey was broke and could not afford the fees charged by top Washington criminal lawyers. The President's attorney offered that she wouldn't need to worry about fees because "we will take care of that."

After that conversation, Gecker reported, he received a call from one of the best criminal lawyers in Washington about representing Kathleen Willey. When Gecker again mentioned that she had no money, the lawyer replied that there would be no fees to pay.

Gecker conveyed this to Willey. She was frightened and convinced that if she testified she would be indicted by Janet Reno's Justice Department. She had seen how Billy Dale of the White House Travel Office had actually been indicted and tried for crimes he had not committed, reportedly because he had gotten in the way of the Clinton administration. She had seen the smears and attacks on Paula Jones. To add to her fears, she felt intimidated by events that followed.

Shortly before her January 10 deposition, Willey came out of her Virginia home to find all of her tires flat. Her mechanic asked, "Who the hell did you tick off? Your tires were flattened with a nail gun."

In another incident, a man called—supposedly from the local electric company—saying her electricity would be turned off that evening so they could run some tests. Later that afternoon, she called the electric company to find out how long the tests would last. She was told there was no plan to interrupt service and no record of anyone calling her.

Kathleen lives in a semirural area. The anonymous caller was reminding her that she was vulnerable and alone.

As the deposition got closer, the intimidation increased. One day her cat, Bullseye, disappeared. On January 8, two days before she was to testify, Willey was walking her dogs in a secluded area early in the morning. A man in a jogging suit approached her.

JOGGER: Good morning, did you ever find your cat?

WILLEY: No, we haven't found her yet.

JOGGER: That's too bad. Bullseye was his name, wasn't it?
[This shocks Willey, because she has not revealed the cat's name to anyone.]
JOGGER: Did you ever get those tires fixed?
WILLEY: They're fine. [Kathleen starts to edge away and look around for help.]
JOGGER: So, —— and —— [Willey's children's first names]?
[Kathleen walks faster toward her house.]
JOGGER: And our attorney, Dan, is he okay?
WILLEY: He's fine.
JOGGER: I hope you're getting the message.

Willey was terrified. She turned and ran. The jogger called after her, "You're just not getting the message, are you?"

As a result of that meeting, Kathleen feared that she, her children, and her lawyer were at risk of physical harm. She told Gecker about the jogger but didn't mention the not-too-veiled threat against Gecker himself. As she put it, "He was my only hope—I didn't want to lose him." Willey confessed that even during the deposition she was contemplating whether to lie or to tell the truth and possibly suffer terrible consequences.

The deposition began as scheduled. However, before the questioning began, the President's lawyer said, "You know, I've talked to the President, and he just thinks the world of you. You don't really think this was sexual harassment. It wasn't unwelcome, was it?"

"Not only was it unwelcome, it was unexpected."

In the room during the deposition were the court reporter, the Jones attorneys, the President's attorney, Daniel Gecker, Kathleen Willey, and the presiding judge.

Gecker saw that Willey was nervous. When the Jones attorneys asked about the incident in the Oval Office, she looked terrified. Gecker asked for a short recess to consult with his client. He took Kathleen aside and told her they were about to go into the heart of the subject.

"Kathleen, there is no turning back, what are you going to do?"

"I'm going to tell the truth, the whole truth," she answered, with tears in her eyes. She went back and answered every question put to her.

The next morning Willey stepped outside to pick up the newspaper. There on the porch, within a few feet of the front door, the skull of a small animal lay facing her.

I asked Willey if she would be willing to testify. As she looked at Gecker, I could see real fear in her eyes. He said it was up to her.

I confessed that we couldn't vouch for the tactics of the President's lawyers, but we would not embarrass her.

"Okay, if I'm subpoenaed, I'll testify."

Because of that meeting, we planned to have Kathleen Willey and Dan Gecker as witnesses at a Senate impeachment trial.

Kathleen Willey wasn't the only woman from President Clinton's past with an outrageous story to tell.

A week or so after the election, Pete Wacks, Diana Woznicki, and I met with Congressman Bob Barr and Larry Klayman. Klayman is a lawyer and the leader of Judicial Watch, which had vigorously pursued Clinton scandals from Filegate to Chinagate, deposing John Huang, the mysterious employee of the Department of Commerce and later of the Democratic National Committee. Barr thought Klayman might be able to help us.

The trick was how to focus our effort.

Klayman had testimony on Filegate that he thought showed clear abuse of power by the President. He was building a case on Commercegate, having uncovered evidence of a scheme by Huang to sell Commerce Department junkets to heavy contributors to the Clinton-Gore campaign. Klayman had developed an informant close to Commerce Secretary Ron Brown who gave testimony showing a pattern of raffling off trips on federally funded trade missions.

Commercegate could have led to possible charges of bribery, an impeachable offense; Filegate could have led to charges of abuse of power, another impeachable offense. But our primary focus wasn't looking for new offenses to prosecute; it was developing the case for the charges we had.

Then Klayman told us about his client Dolly Kyle Browning. If true, her testimony fit perfectly into the pattern of obstruction of justice and perjury charges we had already developed.

A few days later, in the course of our investigation, Diana Woznicki, Pete Wacks, Al Tracy, and I met with Dolly Kyle

Browning. She was a terrific potential witness who spoke directly and succinctly. I was convinced of her candor. Here's what she told us:

Dolly Kyle Browning had known Clinton from childhood. They had attended high school together and had had an "intimate relationship" (that's the phrase we would have used in the Senate if we'd been able to present the case in a real trial). They saw each other socially from the mid-1970s until January 1992.

In January 1992, when Clinton was campaigning for the Presidency, Browning learned that a magazine was preparing to publish an article about her long-standing relationship with him. She had declined to be interviewed for the article but called Clinton to warn him about its appearance. Clinton never returned her call. However, she told us, a Clinton campaign worker called to threaten her: "If you cooperate with the media, we will destroy you." Then another member of the Clinton campaign called her with instructions to deny the story. Clinton was nominated by the Democratic Party and elected President of the United States on November 3, 1992.

Dolly Kyle Browning's sister, Dorcy Kyle Corbin, is a Little Rock attorney who represented Browning's interests. In late fall 1993, an individual close to the White House told her, "We've read your sister's book"—Dolly had been working on an autobiographical novel—"and we don't want it published."

It still hasn't been.

On July 23, 1994, two months after Paula Jones filed her lawsuit against the President, Browning and Clinton attended their thirtieth high school reunion in Hot Springs, Arkansas. At midnight, Clinton approached Browning and engaged her in conversation. They sat down side-by-side in front of a large column in the ballroom where the dance was taking place. A Secret Service agent stood on each side of them. As the President and Browning spoke, their faces were close together. They spoke so that each could hear the other, but so as not to be overheard. At one point, Marsha Scott from the White House momentarily interrupted them to advise the President that the bar was closing. This interruption took less than one minute.

Browning says she and Clinton spoke about a variety of topics, including the "we will destroy you" threat and an offer he'd made to help her find a job in Washington. But she never discussed lying about their relationship for money, as the President later claimed in connection with the Paula Jones lawsuit.

During the Jones lawsuit, the President submitted a three-page handwritten memo that he says he wrote shortly after his conversation with Browning. According to the note, Browning stated that her book was not true but that she needed money. Marsha Scott wrote on the same document that she had been asked by the President to stand immediately behind Dolly so she could hear every word said. Scott claims to have overheard the entire conversation between Browning and the President. She affirmed that the President's account was true in every respect, including that Browning said she wrote the book because she needed money.

During the fall of 1994, Dorcy Kyle Corbin reported to Browning a series of discussions with a White House official. In the conversations, the official outlined precisely what Browning could and could not say about her relationship with Clinton. Under this "understanding," Browning was permitted to state publicly that she and Clinton had a thirty-three–year relationship that, from time to time, included intimacy.

Dolly agreed not to tell the true story about their relationship if he would not tell any lies about her. She further agreed not to use, in public, the "A words," which were defined as "adultery" and "affair." Finally, if she needed to contact Clinton, she would call Dorcy, and Dorcy would call her contact in the White House. She used this method of communication several times over the years.

Browning was served with a subpoena in the Jones case, with her deposition scheduled for October 28, 1997. She was also requested to produce certain documents in her possession. Once the White House learned that Browning had been subpoenaed, White House lawyers immediately prepared and forwarded a number of documents to her. She received a form motion for a protective order and motion to quash. In addition, she received a document entitled "Dolly Kyle Browning's Memorandum of Points and Authorities in Support of Motion for Protective Order and Motion to Quash." In that memorandum, Clinton's lawyers outlined an elaborate strategy to circumvent a deposition and avoid having to turn over documents. Moreover, Clinton's lawyers asked Browning to sign an affidavit that she and Clinton had never had "nonconsensual" sexual relations. Browning didn't sign it.

The President was deposed on January 17, 1998. During that deposition, President Clinton told his story about how after the reunion he had made some handwritten notes regarding his discussion with Browning and had Marsha Scott include her own handwritten notations. Clinton asserted that Browning made up her claims about having had a long-standing sexual relationship with him because she needed money. He further asserted that Browning was "mad at me because I'd never been her lover, and when I told her Gennifer Flowers's story was bogus and that many, many problems with it had already been proven—it's very hard to prove your innocence in a case like this, but that we'd done it—you know, she just was very angry. That's basically what these notes reflect." He further claimed that Browning stated that Gennifer Flowers had received $150,000, "and she needed money, too." Scott's own notes stated that Browning was "very animated and threatening acting."

That description was important to us because it was something we could try to verify or debunk with witnesses.

As a whole, Dolly's story tracked so well with Kathleen Willey's and Monica Lewinsky's experiences that we were convinced it needed further investigation. We had possible evidence here of a conspiracy to obstruct justice and provide false testimony.

Just as with Lewinsky, the President's attorneys provided Browning's attorneys with form affidavits and legal memoranda to support motions to quash their subpoenas. And just as with Lewinsky, when this did not work, President Clinton denied that anything improper had occurred between him and Browning and began a campaign to trash her character.

Browning's interview was possible further evidence of the President's willfully providing perjurious, false, and misleading testimony to a grand jury. As with his deposition testimony concerning Lewinsky, he flatly denied, in a deposition, an improper relationship with Browning.

I asked Dolly if she could give us the names of people who had seen them at the reunion and could verify her version of the story. I told her I didn't want enemies of the President, only neutral or friendly people.

A few days later, we had a list of names and addresses.

I asked John Kocoras and Diana Woznicki to fly down to Little Rock as soon as possible and interview the possible witnesses. I told them it was essential that they identify themselves fully and advise each of the persons interviewed that we were engaged in an impeachment inquiry for the House Judiciary Committee and were trying to establish what happened at the high school reunion. To avoid later recantations under possible pressure, we wanted each witness to sign an affidavit under oath.

John and Diana returned with three affidavits from professed friends of Clinton. They essentially corroborated Dolly Kyle Browning's account of the events. Most significantly, they agreed that Marsha Scott approached Dolly and Clinton just once, and then only for a very short time. In that case, Marsha Scott could not have been standing immediately behind the two and listening to the entire conversation, for the simple reason that they were seated against a four-foot square pillar. We had thus uncovered evidence of blatant perjury on the President's part and witness tampering with Marsha Scott—all in the President's own handwriting. Had there been a real trial in the Senate, the American people would have heard all of this.

During our investigation, we began receiving reports that one of the "Jane Does" mentioned in the Jones case was a woman who might have been assaulted by then–Arkansas Attorney General William Clinton. The event had taken place some twenty years earlier and was far beyond the Arkansas statute of limitations.

But this matter required investigation if we were to exercise due diligence in our inquiry. It could provide yet further confirmation of the pattern that we had seen with Lewinsky, Willey, and Browning. Accordingly, I asked Diana Woznicki to look into the matter.

Within a day or two, Diana reported to me about a woman in Arkansas, Juanita Broaddrick, who alleged that Clinton had raped her years earlier. A shocking story, but nothing in itself that would affect our case in the Senate.

Then Diana dropped the bomb.

"Oh, one more thing that I picked up. She was subpoenaed by the Jones lawyers. She filed an affidavit denying everything."

Bingo! That changed the whole picture. Three questions had to be answered: Was the original assault story true? Where did she get the affidavit? And was she pressured directly or indirectly by the White House to sign a false affidavit?

I asked Diana and John Kocoras to dig deeper and called Bob Bittman at the Independent Counsel's Office to see what I could learn. Earlier, when I had gone through the files that were originally sent over with Starr's referral, I had found two files containing FBI interviews with people whose names I didn't recognize. I read those reports and found that they suggested a possible sexual assault by Clinton earlier in his career. The reports were certainly not complete and raised more questions than they answered, so we just ignored that allegation. A few days after the referral, the Independent Counsel asked us to return the reports, saying that they had been included by mistake. We returned the two files and forgot about them. Now, with the new information gathered by Diana, the issue took a new turn.

Bittman confirmed that his office had investigated the Broaddrick matter. They had interviewed Broaddrick as well as several witnesses. According to Bittman, the Independent Counsel was convinced that the event had actually occurred while Clinton was the Arkansas Attorney General. Bittman also told me that lawyers for Paula Jones had had Broaddrick interviewed. When I asked him whether she had been subpoenaed to give a deposition in the Jones case, he said that she had, but didn't testify.

"Why?"

"She filed a motion to quash, a memorandum of law, and a false affidavit." Because that fit the pattern, I asked Bittman to send over everything in his office concerning the Broaddrick situation. I told him that we were no longer confined to the original referral because the House had voted to have the committee undertake a wide-open impeachment inquiry.

When the material arrived, we found that it consisted of several extensive interviews involving, in addition to Broaddrick, a number of corroborating witnesses. Diana, John Kocoras, and I went into our private office in the secure room, and each of us read and reread every word of every memorandum until we had almost committed the material to memory. Then we met to discuss our next move. We agreed that nothing should be done and no decision would be made until Broaddrick and other witnesses were interviewed and their credibility weighed.

I sent Diana and John to meet with Broaddrick and her lawyer in Arkansas. The meeting, though amicable, did not go well. Diana said Broaddrick appeared to be hiding something. When asked if she had executed a false affidavit in the Jones case, she acknowledged that she had. Her lawyer interrupted, saying that the affidavit wasn't technically false, and Broaddrick retorted, "Yes, it was!"

Later, Broaddrick phoned Diana and unburdened herself for about an hour-and-a-half, telling her the full story.

I asked Diana the critical question, "Do you believe her?"

Diana, who had extensive experience helping rape victims as a Chicago cop, said definitively, "Juanita fits the pattern of the classic rape victim."

Here is the story as told by Juanita Broaddrick to Diana Woznicki as part of our investigation:

Juanita Broaddrick met Bill Clinton in 1978, when he made a campaign stop at a nursing home that she owned. At the time, Broaddrick was a young married woman who worked in the long-term care industry and was involved in running several nursing homes, while Clinton, Arkansas's Attorney General, was campaigning for his first term as Governor. During the visit, Clinton told Broaddrick to call him and visit his headquarters to pick up campaign materials the next time she was in Little Rock.

In the spring of that year, Broaddrick and a female friend attended a health care conference in Little Rock. She remembered Clinton's invitation and called for an appointment. He wasn't there, so she left her number at the hotel.

Clinton called her back and suggested they meet in the hotel coffee shop to talk about his campaign. A few minutes later, he called again. He told Juanita there were reporters in the coffee shop and asked if they could meet in her room so they could talk without interruption. Broaddrick hesitated because she was alone in her room, her roommate having left to attend a session of the conference. In those days it was still considered unusual for a woman to meet a man alone in her hotel room, especially in the South. Then she thought, "This is the Attorney General; if I can't trust him, who can I trust?" So she agreed to the meeting.

When the Attorney General arrived, he was alone. Broaddrick was completely at ease because, after all, this was a business meeting. The two engaged in some general small talk, and Broaddrick ushered Clinton to the window, where the coffee service was laid out.

Suddenly, Clinton began kissing her, at first not forcefully. But then he threw her on the bed and kept kissing her. She struggled to get away, and as she did, he got on top of her and bit her lower lip as a way of controlling her. Every time she struggled, Clinton bit harder to keep control of her. She kept saying no, that she didn't want this to happen. The pain became excruciating. He forced her legs apart and raped her. At one point in the attack, Clinton assured Juanita that there was no danger of her getting pregnant. He said, "I had mumps when I was a kid; I'm sterile." Finally, the ordeal appeared to be completed. Clinton rose up slightly as though he were about to withdraw. Then he said, "My God, I can do it again!" And he did.

When Clinton finally completed the assault, Broaddrick was close to collapse. She was sobbing uncontrollably, afraid of what might happen next, confused, and in a panic. Clinton appeared unfazed. He coolly rose from the bed and went into the bathroom. All the time Juanita was afraid to move. He emerged after a few minutes and started to walk out. When he reached the door, he turned to his sobbing victim, still lying on the bed, smiled, and said, "You better do something about that lip. Get some ice on it." Then he put on his sunglasses and left.

Broaddrick was still sobbing when her friend returned to the room. She took a single look at Juanita and the bed, immediately noticed Juanita's swollen and blue lip, and asked what had happened. Broaddrick told her. Finally, Juanita put a bag of ice to her face, and she and her friend drove all the way across the state to their home in Fort Smith. Typical of that time, she blamed herself, so she felt humiliated and ashamed.

When Broaddrick returned home, she decided that she would tell nobody of her ordeal, including her husband. She asked her friend to forget what she knew and to support her explanation that she received her injury when she ran into a revolving door.

A few weeks following the attack, Juanita's first husband, Gary, told her that they were invited to a Clinton fund-raiser. The last thing Juanita wanted was another confrontation with Clinton, so she tried to beg off by claiming illness. Her husband was insistent, though, and said that they would only put in an appearance. With that assurance, she relented.

They were there for only a few minutes when Bill and Hillary Clinton arrived and began to work the room. Juanita was able to avoid Clinton because he walked away from where she was standing. Hillary, however, paused and appeared to be looking for something. Suddenly she hurried directly to Juanita and gushed, "I've heard so much about you. You've done so much for us." Hillary put her face real close to Juanita's and said, "We appreciate everything you do." Broaddrick thought that was a strange comment, because she had done nothing for the Clintons in the campaign. She told Diana that she wondered if Hillary knew what had happened and was thanking her for keeping her mouth shut.

During the presidential primary campaign in 1991, just before Clinton announced his candidacy, Broaddrick found herself once more in Little Rock attending another health care conference. She was now divorced and remarried to a caring and supportive husband, David Broaddrick, who was aware of the heinous rape. The couple owned and operated two health care facilities in Arkansas.

While she was attending the conference, an announcement came over the loudspeaker that Juanita Broaddrick was wanted outside. She walked out and saw Clinton standing next to the stairs. His first words were, "Can you ever forgive me?" He apologized and said: "That was the old me. I'm not the same now. I'm a new man."

"You can just go to hell," Broaddrick replied, and walked away.

One evening, years before, in 1984 or 1985, Mr. and Mrs. Broaddrick had attended a function in Hot Springs, Arkansas. The couple didn't realize that Clinton was the keynote speaker. When they found out, they returned to their hotel room. In the course of the evening, David went down to the bar and found himself standing next to Clinton. Clinton stuck out his hand and said, "You're with Juanita, aren't you?" Broaddrick squeezed Clinton's hand as hard as he was able. He looked Clinton right in the eye and, continuing his grip, said, "Don't you go near her or near her home; don't you even so much as look at her." Startled, Clinton pulled his hand away and said, "I didn't know she was with you when that happened."

It wasn't until twenty years after the event that rumors began circulating about a possible rape committed by the President. Someone claimed he had a tape recording of Broaddrick giving details of the assault. That, Broaddrick knew, was a lie, but she was afraid that her private trauma might become public knowledge. Her fear was confirmed when investigators working for Paula Jones asked about the encounter. She didn't go beyond admitting that Clinton had acted "horribly" and "inappropriately." That interview was followed by a deposition subpoena.

Broaddrick's lawyer was an acquaintance of Bruce Lindsey, one of Clinton's closest friends and advisors. She didn't know who Lindsey was. Her lawyer told her that he would call Lindsey because "he works with the President, and we'll see how we can keep you out of this."

A few days after talking to Lindsey, Broaddrick's attorney received a package from the President's lawyers. It contained the usual motion to quash the subpoena, a memorandum of law in support of the motion, and a form affidavit for Broaddrick's signature. When she saw the material, Juanita realized that the affidavit was the method by which the other "Jane Does" had avoided testimony and stayed out of the Jones case. This might be the way out, she thought.

Both she and her husband agonized over what to do. She had seen what happened to other women when they gave evidence against Clinton. She didn't want to share their fate. In addition, she and her husband were still engaged in a business that was regulated by the State of Arkansas. The couple feared reprisals. Finally, and perhaps most significantly, she did not want the sordid matter broadcast and her name sullied. So Broaddrick signed the false affidavit and told her lawyer to get the subpoena quashed. Juanita said that she never told her lawyer the truth. When Diana asked if she had received any pressure from Lindsey or the White House to file a knowingly false affidavit, she answered that there was absolutely no pressure from any source. The whole thing was her idea to avoid testifying.

I reported this story to Hyde and some of the other Republican members who came over to the Ford Building to view our evidence. I said that as far as I was concerned, the entire event had no place in our impeachment inquiry or in any trial in the Senate because, though it was a terrible event, it occurred before Clinton was President. Had there been pressure to force her to lie, it would fit into the obstruction charge. But that was not the case. The Managers, who were in shock, agreed that it would do more harm than good, and we let the matter rest. But we also knew that NBC News had interviewed Broaddrick and was ready to run a story on her in a matter of days.

At least we thought we knew that.

In any event, it wasn't until after the President was

acquitted in the Senate that the *Wall Street Journal* finally broke the story, followed the next day by the *Washington Post*. In a classic case of me-too, cover-your-butt journalism at its lowest, NBC, which had the story in the can and had dragged Juanita Broaddrick through emotional hell to get it, only to tell her, after continual delays, that the network wasn't going to air it after all, finally ran its tape. The timing made for a horrible post-impeachment finale. The President that the Senate had refused to remove from office was, the public now knew, an alleged rapist.

CHAPTER 8

Stonewalling

W e continually worried about the accusation that "it's just sex," which would never be defused, no matter how often we emphasized that the issue was perjury, witness tampering, abuse of power, and obstruction of justice.

One issue that we never touched on sex was Chinagate. Its possible national security implications were enormous, and we wanted to make it part of our investigation. But we couldn't because of an obstacle course of stone walls thrown up by Janet Reno's Justice Department and agreed to by the "bipartisan" Republicans.

FBI Director Louis Freeh and Justice Department prosecutor Charles LaBella had testified before Congress earlier in 1998 that existing evidence of White House fund-raising improprieties justified the appointment of an Independent Counsel to investigate the issues further. Congressman Dan Burton had subpoenaed reports written by Freeh and LaBella, but Reno refused to provide them. Burton pushed for a contempt of Congress citation, and Senator Orrin Hatch of Utah stepped in to mediate the dispute. I attended the meeting in Hatch's office with Senator Patrick Leahy of Vermont, Congressman Burton, Hyde, Janet Reno, LaBella, several congressional staffers, and officials from the Department of Justice and the FBI. The office was crowded, and I found myself seated across from Burton and Hyde. On either side of me were Senator Leahy and Janet Reno.

Reno repeatedly refused to provide the reports. She did, however, offer redacted versions—each of which was numbered and would be collected—that we could read now in the room.

With time short, I concentrated on the LaBella report. I soon realized that all the relevant information had been deleted, with page after page of blank space, up to nearly twenty blank pages at a time. I was disgusted—as was Burton—that Congress should be treated this way by Reno's Justice Department.

Hatch, on the other hand, agreed that these redacted versions constituted sufficient compliance to protect Reno from a contempt citation. Here we had it. More bipartisanship, of which the Republican senatorial leadership seemed to be the grand champions.

I turned to Reno and said: "Well, you dodged that bullet. At least you won't be going to the slammer today."

She was not amused.

When we walked out of Senator Hatch's office, I noticed the corridor was packed with lights and cameras. Mobs of reporters were screaming questions. The corridor was jammed to the outer door about a hundred feet away. The media were focused on Hyde and Burton, who were escorted by the Capitol Police. I thought I was safe, until a reporter, followed by about six others, shoved a microphone in my face.

"What went on in there? What was decided?"

"How the hell do I know? I'm just looking for the bathroom."

That sent them scurrying off into someone else's face.

That meeting had occurred in the late summer. Now, four months later, knee-deep in the impeachment inquiry, Hyde was leery of opening up the campaign finance issue. But he agreed that a due diligence investigation required that we see the unredacted Freeh and LaBella reports.

In my presence, Hyde telephoned Janet Reno. He always treated her with the greatest courtesy and respect, but he was also firm, telling her the committee required the memos from Freeh and LaBella to complete its inquiry.

About ten minutes later, one of Reno's aides called. Hyde handed me the phone. I put my hand over the mouthpiece and said to Hyde, sotto voce, "We really need these reports right now."

He nodded.

"How far can I go with this guy?"

"As far as you need to."

"If I have to threaten them, will you back me?"

"To the hilt."

With that assurance, I took my hand off the mouthpiece. The Justice representative began the usual song and dance about privacy and secrecy and the time-consuming procedure for getting judicial approval and the like. I listened for about a minute.

"Time out! This is an impeachment inquiry by the House of Representatives, and we are running out of time. We are sick to death of this constant stonewalling and stalling. We are not going to put up with this garbage any more. We need to see the LaBella and Freeh reports, and we don't want any more lame excuses."

"Well, we will need to discuss this, since there may be a problem with the court."

"Look, no more stalling. If we don't have the reports within twenty-four hours, we will serve a forthwith subpoena [that is, a subpoena that calls for immediate production of the requested material]. And just so you understand, that subpoena won't call for the production only of the reports. It will call for production of every piece of evidence and testimony that the reports rely on. I am not bluffing—this is impeachment!"

He said he would get back to me as soon as possible.

Henry Hyde whistled. "Boy, you were rough. Do you know who that was? The Chief of the Criminal Division, right under Reno."

"Well, maybe we'll get what we want."

By the next day, nobody had heard from Justice, so I drafted five subpoenas for immediate production of records. The first one was addressed to Janet Reno, Attorney General of the United States. The second would be sent to William Jefferson Clinton, President of the United States. The third was to go to Charles LaBella for his unredacted report, the fourth to Louis Freeh for his report, and the fifth to Independent Counsel Kenneth Starr.

The subpoenas to Reno and the President were identical. The President had the power to force Reno to turn over the documents. If he ignored the subpoena, that in itself would constitute an impeachable offense.

The subpoenas read as follows:

Subpoena Duces Tecum

Produce to the Committee in Executive Session the following:

1) Any and all documents and materials of any kind and nature in your possession referred to directly or indirectly in the memoranda, Public Integrity reports, and Addenda prepared by Charles LaBella and FBI Director Louis Freeh concerning campaign finance abuses; including, but not limited to, investigative files, notes of interviews, memoranda of interviews, grand jury testimony transcripts, deposition transcripts, tape recordings, interrogatories, interrogatory answers, proffers, proffer letters, plea agreements, immunity agreements, orders of immunity, transcripts of electronically intercepted conversations (personal, by facsimile, or by wire), consensual and court ordered electronic interception of telephone calls, facsimiles, pagers, and the like, logs, surveillance reports, correspondence, and all other related material;

2) Any and all files directly or indirectly concerning John Huang, Johnny Chung, Charlie Trie, and Mark Middleton, including, but not limited to, notes of interviews, memoranda of interviews, transcripts of depositions, grand jury transcripts, tape recordings, logs, immunity agreements, orders of immunity, and/or proffer letters;

3) The unredacted memorandum of Charles LaBella, together with the Public Integrity Report and all Addenda thereto, concerning the appointment of an Independent Counsel;

4) The unredacted memorandum of Louis Freeh, Director of the FBI, together with all Addenda thereto concerning the appointment of an Independent Counsel.

Before the subpoenas could be signed and served, I received a call from a Justice Department liaison. He asked that I meet that evening in the office of the Chief of the Criminal Division to iron out the LaBella report situation. I agreed, and Jeff Pavletic and I went over to the Justice Department Building at around 6 PM. A lawyer from the Democratic investigative staff met us there.

After about fifteen minutes, the three of us were ushered into a small conference room. We met five or six top officials of Justice. Both Jeff and I knew we were in for the usual con game of "let's talk about this"; "how much do you really need to see?"; "why do you need this?"; "what are you going to do with this material?"; and finally, "how do we know this won't be leaked to the press?" We'd already met with our share of stonewalling from Reno's Justice Department.

We were not disappointed. Once again, in the usual condescending tones, we were instructed that the report contained a great deal of 6E material (Rule 6E of the Federal Rules of Criminal Procedure forbids disclosure of grand jury material). We replied that any information in the report would be held in strictest confidence within the Executive Session Rule of the committee. Then they played the "ongoing investigation" card, suggesting that any leak might compromise possible criminal charges. We were getting the same old story—"you will get nothing and there is nothing you can do about it." Finally, they made a mistake. A Justice lawyer said that getting the District Judge to permit disclosure of the LaBella and Freeh report would be difficult. I shot back that we were dealing with an impeachment inquiry; the House Judiciary Committee would not permit the Justice Department to hide behind a judge.

"I'll make it easy," I said. "We'll just serve a subpoena for all the backup evidence tomorrow." The Justice lawyers caved, promising to go before the Judge the next morning. No judicial permission was required in our opinion, but we agreed that, as a courtesy to the court, the request could be made.

Late the next morning, I learned that the District Judge had denied our request because, according to Justice Department lawyers, "[t]he House has failed to demonstrate sufficient need." To suggest that the House of Representatives in the course of an impeachment inquiry had "failed to demonstrate sufficient need" was the epitome of judicial usurpation.

I told Hyde I wanted to serve an all-encompassing subpoena on both the President and Janet Reno. If the court tried to interfere, we would get a quick and definitive ruling from the Supreme Court that the Judicial Branch was constitutionally prohibited from injecting itself into an impeachment inquiry. With that decided, the committee would finally be free to do its job. We could subpoena everything from the Independent Counsel and investigate Chinagate, Filegate, Travelgate, and the immigration debacle.

I reminded Hyde that we had talked earlier in the investigation about using the House civil contempt power to force compliance and suggested that this would be the right time to test whether we could in fact use that power.

We had come up with the civil contempt method after watching Janet Reno, the Justice Department, and the White House stall any investigation by Congress or anyone else by hiding behind a brick wall of silence and arrogantly refusing any request for testimony or documents.

The Judicial Branch has employed the civil contempt power consistently to enforce its orders, and our extensive research at the Library of Congress indicated that Congress also possesses this power to coerce stubborn witnesses to cooperate. Theoretically, then, if anyone ignored or disobeyed an order by Congress to appear or to produce documents or other evidence under a subpoena, that person could be fined for every day he did not comply—or could even be put in jail until he complied.

Hyde asked me to explain and defend the concept to lawyers from the Judiciary Committee staff and from the House of Representatives. In doing so, I reminded them that judges jail witnesses every day for refusing to testify after being given immunity and that in impeachment the House possessed every tool available to the Judicial Branch.

"Do you honestly believe that the White House or the Justice Department will allow that to happen without taking immediate action?" one of the lawyers asked.

"Of course not," I said. "They will probably be in the District Court with an emergency petition for a writ of habeas corpus." When the lawyers questioned whether that move would disrupt the whole investigation, I explained that the attorney for the House or the Judiciary Committee would inform the District Court that this was a constitutional impeachment process in which the court had no business interfering.

"And what if the court disagrees and issues the writ?"

I told them that we had prepared an emergency petition for a writ of prohibition to be filed in the Supreme Court, asking the court to declare that the Judiciary had no constitutional jurisdiction to act in an impeachment. When we won there, as I felt we would, the House would have plenary power to coerce anyone to cooperate.

"Oh, then what will you do, send the Sergeant-at-Arms up to arrest someone in the White House?" one of the committee staffers laughed.

"If that becomes necessary, yes."

"And what if the President calls out troops to stop him?"

"I hope he does," I said. "George Wallace tried that, and look what it got him in public opinion."

I know I hadn't convinced anyone. This was a totally new and untried maneuver, and such things are not popular among House staffers. I am certain they reported that this was a harebrained idea that would result only in adverse publicity and cries from Democrats of partisanship and gestapo tactics. But as far as I was concerned, the time to fight for the right to use the power of civil contempt had arrived.

Hyde told me to start the ball rolling.

My staff redid the subpoenas and sent them over to the Rayburn Building for the necessary signatures from the Judiciary Committee. Then we waited, and waited, and waited. Finally, we asked for faxed copies of the signed subpoenas. Nothing. Eventually we heard that the committee staffers would serve the subpoenas. I called back and insisted that the original subpoenas had to come back to us and that my agents deserved the honor of serving them.

Again, nothing happened for several hours. I asked Jeff to drive over to Rayburn and pick up the originals. I told him not to leave until he had them.

When Jeff returned, he threw the manila envelope on

my desk and said: "So much for the coercive power of the House. They have cut the heart out of the investigation."

I opened the envelope and looked at the subpoenas. The one for the President was missing. The one for Starr was as we had drafted it. The one for Reno, though, had been completely changed. Now it called only for the production of the LaBella and Freeh reports, but nothing else.

I was enraged. No wonder nobody would fax the subpoenas. No wonder the committee staffers wanted to serve the subpoenas without our seeing them. They wanted to present us with an accomplished fact before we knew what was going on. It also meant we would never get a chance to use our civil contempt power. This was betrayal—by whom, specifically, we were never able to determine.

It was now clear to us that no boats would be rocked, no chances taken. We were going to have a nice, bland, friendly hearing and then be allowed to slither back to Chicago, beaten by the system.

I drafted and signed a letter of resignation, knowing my staff would follow me. I kept it in my pocket—at least for the time being. But it was ready.

We served one of the five subpoenas—to Ken Starr for the John Huang grand jury testimony. As a matter of courtesy, we called first to tell the Independent Counsel that it was coming. Starr's office replied that it could not comply without the approval of the Department of Justice. I asked Bob Bittman on Starr's staff to do his best to expedite a decision.

The next day I received a call from a Justice Department attorney, who said the department was willing to release Huang's testimony. He warned me, however, that if any of the testimony became public, it would compromise several ongoing investigations of serious federal felonies. I assured him that we would keep the material in utmost confidence.

About fifteen minutes later, Bittman called. He said he had been given authority to turn over the grand jury testimony. "I don't want to tell you your business, but do you mind if I say something? Dave, they are setting you up. They will turn over the grand jury testimony. You can bet your life the White House or the Democrats will leak the testimony. The Justice Department will pretend it's outraged that ongoing investigations have been compromised just because the Republicans wanted to prosecute Clinton."

"You mean to tell me they would jeopardize criminal cases for political advantage?"

"What do you think?"

I called the Justice Department attorney. "You know, I've been thinking about what you said. Certainly neither the members of the committee nor I want to jeopardize in the slightest any criminal investigations that are currently pending. We would rather pass up relevant evidence than take even a remote chance of compromising your work. So, the committee has decided to forgo the Huang grand jury testimony. You can inform Judge Starr's office that we are canceling the subpoena."

The attorney sounded disappointed. He asked if I was certain that we didn't need the material, and I assured him that I was. Thanks to the candor of Bob Bittman, we dodged another bullet. But we still faced Janet Reno's stone wall. With the help of "bipartisan" Republicans, she'd won again.

CHAPTER 9

Starr to the Stand

The impeachment hearings began on November 19, 1998, with the arrival of Judge Kenneth Starr before the committee. Hyde called the hearing to order.

Starr's opening statement gave the history of the investigation, described the manner in which it was conducted, and then offered an analysis and explanation of the charges and evidence contained in his referral.

Starr was questioned by the committee—the Democrats hurling accusations and making speeches—and then Minority Special Counsel Abbe Lowell was allowed a period for "cross-examination."

Lowell handed Starr a loose-leaf binder with about two inches of documents in it. Copies of the binder were passed out to the members. Hyde gave me his copy. The binder was nothing but newspaper articles, letters accusing Starr of various illegalities, and other irrelevant documents. Apparently, the binder was for media spin, furthering the White House's main defense strategy, which was attempting to assassinate Ken Starr's character.

Abbe Lowell referred to the documents in the binder only once or twice. Between the committee and Lowell, Starr was interrogated for more than ten hours.

Hyde called a dinner recess. When the committee reconvened, Hyde called on David Kendall, the President's attorney, to begin *his* cross-examination. Kendall gave Starr another loose-leaf binder even thicker than the one Lowell had tendered. Once again, it contained only newspaper articles, magazine articles—all, of course, critical of the Independent Counsel—and self-serving letters from the President's lawyers to various people. Again, the binder was for the media, not the cross-examination.

Kendall then embarked on one of the most accusatory and unfair cross-examinations I have ever heard. Starr fielded the questions with dignity, but in response to one particularly misleading question, Starr snapped, "David, you know perfectly well that I can't talk about that because it's still under investigation." I made a note: Not one question came from Kendall that addressed, even remotely, the facts of the case or the legal basis for the impeachment. Instead, he focused on alleged improprieties by Starr and his staff during the investigation of the Lewinsky matter. Kendall hammered at the fact that a federal judge had ordered an investigation of possible leaks from the Independent Counsel. Kendall was trying to imply that there must be some evidence against Starr's office. But such investigations are automatic once an allegation of leaks is made, and all of the triggering allegations had been made by Kendall.

Starr answered: "You know that we are dealing with a hair-trigger investigation. Besides, Mr. Kendall, the only information that never leaked is the information that was unavailable to the White House." I made another note and underlined the word "hair-trigger."

Later, I read and heard that Kendall had been brilliant and effective in his "crushing" cross-examination of Judge Starr. If the cross-examination I watched was effective and crushing, I'll take vanilla.

Kendall hadn't hurt Starr's credibility or cast doubt on the facts. He didn't even mention them.

It was now very late, and Hyde gave me only thirty minutes to interrogate Starr. I began with the "hair-trigger" investigations. I pointed out through leading questions that Kendall was able to create his own "investigation" of leaks just by writing a letter to the presiding federal judge. I then showed that Kendall had sent twenty-four such letters and had himself included copies of them in his binder as "evidence."

Unfortunately, each time I asked Judge Starr a leading question, he felt compelled to give a full and lengthy answer. I knew that time was short, and I had a great deal to cover, so I began to cut him off. He got the message. I asked for, and was given, an additional fifteen minutes. I knew that was all I would get, so both my questions and Starr's answers got shorter and more pointed. At the end, I felt compelled—given the ordeal to which Starr had just been subjected—to encourage him to speak from the heart.

MR. SCHIPPERS: Now, Judge Starr, I only have a few more questions. You are a senior partner in a major law firm, or you were before you took a leave of absence?

MR. STARR: Yes, past tense.

MR. SCHIPPERS: You are a recognized scholar in constitutional law and in law in general. You have been the Solicitor General of the United States; is that correct?

MR. STARR: That's correct.

MR. SCHIPPERS: Argued a number of cases before the Supreme Court of the United States?

MR. STARR: That's correct.

MR. SCHIPPERS: You have received honorary doctor of law degrees from six universities?

MR. STARR: I think that is right.

MR. SCHIPPERS: You have written numerous articles in various scholarly journals?

MR. STARR: Yes. I have written a number.

MR. SCHIPPERS: You have a completely unblemished career for your entire life as a lawyer, and you are looked upon in the profession as a man of honor, integrity, and decency, is that right?

MR. SCHIPPERS: Well, I would like to think that at least once upon a time, that was the reputation.

MR. SCHIPPERS: For the past year, you have been trashed in the newspapers, on television, and with snide backward remarks to which you could not reply, isn't that right, Judge Starr?

MR. STARR: Well, I have chosen until now not to reply, but I think the code of silence at some times in terms of basic fairness gets to come to an end.

MR. SCHIPPERS: And you have been pilloried and excoriated, charged with unbelievable things of which you are incapable of being guilty?

MR. STARR: I cannot imagine me and my colleagues engaging in some of the suggested activities that have been described here seriously.

MR. SCHIPPERS: And the Independent Counsel job, you didn't seek that, did you?

MR. STARR: Absolutely not.

MR. SCHIPPERS: You were asked to take it, and you tried to leave and your staff begged you to stay and you did stay; is that right?

MR. STARR: All of that is true. I never sought this job.

MR. SCHIPPERS: You have been given a duty that you did not seek, and you have performed that duty to the best of your ability; is that correct, sir?

MR. STARR: I have certainly tried, and I do it to the best of my ability, and I am proud of what we have been able to accomplish. As I indicated earlier, the records of convictions obtained, but also, the decisions not to seek an indictment, the decision to issue thorough reports, all of that is part of what we have co-labored together, with Mr. Kendall pointing out the number of persons involved in the investigation. I am proud of those persons. They are my colleagues, and they have become my friends, and they have worked very long and very hard under very difficult circumstances, and recognizing, and we are big, big boys, and I mean that in a gender-neutral way. So, when we were accused in Arkansas of a political witch-hunt, we took it, and we did our arguing in court, and we proved, to the satisfaction of a fair-minded jury with a very distinguished judge, that the sitting Governor and President and the First Lady's business partners were guilty of serious felonies, and we had been listening month after month to it as a political witch-hunt, and that was unfair, but we learned that goes with this territory.

MR. SCHIPPERS: Judge, for all that doing your duty, you have been pilloried and attacked from all sides, is that right?

MR. STARR: I would hope not all sides, but yes, that's...

MR. SCHIPPERS: Well, sometimes it seems like all sides. How long have you been an attorney, Judge Starr?

MR. STARR: Twenty-five years.

MR. SCHIPPERS: Well, I have been an attorney for almost forty years, and I want to say I am proud to be in the same room with you and your staff.

MR. STARR: Thank you, Mr. Schippers.

MR. SCHIPPERS: Thank you.

When I had finished, the room erupted in applause. The Democratic members and the President's people were noticeably silent, but the applause got louder as everyone stood and gave Ken Starr a well-deserved standing ovation. Even the Republican members of the committee stood and applauded—it was the most emotional and moving thing that had occurred since we had gotten to Washington.

The committee stayed in session for some time after Starr's testimony ended. I left the committee chamber and went back into the majority offices. I shook hands with Ken Starr and some of his staff. Then my wife and I decided to go home. When we reached the Rayburn Building's main entrance, it was all but deserted, save for the guards and one or two television cameramen. As we were leaving, I was approached by three lovely young women. One asked if I was Mr. Schippers, and I acknowledged that I was. With that, the oldest of the three women held out her hand and said, "Mr. Schippers, I am Mrs. Starr. I want to thank you for what you just did." That moment is still the highlight of my entire stay in Washington.

I was still hoping that before the actual final argument and vote on the articles of impeachment, I could call other witnesses. Hyde discussed the issue with the Republican leadership and came back to tell me, no. The problem, again, was "fairness" and "bipartisanship." The President's attorneys and the Democrats had already been told that no new evidence would be admitted. If we changed the plan, the White House and the Democrats would whine "unfair, unfair," and "partisan, partisan."

"No matter what you do this side of refusing to impeach, the White House and the Democrats will holler 'partisan' and 'unfair,'" I told Chairman Hyde. "Maybe this is the time to be a little partisan."

Hyde laughed, but said that if we introduced evidence, the President would be entitled to put on evidence, too, and the hearings could last a month.

"Who will they put on—Currie, Jordan, Blumenthal, Lindsey? I don't think so. They won't want their people cross-examined on national television. Believe me, Mr. Chairman, they will threaten, but when it comes right down to it, they won't have anyone testify for them." But by the close of our conversation the decision had been made. There would be no live testimony on evidence, all because the Republicans wanted so badly to look "fair"—a word that I instantly came to be wary of.

From the very beginning of the Independent Counsel's investigation, the wail went up from the President, his aides, his lawyers, and his supporters that everyone was treating poor President Clinton oh so unfairly. The Independent Counsel, the prosecutors, the judges, the Republican members of the House of Representatives, and, well, Republicans in general were all blinded—they said—by their hatred and partisanship. As a result, they were descending to low chicanery and suspect methods to beset the Clinton administration with unfair investigations, unfair comments, unfair procedures, unfair treatment of witnesses, unfair votes in committee, unfair votes on the floor of the House, and unfair charges against the White House and the President.

And all of this unfairness, it was claimed, was calculated to undo the verdict of the people, to satisfy what Mrs.

Clinton called the "vast right-wing conspiracy." To question motives, to suggest criminal activity, to ask embarrassing questions, or to seek the truth was sufficient to place one in that conspiracy.

I have no doubt that immediately after my report to the Judiciary Committee listing fifteen possible felonies committed by the President, I was promptly enrolled in that amorphous but far-reaching cabal.

On the other hand, if you were to listen to the White House spinmeisters and their congressional toadies, the President, his followers, and the Democratic members of Congress were the models of fairness. They rose above partisan politics solely to enforce the will of the people, as evidenced by numerous polls. Confronted with an obsessed and out-of-control prosecutor like Ken Starr, the "poor victims" could only sigh and act statesmanlike. Fairness and cooperation were their watchwords, and bipartisanship was their goal.

What a plateful of meadow muffins! Let's see who was fair, who was unfair, and who were the real victims in all this sordid mess.

We begin with the Independent Counsel. The White House unleashed a brutal spin campaign to discredit Ken Starr. As the investigation progressed, so did the attacks. Witnesses from the White House appeared before the grand jury and then met with the press to tell of the horrors and the unfairness they had encountered at the hands of smirking prosecutors. Remember Sidney Blumenthal raving into the cameras about his treatment in the grand jury and of the highly personal and sexual content of the questions? Oh, how the media lapped it up. Of course, when it was later alleged that Blumenthal had been lying through his teeth to the press about the subject of his grand jury testimony, the media suddenly lost its collective appetite and glossed over that little accusation.

In any event, the White House fed the media and the media fed the public the "unfair" spin, until much of America bought into it. The American public began to believe that the President was indeed a victim of a vicious, un-American attack. At one point, I recall, the President's approval ratings were in the high 60s; Judge Starr was riding along at about 15 percent.

Starr, of course, was a sitting duck. By law, he couldn't fight back. If a witness lied to the press, Starr couldn't respond and set the record straight because it would mean revealing grand jury and other confidential materials. He couldn't talk to the press. He couldn't buy the media's favor. He couldn't use the press against the President the way the White House attack machine was using it against him.

When some of the Starr referral was made public, the White House's focus shifted. To further demonize the Office of the Independent Counsel (OIC), the spinmeisters made the treatment of Monica Lewinsky the subject of their strident criticism. Starr had brutalized the poor girl, they wailed; she was held incommunicado for hours and hours. She was kept from her lawyer and not even allowed to talk to her mother. No wonder she was cowed and had her will broken so that she would say anything they wanted to hear. She probably made up things about the poor President, just to get released from such gestapo tactics. The story sounded plausible, because, at that time, the White House was still portraying Monica Lewinsky as a "love-crazed stalker" who was angry because Clinton wouldn't have an affair with her.

That was the spin; now here's the truth, as documented in the Starr referral. On January 12, 1998, Linda Tripp provided the OIC with extensive evidence of criminal wrongdoing involving Monica Lewinsky and others. It included hours of taped conversations between Lewinsky and Tripp in which Lewinsky admitted that she intended to lie and asked Tripp to lie also if she were called to testify in the Jones case. At that point the OIC had enough evidence to indict Lewinsky based on her own admission and other evidence. They chose not to, though, and instead brought her in and confronted her with the evidence. Contrary to the charge that the prosecutors "bullied" Monica Lewinsky, I was convinced, after reviewing all the evidence and the detailed logs kept by the agents while they were with Lewinsky, that the OIC personnel acted with restraint and professionalism. She was not held incommunicado. The reason it took so long for her mother to arrive is that she refused to fly and instead took the train from New York to Washington, as the referral noted.

Lewinsky was neither "seized" nor arrested, though there was ample probable cause to do so. According to the Starr report, she and her mother, after calling their lawyer,

William Ginsburg, were both allowed to go home, even though Lewinsky had refused to cooperate.

Concerning the allegation that Starr violated Justice Department regulations by confronting Lewinsky when they knew she was represented by a lawyer, the critics overlooked the definition of a "Represented Person" as one who "has been arrested or charged in a federal criminal case, or is a defendant in a civil law enforcement proceeding concerning the subject matter of the representation." Monica Lewinsky did not fall within that definition. Besides, she is the one who should have brought any complaint against Starr, and she didn't. Finally, Lewinsky testified that she was never told that she could not call her lawyer. She was told only that if she did so, it might make an immunity agreement less likely. Actually, after talking to her mother—when she finally arrived—Monica Lewinsky contacted Mr. Ginsburg that night, as documented in the referral.

Another of the charges by the President's people was that Ken Starr and his prosecutors treated Clinton unfairly prior to and during his grand jury testimony. Let's see if that's true.

Originally the President was *invited* on six separate occasions to testify before the grand jury that was investigating him. Each time he refused. Finally, and as a last resort when the jury's business was winding down, the Independent Counsel served a subpoena on President Clinton. The only alternative was to proceed without any testimony from the President personally.

Usually the target of a grand jury is not called to testify in federal investigations. If he is subpoenaed, he can usually avoid an appearance by indicating that he intends to assert his Fifth Amendment privilege not to provide evidence tending to incriminate him. The prosecutors have the right even then to require the witness to appear before the jury and assert his privilege to each question. As a rule, however, an honorable prosecutor will not do that. While jurors aren't supposed to assume somebody is guilty because he takes the Fifth Amendment, human beings may be unconsciously prejudiced against a witness by listening to a litany of Fifth Amendment answers. There are rare cases in which a target believes that, by going before the grand jury and answering questions, he will be able to convince the jurors not to take action against him. Then it is incumbent upon the witness, usually through his attorney, to *request* an opportunity to appear, which may or may not be granted.

Then why did the Independent Counsel *invite* Mr. Clinton to appear six times? Was it an unfair effort to bring the President before the grand jury and pepper him with salacious and embarrassing questions? Absolutely not. When Mr. Clinton did finally appear, he was treated with extraordinary dignity and respect by the jurors and the prosecutors. Actually, the invitations and eventual subpoena indicate Judge Starr's intention to bend over backwards to be *fair* with the President. The jurors were hearing only evidence tending to prove guilt. The Independent Counsel had every right to submit a referral based only on that testimony, but that is not Judge Starr's style. He wanted to give the President every opportunity to answer the allegations in the privacy of a secret grand jury room. But Mr. Clinton had no interest in availing himself of that opportunity. He chose instead to take the much less dangerous course of lying to the grand jury indirectly—by relating elaborate falsehoods to his aides and advisors and then relying on them to convey those lies to the grand jury. (This was a tactic I described in my October 5, 1998, report to the Judiciary Committee, and about which we will see more later.)

If Mr. Clinton declined the invitations, then why the subpoena? In my opinion, it was an exercise in self-protection by the Office of the Independent Counsel. Just imagine the outcry from the White House and the spinners if Judge Starr sent even a referral to the House without bringing the President before the grand jury. We would have been bombarded with accusations that Starr never allowed the President to deny the charges, that he poisoned the minds of the grand jurors against the President, that he was afraid to let the President speak to the jurors, and so on and so on. By subpoenaing Mr. Clinton, Starr avoided that firefight.

The President's people still cried foul, as usual. The Independent Counsel could well have forced compliance with the subpoena and required Mr. Clinton to appear. Instead, Starr afforded the President the uncommon courtesy of withdrawing the subpoena and allowing Mr. Clinton to testify voluntarily. Even more, the President was permitted to testify not in the grand jury room but from the White House by closed-circuit television. He was allowed to have his lawyers present, and the time allotted for questioning was limited. Mr. Clinton was granted accommodations far beyond those given to any other witness before a federal grand jury.

Once a witness is sworn to tell the truth, the whole truth, and nothing but the truth, he has three, and only three, options. He can act true to his oath and truthfully answer the questions; he can lie and thereby commit the crime of perjury; or he can assert his Fifth Amendment privilege against self-incrimination. President Clinton, though, was granted a fourth alternative, which he used to great advantage. The prosecutors allowed him to read a self-serving statement to the jurors at the very outset of his testimony. Then, whenever a sticky question was asked, one that might be dangerous to answer truthfully and perilous to lie about directly, he merely reread his statement. He did that on some nineteen occasions, each time taking up more of the limited time available for questioning. Despite all of these accommodations, the White House nonetheless incessantly accused Ken Starr of unfairness.

Starr was not alone in being a target of White House attacks. As soon as the inquiry began in the Judiciary Committee, the cries of unfairness began against the Republicans and continued on a daily basis until the vote in the Senate. It was "unfair" to investigate beyond the referral, vote against the Democrats' amendments, interview prospective witnesses without the President's lawyers, keep the secure room closed to the public, release material, not release more material, ask for witnesses before the committee, not present witnesses before the committee, invite Judge Starr to testify, not invite Judge Starr to testify, and many more accusations—some, like those above, actually contradictory. But contradictions and diametrically opposed charges didn't seem to faze the President's supporters so long as they could append the phrase "and that's just unfair."

In fact, as in his dealings with the Independent Counsel, the President was treated with exceptional courtesy and fairness by the Republican majority on the House Judiciary Committee. For example, from the beginning the Watergate format was adopted, giving the White House the privilege of responding to any evidence received and testimony given during the inquiry; suggesting any additional testimony, other evidence, or leads to make a complete record; attending all executive or open hearings at which witnesses would be called; and presenting and questioning all witnesses. Further, when Judge Starr appeared, the President's counsel was permitted to cross-examine him for over an hour. That was in addition to the cross-examination by Abbe Lowell on behalf of the committee's Democrats and the hours of questioning by the Democrats themselves. Moreover, the Republicans on the committee acceded to a White House request and held an all-day hearing concerning the legal and factual standards for impeachment. And the President's counsel was given access to the secure room to assist him in preparing his defense prior to the final hearing.

At the impeachment hearing itself, the President was afforded thirty hours, or the equivalent of four working days, to present witnesses or other evidence for the defense. By comparison, I took a mere two-and-a-half hours to present the case for impeachment. Throughout the inquiry, the preparation for the hearing, and the hearing itself, Hyde repeatedly asked the President to submit any exculpatory evidence. None was forthcoming. Significantly, President Clinton's lawyers didn't call a single witness who dealt with the actual facts of the case. In addition, our staff met with the White House counsel on more than one occasion to try to work out a method of cooperation so as to narrow the issues and streamline the hearing. Hyde's reward for his scrupulous fairness? Vilification.

But let's take a look at the honesty and fair dealing of the President and his supporters prior to and during the impeachment hearing. Was it fair to seek false affidavits from prospective witnesses in the Jones case and subject those witnesses to the risk of prosecution for perjury? How about using the power of the Presidency, and other means—including perjury, witness tampering, and planting the seeds of false evidence—to defeat the constitutional rights of a single woman who claimed she had been "wronged"? How fair and gallant was it of President Clinton to stand by silently while a friend attacked that woman's character and reputation with remarks like, "Drag a $100 bill through a trailer park and there's no telling what you'll find"?

What extreme fairness the President displayed when he constructed a grandiose lie about Monica Lewinsky. He told his aides that Lewinsky was a predator who had threatened to lie about a sexual encounter unless the President succumbed to her advances. As we will see, he set the stage for later grand jury or deposition appearances by those aides, and he gave them their lines. I am thoroughly convinced that, had the stained dress not surfaced, the Monica-as-sexual-predator story would have been the President's account before the grand jury and would still be his story. That is not idle speculation; it is based on a pattern of behavior. Remember that Dolly Kyle Browning—according to Clinton—threatened to lie about him unless he met her demands. Indeed, the scenario was almost identical to Lewinsky's, at least until the blue dress came along.

President Clinton was fair to Betty Currie, wasn't he? All he did was coach her, more directly than his other aides, in order to confirm the lies that he had told in his Jones deposition. It didn't matter to him that Betty Currie would likely testify accordingly under oath and expose herself to possible perjury charges. And how about the constant trashing of anyone who had the courage to criticize or to refuse to go along with the game plan?

The lack of candor and fair dealing continued right through the Judiciary Committee's impeachment hearing. Immediately before the hearing, the President's counsel filed a "Submission" of nearly two hundred pages. Stripped to its basic elements, the Submission merely reiterated the old party line: The President lied, but it was all right to lie to the people, because what he lied about was nobody's business but his

own. Anyhow, what he did isn't a "high crime or misde-
meanor." The President would never be indicted or convicted
of perjury or obstruction of justice in a court of law. The Jones
suit was bogus, and therefore his testimony did not matter.
(By the way, you don't settle "bogus" cases for $700,000,
especially after you win in the trial court.) Kenneth Starr is a
prosecutor most foul, who purposefully hid testimony exculpatory of President Clinton. Finally, impeachment is such a
big step that the country should not have to endure it.

The Submission was, then, a classic example of the "legal
technicality concept" that was so typically employed by
President Clinton. But worse, we were again presented with
the predictable misstatements and half-truths.

Consider a few examples. First, concerning the President's
and Monica Lewinsky's testimony, the Submission stated
that the President answered "yes" to the question "your testimony is that it was possible, then, that you were alone with
her [Ms. Lewinsky]." Actually both the question and the
answer are misleading as stated. Here's the full testimony:

> **Q.** So I understand your testimony is that it was possible, then,
> that you were alone with her, *but you have no specific recollec-
> tion* of that ever happening.
> **A.** Yes, that's correct. It's possible that she, while she was work-
> ing there, she brought something to me and that at the time she
> brought it to me, she was the only person there. That's possible.

The White House Submission noted that Lewinsky had stated that no one had asked her to lie. The Independent Counsel's referral made this very point but pointed out that the President had suggested false and misleading cover stories that Lewinsky could include in an affidavit designed to keep her from testifying. Lewinsky testified in the grand jury that the affidavit was false and misleading. Moreover, the President's attorney used this false affidavit during the President's deposition in an attempt to cut off questioning about Lewinsky. In criminal law terms, this activity evidences a conspiracy to lie or to obstruct justice; Starr's referral had it right.

Another example concerns Ken Starr and the referral. On evidence regarding the transfer of gifts, the White House contended that the referral omitted a "fundamental and important fact"—that it was Lewinsky who, in her December 28 conversation with the President, first mentioned Betty Currie as a possible holder of the gifts. In fact, the referral twice quoted Lewinsky's testimony that she asked the President if "I should put the gifts outside my house somewhere or give them to someone, maybe Betty."

The White House Submission asserted that "a wealth of information contradict[s]" the allegation that the President obstructed justice with regard to gifts he had given Ms. Lewinsky. In the most dramatic contradiction, highlighted as the epigraph to the section, the Submission juxtaposed (1) the Independent Counsel's statement that the "President and Ms. Lewinsky met and discussed what should be done with the gifts subpoenaed from Ms. Lewinsky," and (2) Ms. Lewinsky's statement in the grand jury that "he really didn't—he didn't really discuss it." In truth, "he didn't really discuss it" came in response to a second, more specific question, *after* Ms. Lewinsky had spent several hundred words recounting her conversation with the President about the gifts. The full excerpt shows that the White House's quotation was misleading:

JUROR: Retell for me the conversation you had with the President about the gifts.

WITNESS [MS. LEWINSKY]: Okay. It was December 28 and I was there to get my Christmas gifts from him.... And we spent maybe about five minutes or so, not very long, talking about the case. And I said to him, "Well, do you think—" What I mentioned—I said to him that it had really alarmed me about the hat pin being in the subpoena and I think he said something like, "Oh," you know, "that sort of bothered me, too," you know, "That bothers me." Something like that.

And at one point, I said, "Well, do you think I should"—I don't think I said "get rid of," I said, "But do you think I should put away or maybe give to Betty or give to someone the gifts?"

And he—I don't remember his response. I think it was something like, "I don't know," or "Hmm" or—there really was no response. I know that I didn't leave the White House with any notion of what I should do with them, that I should do anything different than that they were sitting in my house. And then later I got the call from Betty.

JUROR: Now, did you bring up Betty's name or did the President bring up Betty's name?

WITNESS: I think I brought it up. The President wouldn't have brought up Betty's name because he really didn't—he didn't really discuss it, so either I brought up Betty's name, which I think is probably what happened, because I remember not being too, too shocked when Betty called.

But the Submission contained even more examples of hocus-pocus. Using words like "insidious," "extraordinary," and "wholly unfair," the Submission charged that the referral never attempted to rebut Ms. Currie's assertion that Ms. Lewinsky had wanted to get rid of the gifts because, in Ms. Currie's words, "people were asking questions about the stuff he had gotten." In fact, the referral outlined Ms. Currie's understanding of these "questions" and pointed out contradictory evidence.

According to the White House, the referral omitted "important testimony" from Ms. Currie to the effect that Ms. Lewinsky asked her to pick up the box of gifts. In fact, the referral included Ms. Currie's recollection three times.

The White House suggested that the referral inaccurately indicated that Ms. Currie said that the gift transfer occurred on December 28. In fact, the referral said that "Ms. Currie stated, at various times, that the transfer occurred sometime in late December 1997 or early January 1998."

The White House alleged that the OIC waited "two full months to question [Clinton aide] Nancy Hernreich after the withdrawal of executive privilege," thus showing that meritless assertions of executive privilege did not delay the OIC investigation. In fact, Ms. Hernreich testified within two weeks of the White House's withdrawal of the privilege claim.

The President's people even resorted to misleading statements in their legal analysis. The Submission made reference to Raoul Berger's authoritative treatise *Impeachment: The Constitutional Problems* (1973). But the White House deliberately avoided comment on Professor Berger's analysis of the precise question under consideration by the Judiciary Committee—whether private misconduct, including perjury, could support an impeachment: "To conclude that the Founders would have impeached a Judge who accepted a bribe of $100 but would shield one who forged a note for $10,000 or *who filed a perjured affidavit in a private transaction*, would attribute to them a thralldom to concepts from which they were far removed [emphasis added]."

To put it in modern-day Chicago-ese, the Founding Fathers would have been afflicted with wooden heads to come up with such a ridiculous distortion.

Fair? Honest? Candid? No way! The White House never ceased to astound and dismay me in the extent to which it demonstrated its utter contempt for the Judiciary Branch, the Legislative Branch, and the American people.

CHAPTER 10

Abuse of Power

W hile the proposed articles of impeachment were being drafted for presentation to the Judiciary Committee, there was a great deal of infighting both between the Democrats and Republicans, and among the Republican members themselves. The Democrats pulled out all stops in an attempt to make the charges as limited and detailed as possible. The more detailed each charge, the more limited would be the evidence that we could produce to prove our charges in the Senate. They demanded that a perjury article, for example, must identify specifically the precise perjurious statement. The Democrats also argued that any article of impeachment must be as specific and detailed as a criminal indictment. This was the opening salvo in a campaign that was to haunt the Managers in the Senate. Once you begin applying criminal law principles to an impeachment proceeding, you raise the proof standard from clear and convincing to beyond a reasonable doubt, which is not the standard for impeachment. With these demands, the Democrats were setting a trap that my staff and I begged the Republican members to avoid.

I met with Hyde and some of the staffers who were working on the articles. We agreed that the fifteen felonies set out in my October 5 talk were just too many to be manageable for a committee vote or for the full House. Some of the Republicans on the committee, including Hyde, thought we should adopt the Democrats' theory of very specific and detailed charges to encourage "bipartisanship" and perhaps win a Democratic vote or two. The majority of the members and my staff urged that the articles be drafted in a wide-open manner with the fewest possible details. That way, if additional evidence were developed after the vote, it could be plugged into a general article. It was also vital that the articles not be drafted as a criminal indictment and that no reference be made to criminal statutes or even to criminal titles, such as perjury. That would lead directly to a requirement that we prove the President guilty beyond a reasonable doubt. I argued that, as a compromise, the charges against the President of making false statements could be quite specific and detailed. But it was absolutely essential that the obstruction of justice and abuse of power articles be extremely broad.

Finally, it was agreed that four articles would be presented to the Judiciary Committee for debate. Article One charged perjury in the grand jury. Article Two charged perjury in the Paula Jones deposition. Article Three charged obstruction of justice. Article Four charged abuse of power. When I read the final draft, I was happy to see that the obstruction charge was very broadly drafted. The abuse of power article had more detail but was still broad enough to encompass the proof that we anticipated producing. I was convinced that the strongest article was the one charging abuse of power by the President.

The charges against President Clinton have been compared with those against President Nixon (which, of course, Nixon avoided facing by resigning in August 1974). Those opposing the Clinton impeachment often suggest that the President's actions, though tawdry and perhaps criminal, did not rise to the level of the "high crimes and misdemeanors" necessary to support impeachment. His lies and obstruction were purely personal failings and did not affect the Constitution, the Office of the President, or affairs of state. Nixon, on the other hand, employed his high office to obstruct justice, suborn perjury, and otherwise affect the constitutional rights and privileges of American citizens.

But in my opinion, what Nixon did—and it was bad—did not remotely approach the abuses of office perpetrated by Clinton and his cronies. Nor did President Nixon attack the constitutional rights of private citizens the way Clinton did.

Republican Congressman George Gekas of Pennsylvania announced that he could not vote for Article Four in its present form. At a caucus of the Republican members, Gekas said he didn't think the President's manipulation of the judicial process rose to abuse of power. He had an alternative amendment that he thought would be more acceptable to the Democrats. There was a short debate. Hyde suggested that, in the interest of unity, all Republican members join with the Democrats in voting for Gekas's amendment rather than the original article. The Republican members readily agreed. Later, when I had a chance to read the Gekas amendment, I realized that it had completely emasculated Article Four and that there would be no chance of its passage on the floor of the House.

Here is why I thought it so important to retain a strong and broadly drafted abuse of power article of impeachment.

Our Founders decided in the Constitutional Convention that one of the duties imposed upon the President is to "take care that the laws be faithfully executed." Furthermore, he is required to take an oath to "preserve, protect, and defend the Constitution of the United States." Twice this President stood on the steps of the Capitol, raised his right hand to God, and repeated that oath.

Now, the Fifth Amendment to the Constitution of the United States provides that no person shall "be deprived of life, liberty, or property without due process of law," the Seventh Amendment ensures that in civil suits "the right of trial by jury shall be preserved," and the Fourteenth Amendment guarantees due process of law and equal protection of the laws. We examined the concepts of due process, equal protection, and the right to trial by jury as practiced by the President to determine whether he had kept his oath to preserve, protect, and defend the law and whether he had abused his office for purely personal gain.

As soon as Paula Jones filed her lawsuit, President Clinton, rather than confronting the charges, tried to get them dismissed. To do so he used the power and dignity of the Office of President in an attempt to deny Ms. Jones her day in court. He argued that, as President, he was immune from a lawsuit during his tenure in office—that is, that the President while in office is immune from the civil law of the land. More interesting is the rationale given by the President for that immunity: "The broad public and constitutional interests that would be placed at risk by litigating such claims against an incumbent President *far outweigh* the asserted *private interest* of a plaintiff who seeks civil damages for an alleged past injury [emphasis added]."

There you have it. Sorry, Ms. Jones, because William Jefferson Clinton occupies the Office of President, your lawsuit against him, not as President, but *personally*, must be set aside. The President's lawyers are referring to the most basic civil rights of an American citizen to due process of law and to the equal protection of the laws—those same rights that President Clinton had taken an oath to preserve and protect. Or is it that some people are more equal than others? Here is a clear example of the President's abusing the power and majesty of his office to obtain a purely personal advantage over Ms. Jones and avoid having to pay damages. The case was, in fact, stalled for several years until the Supreme

Court ruled. If there is one statement that might qualify as the motto of this Presidency, it is that contained in one of the briefs filed on behalf of Mr. Clinton: "In a very real and significant way, the objectives of William J. Clinton, the person, and his Administration (the Clinton White House) are one and the same."

The President was just getting started: He employed the power and prestige of his office and of his cabinet officers to mislead and to lie to the American people about the Paula Jones case and the Monica Lewinsky matter. But more: Throughout the grand jury investigation and various other investigations, the President tried to extend the relatively narrow bounds of presidential privilege to unlimited, if not bizarre, lengths, again for his own personal purposes. For instance, according to the Starr referral, on August 28, 1998, when Deputy White House Counsel Bruce Lindsey appeared before the grand jury, "the President again asserted executive privilege with respect to his testimony—even though the President had dropped the claim of executive privilege while the case was pending before the Supreme Court of the United States in June." The plan was to delay, obstruct, and detour the investigations, not to protect the Presidency, but to protect Mr. Clinton personally. It is bad enough that the office was abused for that reason, but the infinite harm done to the Presidency by those frivolous and dilatory tactics is irreparable. The courts routinely rejected the President's array of immunity and privilege claims, with one notable exception. Future presidents will be forced to operate within these strictures because one person assumed that the office put him above the law.

Furthermore, the power and the prestige of the Office of the President were marshaled to destroy the character and reputation of Monica Lewinsky, a young woman who had been ill-used by the President. As soon as her name surfaced, the campaign began to muzzle any possible testimony and to attack the credibility of witnesses in a concerted effort to insulate the President from the lawsuit filed by another woman allegedly misused by Bill Clinton, Paula Jones. It almost worked.

When the President testified at his deposition that he had had no sexual relations with Monica Lewinsky, he felt secure. Monica Lewinsky, the only other witness, was in the bag. She had furnished a false affidavit also denying everything. Later, when he realized from the January 18, 1998, *Drudge Report* that there were taped conversations between Ms. Lewinsky and Linda Tripp, he had to come up with a new story, and he did. In addition, he recounted that story to White House aides, who passed it on to the grand jury.

On Wednesday, January 21, 1998, the *Washington Post* published a story entitled "Clinton Accused of Urging Aide to Lie; Starr Probes Whether President Told Woman to Deny Alleged Affair to Jones' Lawyers." The White House learned the substance of the *Post* story on the evening of January 20, 1998. After the President knew of the existence of that story, he made a series of telephone calls. At

12:08 AM, according to the Starr referral, he called his attorney, Robert Bennett. The next morning, Mr. Bennett was quoted in the *Post* stating: "The President adamantly denies he ever had a relationship with Ms. Lewinsky and she has confirmed the truth of that. This story seems ridiculous and I frankly smell a rat."

The Starr report laid out the chronology. After his conversation with Bennett, the President had a half-hour conversation with Deputy White House Counsel Bruce Lindsey. At 1:16 AM, the President called Betty Currie and spoke to her for twenty minutes. He then called Bruce Lindsey again. At 6:30 AM the President called Vernon Jordan. After that, the President again spoke with Lindsey. This flurry of activity was a prelude to the stories that the President would soon inflict upon top White House aides and advisors.

On the morning of January 21, 1998, the President met with White House Chief of Staff Erskine Bowles and his two deputies, John Podesta and Sylvia Matthews. Bowles recalled entering the President's office at 9 AM. He then recounted to the grand jury the President's immediate words as he and two others entered the Oval Office: "And he looked up at us and he said the same thing he said to the American people. He said, 'I want you to know I did not have sexual relationships with this woman, Monica Lewinsky. I did not ask anybody to lie. And when the facts come out, you'll understand.'"

Mr. Bowles recalled that, after the President made that blanket denial, "I said, 'Mr. President, I don't know what the facts are. I don't know if they're good, bad, or indifferent. But whatever they are, you ought to get them out. And you ought to get them out right now.'"

When counsel asked whether the President responded to Bowles's suggestion that he tell the truth, Bowles answered, "I don't think he made any response, but he didn't disagree with me."

Deputy Chief of Staff John Podesta also recalled a meeting with the President on the morning of January 21, 1998. He testified before the grand jury as to what occurred in the Oval Office that morning:

> **A.** And we started off meeting—we didn't—I don't think we said anything. And I think the President directed this specifically to Mr. Bowles. He said, "Erskine, I want you to know that this story is not true."
> **Q.** What else did he say?
> **A.** He said that—that he had not had a sexual relationship with her, and that he never asked anybody to lie.

Mr. Podesta told the grand jury that two days later, on January 23, 1998, he had another discussion with the President:

> I asked him how he was doing, and he said he was working on this draft and he said to me that he never had sex with her, and that—and that he never asked—you know, he repeated the denial, but he was extremely explicit in saying he never had sex with her.

Podesta was asked to elaborate on his statement:

> **Q.** Okay. Not explicit, in the sense that he got more specific
> than sex, than the word "sex."
> **A.** Yes, he was more specific than that.
> **Q.** Okay. Share that with us.
> **A.** Well, I think he said—he said that—there was some spate of,
> you know, what sex acts were counted, and he said that he had
> never had sex with her in any way whatsoever—
> **Q.** Okay.
> **A.** —that they had not had oral sex.

Later in the day on January 21, 1998, the President called
White House aide Sidney Blumenthal to his office. It is interesting to note how the President's lies become more elaborate and pronounced when he has time to concoct his newest
line of defense. When the President spoke to Mr. Bowles and
Mr. Podesta, he simply denied the story. But, by the time he
spoke to Mr. Blumenthal, the President had added three new
angles to his defense strategy: (1) he now portrayed Monica
Lewinsky as the aggressor; (2) he launched an attack on her
reputation by portraying her as a "stalker"; and (3) he presented himself as the innocent victim being attacked by the
forces of evil.

Note well this recollection by Sidney Blumenthal in his
June 4, 1998, testimony:

> And it was at this point that he gave his account of what had
> happened to me and he said that Monica—and it came very

fast. He said, "Monica Lewinsky came at me and made a sexual demand on me." He rebuffed her. He said, "I've gone down that road before, I've caused pain for a lot of people and I'm not going to do that again."

She threatened him. She said that she would tell people they'd had an affair, that she was known as the stalker among her peers, and that she hated it and if she had an affair or said she had an affair then she wouldn't be the stalker anymore.

And then consider Mr. Blumenthal's recollection of what the President told him moments later:

And he said, "I feel like a character in a novel. I feel like some-body who is surrounded by an oppressive force that is creating a lie about me and I can't get the truth out. I feel like the character in the novel *Darkness at Noon*." And I said to him, "When this happened with Monica Lewinsky, were you alone?" He said, "Well, I was within eyesight or earshot of someone."

At one point, Mr. Blumenthal was asked by the grand jury to describe the President's manner and demeanor during the exchange:

Q. In response to my question how you responded to the President's story about a threat or discussion about a threat from Ms. Lewinsky, you mentioned you didn't recall specifically. Do you recall generally the nature of your response to the President?

A. It was generally sympathetic to the President. And I certainly believed his story. It was a very heartfelt story, he was pouring out his heart, and I believed him.

When asked in the grand jury about his conversations with Podesta, Bowles, and Blumenthal, President Clinton said that he had been very careful with his wording in those conversations. He asserted that he wanted his statement regarding "sexual relations" to be literally true because he was referring only to intercourse. Really? Then why did he tell John Podesta that he denied sex "in any way whatsoever," including oral sex?

When Betty Currie testified before the grand jury, she could not recall whether she had another one-on-one discussion with the President on Tuesday, January 20, or Wednesday, January 21. But she did state that on one of those days, the President summoned her back to his office. At that time, the President recapped their now-infamous Sunday afternoon post-deposition discussion in the Oval Office. That's when the President made a series of statements to Ms. Currie, including some to which Ms. Currie could not possibly have known the answers (for example, "Monica came on to me, and I never touched her, right?"). When he spoke to her on January 20 or 21, the referral noted, he spoke in the same tone and demeanor that he had used in his Sunday, January 18, session. Ms. Currie stated that the President may have mentioned that she might be asked about Monica Lewinsky.

It is clear that the President's assertions to staff were designed for dissemination to the American people. But it is equally important to understand that the President intended his aides to relate those false stories to investigators and grand jurors alike.

We know that this is true for the following reasons: The Special Division had recently appointed the Office of the Independent Counsel to investigate the Monica Lewinsky matter; the President realized that Jones's attorneys and investigators were investigating this matter; the *Washington Post* journalists and investigators were exposing the details of the Lewinsky affair; and an investigation relating to perjury charges based on presidential activities in the Oval Office would certainly lead to interviews with West Wing employees and high-level staffers. Because the President would not appear before the grand jury, his version of events would be supplied by those staffers to whom he had lied.

The President actually acknowledged in his grand jury testimony that he knew his aides might be called before the grand jury. In addition, Mr. Podesta testified before the grand jury that he knew that he was likely to be a witness in the ongoing grand jury criminal investigation. He said that he was "sensitive about not exchanging information because I knew I was a potential witness." He also recalled that the President volunteered to provide information about Ms. Lewinsky to him even though Mr. Podesta had not asked for these details.

In other words, the President's lies and deceptions to his

White House aides, coupled with his steadfast refusal to testify, had the effect of presenting a false account of events to investigators and grand jurors. The President's aides believed the President when he told them his contrived account. The aides' eventual testimony provided the President's calculated falsehoods to the grand jury, which, in turn, gave the jurors an inaccurate and misleading set of facts upon which to base any decisions. That is abuse of the Presidency and use of the power of the office to obstruct justice.

President Clinton also implemented a win-at-all-costs strategy. We know this because of testimony presented by Dick Morris to the federal grand jury. Mr. Morris, a former presidential advisor, testified before the grand jury that on January 21, 1998, he met President Clinton to discuss the turbulent events of the day. The President again denied the accusations against him. After further discussions, they decided to have an overnight poll taken to determine if the American people would forgive the President for adultery, perjury, and obstruction of justice. When Mr. Morris received the results, he called the President. As he told the grand jury:

> And I said, "They're just too shocked by this. It's just too new, it's too raw." And I said, "And the problem is they're willing to forgive you for adultery, but not for perjury or obstruction of justice or the various other things."

Morris further recalled the following exchange:

MORRIS: And I said, "They're just not ready for it," meaning
the voters.
PRESIDENT: Well, we just have to win, then.

In order to win, the White House had to convince the pub-
lic, and the grand jurors who read the newspapers, that
Monica Lewinsky was unworthy of belief. If the account
Lewinsky gave to Linda Tripp was believed, then there
would emerge a tawdry affair in and near the Oval Office.
Moreover, the President's own perjury and that of Monica
Lewinsky would surface. How do you counter this? You
employ the full power and credibility of the White House
and its admirers in the press corps to destroy the witness.
Thus on January 29, 1998, the *Cleveland Plain Dealer*
wrote:

> Inside the White House, the debate goes on about the best way
> to destroy "that woman," as President Bill Clinton called
> Monica Lewinsky. Should they paint her as a friendly fantasist
> or a malicious stalker?

The *Plain Dealer* added:

> "That poor child has serious emotional problems," Rep.
> Charles Rangel, Democrat of New York, said Tuesday night
> before the State of the Union. "She's fantasizing. And I haven't
> heard that she played with a full deck in her other experiences."

Listen to Gene Lyons, an Arkansas columnist, on January 30:

> But it's also very easy to take a mirror's eye view of this thing, look at this thing from a completely different direction and take the same evidence and posit a totally innocent relationship in which the President was, in a sense, the victim of someone rather like the woman who followed David Letterman around.

From another White House "source," which appeared in the *Los Angeles Times* on February 1:

> Monica had become known at the White House, says one source, as "the stalker."

And on February 4 the *Buffalo News* added:

> The media have reported that sources describe Lewinsky as "infatuated" with the President, "star struck" and even "a stalker."

And this from the *Toronto Sun* on January 31:

> One White House aide called reporters to offer information about Monica Lewinsky's past, her weight problems and what the aide said was her nickname—"The Stalker."
>
> Junior staff members, speaking on the condition that they not be identified, said she was known as a flirt, wore her skirts too short, and was "a little bit weird."
>
> Little by little, ever since allegations of an affair between U.S. President Bill Clinton and Lewinsky surfaced 10 days ago,

White House sources have waged a behind-the-scenes campaign to portray her as an untrustworthy climber obsessed with the President.

Just hours after the story broke, one White House source made unsolicited calls offering that Lewinsky was the "troubled" product of divorced parents and may have been following the footsteps of her mother, who wrote a tell-all book about the private lives of three famous opera singers....

One story had Lewinsky following former Clinton aide George Stephanopoulos to Starbucks. After observing what kind of coffee he ordered, she showed up the next day at his secretary's desk with a cup of the same coffee to "surprise him."

Sound familiar? It ought to, because that is the same type of tactic used in Clinton's attempt to destroy Paula Jones and Dolly Kyle Browning. The difference is that these evil rumors were emanating from the White House, the bastion of the free world, to protect one man from being forced to answer for his deportment in the highest office in the land. And don't forget that the release of Kathleen Willey's letters to the President arguably violated federal privacy laws. But then, what's another unlawful act when you need to destroy a witness?

Let's turn to President Clinton's grand jury appearance.

On August 16, 1998, the day before that scheduled appearance, the President's personal attorney, David Kendall, provided the following statement: "There is apparently an enormous amount of groundless speculation about the President's testimony tomorrow. *The truth is the truth. Period. And that's how the President will testify* [emphasis added]."

On August 17, 1998, the President testified. He admitted to the grand jury that, after the allegations were publicly reported, he made "misleading" statements to particular aides who he knew would likely be called to testify before the grand jury:

> **Q.** Do you recall denying any sexual relationship with Monica Lewinsky to the following people: Harry Thomason, Erskine Bowles, Harold Ickes, Mr. Podesta, Mr. Blumenthal, Mr. Jordan, Ms. Betty Currie? Do you recall denying any sexual relationship with Monica Lewinsky to those individuals?
>
> **WJC [PRESIDENT CLINTON].** I recall telling a number of those people that I didn't have, either I didn't have an affair with Monica Lewinsky or didn't have sex with her. And I believe, sir, that— you'll have to ask them what they thought. But I was using those terms in the normal way people use them. You'll have to ask them what they thought I was saying.
>
> **Q.** If they testified that you denied [a] sexual relationship with Monica Lewinsky, or if they told us that you denied that, do you have any reason to doubt them, in the days after the story broke; do you have any reason to doubt them?
>
> **WJC.** No.

The President was then specifically asked whether he knew that his aides were likely to be called before the grand jury:

Q. It may have been misleading, sir, and you knew though, after January 21 when the *Post* article broke and said that Judge Starr was looking into this, you knew that they might be witnesses. You knew that they might be called into a grand jury, didn't you?

WJC. That's right. I think I was quite careful what I said after that. I may have said something to all these people to that effect, but I'll also—whenever anybody asked me any details, I said, look, I don't want you to be a witness or turn you into a witness or give you information that would get you in trouble. I just wouldn't talk. I, by and large, didn't talk to people about it.

Q. If all of these people—let's leave Mrs. Currie for a minute— Vernon Jordan, Sid Blumenthal, John Podesta, Harold Ickes, Erskine Bowles, Harry Thomason, after the story broke, after Judge Starr's involvement was known on January 21, have said that you denied a sexual relationship with them. Are you denying that?

WJC. No.

Q. And you've told us that you—

WJC. I'm just telling you what I meant by it. I told you what I meant by it when they started this deposition.

Q. You've told us now that you were being careful, but that it might have been misleading. Is that correct?

WJC. It might have been.... So, what I was trying to do was to give them something they could—that would be true, even if misleading in the context of this deposition, and keep them out of trouble, and let's deal—and deal with what I thought was the almost ludicrous suggestion that I had urged someone to lie or tried to suborn perjury, in other words.

We're all free to call the President's actions anything we like. I call them abuse of power. I believe most Americans, given all the facts, would do the same.

CHAPTER 11

A Lie Is a Lie

Just before the final argument and debate on the articles of impeachment, on November 27, the President finally got around to answering the eighty-one questions that the committee had served right after the November 3 election. The answers were accompanied by a letter from David Kendall that stated, "I want to emphasize again the point I made in the Preliminary Memorandum we submitted to the Committee more than two months ago: The President did *not* commit or suborn perjury, tamper with witnesses, obstruct justice, or abuse power." Now, if Mr. Clinton himself, under his own signature, had made that categorical denial, we would have a direct and easily provable false statement to Congress. But that was the only cold denial in the entire package, and you can't charge a person with making a false statement if the statement is made by a third person.

The actual answers to the eighty-one questions were classic Clintonese. He wouldn't even admit that he was the chief law enforcement officer of the United States. Instead he answered, in response to Request No. 1: "The President is frequently referred to as the chief law enforcement officer, although nothing in the Constitution specifically designates the President as such. Article II, Section 1 of the United States Constitution states that '[t]he Executive Power shall be vested in a President of the United States of America.' And the law enforcement function is a component of the executive power."

The remaining questions were typical examples of Clinton word parsing, dodging, and obfuscation:

28. Do you admit or deny that you had a telephone conversation on January 6, 1998, with Vernon Jordan during which you discussed Monica Lewinsky's affidavit, yet to be filed, in the case of *Jones* v. *Clinton*?

Response to Request No. 28:

White House records included in the OIC Referral reflect that I spoke to Mr. Jordan on January 6, 1998. Supp. at 1886. I do not recall whether we discussed Ms. Lewinsky's affidavit during a telephone call on that date.

34. Do you admit or deny that you had knowledge that any facts or assertions contained in the affidavit executed by Monica Lewinsky on January 7, 1998, in the case of *Jones* v. *Clinton* were not true?

40. Do you admit or deny that during your deposition in the case of *Jones* v. *Clinton* on January 27, 1998, you affirmed that the facts or assertions stated in the affidavit executed by Monica Lewinsky on January 7, 1998, were true?

Response to Requests Nos. 34 and 40:

I was asked at my deposition in January about two paragraphs of Ms. Lewinsky's affidavit. With respect to Paragraph 6, I explained the extent to which I was able to attest to its accuracy. Dep. at 202–03.

With respect to Paragraph 8, I stated in my deposition that it was true. Dep. at 204. In my August 17th grand jury testimony, I sought to explain the basis for that deposition answer: "I believe at the time that she filled out this affidavit, if she believed that the definition of sexual relationship was two people having intercourse, then this is accurate." App. at 743.

42. Do you admit or deny that when asked on January 17, 1998, in your deposition in the case of *Jones* v. *Clinton* if you had ever given gifts to Monica Lewinsky, you stated that you did not recall, even though you actually had knowledge of giving her gifts in addition to gifts from the "Black Dog"?

Response to Request No. 42:

In my grand jury testimony, I was asked about this same statement. I explained that my full response was "I don't recall. *Do you know what they were?*" By that answer, I did not mean to suggest that I did not recall giving gifts, rather, I meant that I did not recall what the gifts were, and I asked for reminders. *See* App. at 502–03.

When pressed, though, the President did not hesitate to mislead, if not actually restate previous lies:

> **52.** Do you admit or deny that on January 18, 1998, at or about 5 PM, you had a meeting with Betty Currie at which you made statements similar to any of the following regarding your relationship with Monica Lewinsky?
>> **a.** "You were always there when she was there, right? We were never really alone."
>> **b.** "You could see and hear everything."
>> **c.** "Monica came on to me, and I never touched her, right?"
>> **d.** "She wanted to have sex with me and I couldn't do that."
>
> **Response to Request No. 52:**
> When I met with Ms. Currie, I believe that I asked her certain questions, in an effort to get as much information as quickly as I could, and made certain statements, although I do not remember exactly what I said. *See* App. at 508.
>
> Some time later, I learned that the Office of Independent Counsel was involved and that Ms. Currie was going to have to testify before the grand jury. After learning this, I stated in my grand jury testimony, I told Ms. Currie, "Just relax, go in there and tell the truth." App. at 591.
>
> **53.** Do you admit or deny that you had a conversation with Betty Currie within several days of January 18, 1998, in which you made statements similar to any of the following regarding your relationship with Monica Lewinsky?
>> **a.** "You were always there when she was there, right? We were never really alone."

b. "You could see and hear everything."

c. "Monica came on to me, and I never touched her, right?"

d. "She wanted to have sex with me and I couldn't do that."

Response to Request No. 53:

I previously told the grand jury that "I don't know that I" had another conversation with Ms. Currie within several days of January 18, 1998, in which I made statements similar to those quoted above. "I remember having this [conversation] one time." App. at 592. I further explained, "I do not remember how many times I talked to Betty Currie or when. I don't. I can't possibly remember that. I do remember, when I first heard about this story breaking, trying to ascertain what the facts were, trying to ascertain what Betty's perception was. I remember that I was highly agitated, understandably, I think." App. at 593.

I understand that Ms. Currie has said a second conversation occurred the next day that I was in the White House. Supp. at 535–36. This would have been Tuesday, January 20, before I knew about the grand jury investigation.

Perhaps the most blatant attempt to dodge the truth, yet not put himself in the position of contradicting his aides, came near the end:

62. Do you admit or deny that on January 21, 1998, the day the Monica Lewinsky story appeared for the first time in the *Washington Post*, you had a conversation with Sidney Blumenthal, in which you stated that you rebuffed alleged advances from Monica Lewinsky and in which you made a statement similar to the following?: "Monica Lewinsky came at me and made a sexual demand on me."

63. Do you admit or deny that on January 21, 1998, the day the Monica Lewinsky story appeared for the first time in the *Washington Post*, you had a conversation with Sidney Blumenthal, in which you made a statement similar to the following in response to a question about your conduct with Monica Lewinsky?: "I haven't done anything wrong."

64. Do you admit or deny that on January 21, 1998, the day the Monica Lewinsky story appeared for the first time in the *Washington Post*, you had a conversation with Erskine Bowles, Sylvia Matthews, and John Podesta, in which you made a statement similar to the following?: "I want you to know I did not have sexual relationships with this woman, Monica Lewinsky. I did not ask anybody to lie. And when the facts come out, you'll understand."

65. Do you admit or deny that on or about January 23, 1998, you had a conversation with John Podesta, in which you stated that you had never had an affair with Monica Lewinsky?

66. Do you admit or deny that on or about January 23, 1998, you had a conversation with John Podesta, in which you stated that you were not alone with Monica Lewinsky in the Oval Office, and that Betty Currie was either in your presence or outside your office with the door open while you were visiting with Monica Lewinsky?

67. Do you admit or deny that on or about January 26, 1998, you had a conversation with Harold Ickes in which you made

statements to the effect that you did not have an affair with
Monica Lewinsky?

68. Do you admit or deny that on or about January 26, 1998,
you had a conversation with Harold Ickes, in which you made
statements to the effect that you had not asked anyone to change
their story, suborn perjury, or obstruct justice if called to testify
or otherwise respond to a request for information from the
Office of Independent Counsel or in any other legal proceeding?

Response to Requests Nos. 62–68:

As I have previously acknowledged, I did not want my family,
friends, or colleagues to know the full nature of my relationship
with Ms. Lewinsky. In the days following the January 21, 1998,
Washington Post article, I misled people about this relationship.
I have repeatedly apologized for doing so.

Now that answer contains the truth, the whole truth, and
nothing but the truth, doesn't it? Clinton did not hesitate to
adopt his pattern of false, misleading, and nonresponsive
answers even when dealing with the United States Congress.
That, too, went into our preparation for impeachment.

When the staff and the members returned after Thanksgiving, Hyde told me that the hearing and debate on the
four impeachment articles would begin on Monday,
December 7, and continue until a vote in committee could
take place, he hoped, by the end of the week. Our evidence
was limited to Ken Starr's testimony, but Hyde decided to
give the President's counsel, Mr. Kendall, thirty hours to

present whatever evidence he might deem relevant. The two staff lawyers, Abbe Lowell and I, would give closing arguments. The members would then debate the articles and vote.

When the hearings began, I again asked Hyde for at least one day to present additional evidence. I told him that Dolly Kyle Browning had flown to Washington at her own expense to testify. Hyde said no. If we called witnesses, then the President would want to call rebuttal witnesses. We didn't have the time. If we didn't finish in the 105th Congress, there would be no reauthorization in the 106th Congress.

I called Larry Klayman and asked him to break the bad news to Dolly. Larry rarely raises his voice, but he was livid. "What am I going to tell her, that the Republicans on the committee were too timid to take on the President and the House Democrats?"

"It's not that. We simply have no time."

"This is nonsense. Dolly may show up on the steps of the Capitol and hold a news conference, or she may show up in the committee room and demand to be heard."

I told Larry I hoped she would do both, and hung up.

As it turned out, Ms. Browning did neither. She did, however, send a letter to Mr. Hyde the day the hearings ended, December 11. In it, she noted that she had been asked by my staff to come to testify before the committee, but for some reason "the leadership decided against it." She enclosed thirty-five copies of a declaration and supporting materials and asked that they be distributed to all the committee members. I don't know if they ever were.

On Thursday, December 10, I was called into Hyde's office. It was time for me to present our case before the committee. Hyde shook my hand. "No matter what happens, the country owes you and your staff a vote of thanks," he said.

I went into the conference room to get a soda and found Jim Rogan and Mary Bono just walking out. "Go get 'em, tiger," Jim said. "We're all counting on you."

Ms. Bono smiled and said, "You know what they say in show business?"

"Break a leg?" I responded.

"No—don't screw up."

Then I was alone. I stood for a good five minutes just looking out the window where the cars were driving by. Lindsey Graham's voice interrupted my thoughts. "Come on, partner, show time!" I muttered a short prayer to my patron saint, Thomas More, and walked into the committee room.

What follows are portions of what I said:

On October 5, 1998, I came before this Committee to advise you of the results of our analysis and review of the Referral from the Office of the Independent Counsel. We concluded that there existed substantial and credible evidence of several separate events directly involving the President that could constitute grounds for impeachment. At that time I specifically limited my review and report to evidence of possible felonies. In addition, I asserted that the report and analysis were merely a litany of crimes that might have been committed.

On October 8, the House of Representatives passed Resolution 581 calling for an inquiry to determine whether the House should exercise its constitutional duty to impeach President William Jefferson Clinton.

Thereafter, this Committee heard testimony from several experts and other witnesses, including the Independent Counsel, Kenneth Starr.

Since that time, my staff and I, as requested, have conducted ongoing investigations and inquiries. We have received and reviewed additional information and evidence from the Independent Counsel and have developed additional information from diverse sources.

Unfortunately, because of the extremely strict time limits placed upon us, a number of very promising leads had to be abandoned. We just ran out of time. In addition, many other allegations of possible serious wrongdoing cannot be presented publicly at this time by virtue of circumstances totally beyond our control.

For example, we uncovered more incidents involving probable direct and deliberate obstruction of justice, witness tampering, perjury, and abuse of power. We were, however, informed both by the Department of Justice and by the Office of the Independent Counsel that to bring forth publicly that evidence at this time would seriously compromise pending criminal investigations that are nearing completion. We have bowed to their suggestion.

First of all, allow me to assert my profound and unqualified respect for the Office of the President of the United States. It represents to the American people and to the world the strength, the philosophy, and, most of all, the honor and integrity that makes us a great nation and an example for developing people.

Because all eyes are focused upon that high office, the character and credibility of any temporary occupant of the office is vital to the domestic and foreign welfare of the citizens. Consequently, serious breaches of integrity and duty of necessity adversely influence the reputation of the United States.

When I appeared in this Committee Room a little over two months ago, it was merely to analyze the Referral and to report. Today, after our investigation, I have come to a point that I prayed I would never reach. It is my sorrowful duty now to accuse President William Jefferson Clinton of the following crimes: obstruction of justice, false and deliberately misleading statements under oath, witness tampering, abuse of power, and false statements to and obstruction of the Congress of the United States in the course of this very impeachment inquiry. Whether these charges are high crimes and misdemeanors and whether the President should be impeached is not for me to say or even to give an opinion. That is your job. I am merely going to set forth the evidence and testimony before you so that you can judge.

As I stated earlier, this is not about sex or private conduct, it is about multiple obstructions of justice, perjury, false and misleading statements, witness tampering, and abuses of power, all committed or orchestrated by the President of the United States.

Before we get into the President's lies and obstruction, it is important to place the events in the proper context. We have acknowledged all along that if this were only about sex, you would not now be engaged in this debate. But the manner in which the Lewinsky relationship arose and continued is important. It is illustrative of the character of the President and the decisions he made.

Monica Lewinsky, a twenty-two-year-old intern, was working at the White House during the government shutdown in 1995. Prior to their first intimate encounter, she had never even spoken with the President. Sometime on November 15, 1995, Ms. Lewinsky made an improper gesture to the President. What did the President do in response? Did the President immediately confront her or report to her supervisor as you would expect? Did he make it clear that such conduct would not be tolerated in the White House?

That would have been an appropriate reaction, but it was not the one the President took. Instead, the President of the United States of America invited this unknown young intern into a private area off the Oval Office, where he kissed her. He then invited her back later, and when she returned, the two engaged in the first of many acts of inappropriate contact.

Thereafter, the two concocted a cover story. If Ms. Lewinsky were seen, she was bringing papers to the President. That story was totally false. The only papers she brought were personal messages having nothing to do with her duties or those of the President. After Ms. Lewinsky moved from the White House to the Pentagon, her frequent visits to the President were disguised as visits to Betty Currie. Those cover stories are important because they play a vital role in the later perjuries and obstructions.

Over the term of their relationship the following significant matters occurred:

1) Monica Lewinsky and the President were alone on at least twenty-one occasions;

2) They had at least eleven personal sexual encounters, excluding phone sex: three in 1995, five in 1996, and three in 1997.

3) They had at least fifty-five telephone conversations, of which at least seventeen involved phone sex;

4) The President gave Ms. Lewinsky twenty presents; and,

5) Ms. Lewinsky gave the President forty presents.

These are the essential facts that form the backdrop for all of the events that followed. During the fall of 1997, things were relatively quiet. Monica Lewinsky was working at the Pentagon and looking for a high-paying job in New York. The President's attempt to stall the Paula Jones case was still pending in the Supreme Court, and nobody seemed to care one way or another what the outcome would be. Then, in the first week of December 1997, things began to unravel.

I do not intend to discuss the sexual details of the President's encounters with Ms. Lewinsky. However, I do not want to give this Committee the impression that those encounters are irrelevant. In fact, they are highly relevant because the President repeatedly lied about that sexual relationship in his deposition, before the grand jury, and in his responses to this Committee's questions. He has consistently maintained that Ms. Lewinsky performed acts on him, while he never touched her in a sexual manner. This characterization not only directly contradicts Ms. Lewinsky's testimony, but it also contradicts the sworn grand jury testimony of three of her friends and the statements by two professional counselors with whom she contemporaneously shared the details of her relationship.

While his treatment of Ms. Lewinsky may be offensive, it is much more offensive for the President to expect this Committee to believe that in 1996 and 1997 his intimate contact with Ms. Lewinsky was so narrowly tailored that it conveniently escapes his strained interpretation of a definition of "sexual relations" which he did not conceive until 1998.

A few words of caution:

The evidence and testimony must be viewed as a whole; it cannot be compartmentalized. Please do not be cajoled into considering each event in isolation and then treating it separately. That is the tactic employed by defense lawyers in every conspiracy trial that I have ever seen. Remember, events and words that may seem innocent or even exculpatory in a vacuum may well take on a sinister or even criminal connotation when observed in the context of the whole plot. For example, everyone agrees that Monica Lewinsky testified, "No one ever told me to lie; nobody ever promised me a job."

When considered alone this would seem exculpatory. In the context of the other evidence, we see that this is again technical parsing of words to give a misleading inference. Of course no one said, "Now, Monica, you go in there and lie." They didn't have to; Monica knew what was expected of her. Similarly, nobody *promised* her a job, but once she signed the false affidavit, she got one, didn't she?

Likewise, please don't permit the obfuscations and legalistic pyrotechnics of the President's defenders to distract you from the real issues here. A friend of mine flew bombers over Europe in the Second World War. He once told me that the planes would carry packages of lead-based tinfoil strips. When the planes flew into the perimeter of the enemy's radar coverage, the crews would release that tinfoil. It was intended to confuse and distract the radar operators from the real target.

Now, the treatment that Monica Lewinsky received from the Independent Counsel, the legality of Linda Tripp's taping, the motives of some of the witnesses, and those who helped finance the Paula Jones lawsuit—that's tinfoil. The real issues are whether the President of the United States testified falsely under oath; whether he engaged in a continuing plot to obstruct justice, to hide evidence, to tamper with witnesses, and to abuse the power of his office in furtherance of that plot. The ultimate issue is whether the President's course of conduct was such as to affect adversely the Office of the President by bringing scandal and disrespect upon it and also upon the administration of justice, and whether he has acted in a manner contrary to his trust as President and subversive to the rule of law and constitutional government.

Finally, the truth is not decided by the number of scholars with different opinions, the outcome of polls, or by the shifting winds of public opinion. Moreover, you often possess information that is not generally available to the public. As Representatives of the people you must honestly and thoroughly examine all the evidence, apply the applicable constitutional precepts, and vote your conscience—independently and without fear or favor. As Andrew Jackson said: "One man with courage makes a majority."

The events that form the basis of these charges actually began in late 1995. They reached a critical stage in the winter of 1997 and the first month of 1998. The final act in this sordid drama took place on August 17, 1998, when the President of the United States appeared before a federal grand jury, raised his right hand to God, and swore to tell the truth. Did he? We shall see.

This Committee has been asked to keep an open heart and mind and focus on the record. I completely agree. So, in the words of Al Smith, a good Democrat, let's look at the record.

December 5–6, 1997

On Friday, December 5, 1997, Monica Lewinsky asked Betty Currie if the President could see her the next day, Saturday, but Ms. Currie said that the President was scheduled to meet with his lawyers all day. Later that Friday, Ms. Lewinsky spoke briefly to the President at a Christmas party.

That evening, Paula Jones's attorneys faxed a list of potential witnesses to the President's attorneys. The list included Monica Lewinsky. However, Ms. Lewinsky did not find out that her name was on the list until the President told her days later, on December 17. That delay is significant.

After her conversation with Ms. Currie and seeing the President at the Christmas party, Ms. Lewinsky drafted a letter to the President terminating their relationship. The next morning, Saturday, December 6, Ms. Lewinsky went to the White House to deliver the letter and some gifts for the President to Ms. Currie. When she arrived at the White House, Ms. Lewinsky spoke to several Secret Service officers, and one of them told her that the President was not with his lawyers, as she thought, but rather, he was meeting with Eleanor Mondale. Ms. Lewinsky called Ms. Currie from a pay phone, angrily exchanged words with her, and went home. After that phone call, Ms. Currie told the Secret Service watch commander that the President was so upset about the disclosure of his meeting with Ms. Mondale that he wanted somebody fired.

At 12:05 PM, records demonstrate that Ms. Currie paged Bruce Lindsey with the message: "Call Betty ASAP." Around that same time, according to Ms. Lewinsky, while she was back at her apartment, Ms. Lewinsky and the President spoke on the telephone. The President was very angry; he told Ms. Lewinsky that no one had ever treated him as poorly as she had. The President acknowledged to the grand jury that he was upset about Ms. Lewinsky's behavior and considered it inappropriate. Nevertheless, in a sudden change of mood, he invited her to visit him at the White House that afternoon.

Monica Lewinsky arrived at the White House for the second time that day and was cleared to enter at 12:52 PM. Although, in Ms. Lewinsky's words, the President was "very angry" with her during their recent telephone conversation, he was "sweet" and "very affectionate" during this visit. He also told her that he would talk to Vernon Jordan about her job situation.

The President also suddenly changed his attitude toward the Secret Service. Ms. Currie informed some officers that if they kept quiet about the Lewinsky incident, there would be no disciplinary action. According to the Secret Service watch commander, Captain Jeffrey Purdie, the President personally told him, "I hope you use your discretion" or "I hope I can count on your discretion." Deputy Chief Charles O'Malley, Captain Purdie's supervisor, testified that he knew of no other time in his fourteen years of service at the White House where the President raised a performance issue with a member of the Secret Service uniformed division. After his conversation with the President, Captain Purdie told a number of officers that they should not discuss the Lewinsky incident.

When the President was before the grand jury and questioned about his statements to the Secret Service regarding this incident, the President testified, "I don't remember what I said and I don't remember to whom I said it." When confronted with Captain Purdie's testimony, the President testified, "I don't remember anything I said to him in that regard. I have no recollection of that whatever."

President Clinton testified before the grand jury that he learned that Ms. Lewinsky was on the Jones witness list that evening, Saturday, December 6, during a meeting with his lawyers. He stood by this answer in response to Request Number 16 submitted by this Committee. The meeting occurred around 5 PM, after Ms. Lewinsky had left the White House.

According to Bruce Lindsey, at the meeting, Bob Bennett [Clinton's attorney] had a copy of the Jones witness list faxed to him, Bennett, the previous night.

However, during his deposition, the President testified that he had heard about the witness list *before* he saw it. In other words, if the President testified truthfully in his deposition, then he knew about the witness list before the 5 PM meeting. It is valid to infer that hearing Ms. Lewinsky's name on a witness list prompted the President's sudden and otherwise unexplained change from "very angry" to "very affectionate" that Saturday afternoon. It is also reasonable to infer that it prompted him to give the unique instruction to a Secret Service watch commander to use "discretion" regarding Ms. Lewinsky's visit to the White House, which the watch commander interpreted as an instruction to keep the incident under wraps.

The Job Search

Now to go back a little, Monica Lewinsky had been looking for a good-paying and high-profile job in New York since the previous July. She wasn't having much success despite the President's promise to help. In early November, Betty Currie arranged a meeting with Vernon Jordan, who was supposed to help.

On November 5, Monica met for twenty minutes with Mr. Jordan. No action followed, no job interviews were arranged, and there were no further contacts with Mr. Jordan. It was obvious that Mr. Jordan made no effort to find a job for Ms. Lewinsky. Indeed, it was so unimportant to him that he "had no recollection of an early November meeting" and that finding a job for Ms. Lewinsky was not a priority. Nothing happened throughout the month of November because Mr. Jordan was either gone or would not return Monica's calls.

During the December 6 meeting with the President, she mentioned that she had not been able to get in touch with Mr. Jordan and that it did not seem he had done anything to help her. The President responded by stating, "Oh, I'll talk to him. I'll get on it," or something to that effect. There was obviously still no urgency to help Monica. Mr. Jordan met the President the next day, December 7, but the meeting had nothing to do with Ms. Lewinsky.

The first activity calculated to help Monica actually procure employment took place on December 11. Mr. Jordan met with

Ms. Lewinsky and gave her a list of contact names. The two also discussed the President. That meeting Mr. Jordan remembered. Vernon Jordan immediately placed calls to two prospective employers. Later in the afternoon, he even called the President to give him a report on his job search efforts. Clearly, Mr. Jordan and the President were now *very* interested in helping Monica find a good job in New York.

But why the sudden interest, why the total change in focus and effort? Nobody but Betty Currie really cared about helping Ms. Lewinsky throughout November, even after the President learned that her name was on the prospective witness list. Did something happen to move the job search from a low to a high priority on that day? Oh yes, something happened. On the morning of December 11, 1997, Judge Susan Webber Wright ordered that Paula Jones was entitled to information regarding any state or federal employee with whom the President had sexual relations or proposed or sought to have sexual relations. To keep Monica on the team was now of critical importance. Remember, they already knew that she was on the witness list, although nobody bothered to tell her.

December 17, 1997

That was remedied on December 17, 1997. Between 2:00 and 2:30 in the morning, Monica Lewinsky's phone rang unexpectedly. It was the President of the United States. The President said that he wanted to tell Ms. Lewinsky two things: one was that Betty Currie's brother had been killed in a car accident; secondly, the President said that he "had some more bad news," that he had seen the witness list for the Paula Jones case and her name was on it. The President told Ms. Lewinsky that seeing her name on the list "broke his heart." He then told her that "if [she] were to be subpoenaed, [she] should contact Betty and let Betty know that [she] had received the subpoena." Ms. Lewinsky asked what she should do if subpoenaed. The President responded, "Well, maybe you can sign an affidavit." Both parties knew that the affidavit would need to be false and misleading to accomplish the desired result.

Then the President had a very pointed suggestion for Monica Lewinsky, a suggestion that left little room for compromise. He did not say specifically "go in and lie." What he did say is, "You know, you can always say you were coming to see Betty or that you were bringing me letters."

In order to understand the significance of this statement, it is necessary to recall the "cover stories" that the President and Ms. Lewinsky had previously structured in order to deceive those who protected and worked with the President.

Ms. Lewinsky said she would carry papers when she visited the President. When she saw him, she would say: "Oh, gee, here are your letters," wink, wink, wink, and he would answer, "Okay that's good." After Ms. Lewinsky left White House employment, she would return to the Oval Office under the guise of visiting Betty Currie, not the President.

Moreover, Monica promised him that she would always deny the sexual relationship and always protect him. The President would respond "that's good" or similar language of encouragement.

So, when the President called Monica at 2 AM on December 17 to tell her she was on the witness list, he made sure to remind her of those prior "cover stories." Ms. Lewinsky testified that when the President brought up the misleading story, she understood that the two would continue their preexisting pattern of deception.

It became clear that the President had no intention of making his sexual relationship with Monica Lewinsky a public affair. And he would use lies, deceit, and deception to ensure that the truth would not be known.

It is interesting to note that when the President was asked by the grand jury whether he remembered calling Monica Lewinsky at 2 AM, he responded: "No sir, I don't. But it would—it is quite possible that that happened." And when he was asked whether he encouraged Monica Lewinsky to continue the cover stories of "coming to see Betty" or "bringing the letters," he answered, "I don't remember exactly what I told her that night."

Six days earlier, he had become aware that Paula Jones's lawyers were now able to inquire about other women. Monica could file a false affidavit, but it might not work. It was absolutely essential that both parties told the same story. He knew that he would lie if asked about Ms. Lewinsky, and he wanted to make certain that she would lie also. Why else would the President of the United States call a twenty-four-year-old woman at 2:00 in the morning?

But the President had an additional problem. It was not enough that he [and Ms. Lewinsky] simply deny the relationship. You see, ladies and gentlemen, the evidence was beginning to accumulate. And it was the evidence that was driving the President to reevaluate his defense. By this time, the evidence was establishing, through records and eyewitness accounts, that the President and Monica Lewinsky were spending a significant amount of time together in the Oval Office complex. It was no longer expedient simply to refer to Ms. Lewinsky as a "groupie," "stalker," "clutch," or "home wrecker," as the White House first attempted to do. The unassailable facts were forcing the President to acknowledge the relationship. But at this point, he still had the opportunity to establish a nonsexual explanation for their meetings. You see, he still had this opportunity because his DNA had not yet been identified on Monica Lewinsky's blue dress.

Therefore, the President needed Monica Lewinsky to go along with the cover story in order to provide an innocent, intimate-free explanation for their frequent meetings. And that innocent explanation came in the form of "document deliveries" and "friendly chats with Betty Currie."

It is also interesting to note that when the President was deposed on January 17, 1998, he used the exact same cover stories that had been utilized by Ms. Lewinsky. In doing so, he stayed consistent with any future Lewinsky testimony while still maintaining his defense in the Jones lawsuit.

In the President's deposition he was asked whether he was ever alone with Monica Lewinsky. He responded, "I don't recall."

"She—it seems to me she brought things to me once or twice on the weekends. In that case, whatever time she would be in there, drop it off, exchange a few words, and go, she was there."

You will also notice that whenever questions were posed regarding Ms. Lewinsky's frequent visits to the Oval Office, the President never hesitated to bring Betty Currie's name into his answers:

A. And my recollection is that on a couple of occasions after [the pizza party meeting] she was there [in the Oval Office] but my secretary, Betty Currie, was there with her.

Q. When was the last time you spoke with Monica Lewinsky?

A. I'm trying to remember. Probably some time before Christmas. She came by to see Betty sometime before Christmas. And she was there talking to her, and I stuck my head out, said hello to her.

Life was so much simpler before the dress was discovered.

The President's and Ms. Lewinsky's greatest fears were realized on December 19, 1997, when Monica was subpoenaed to testify in a deposition on January 23, 1998, in the Jones case. Extremely distraught, she immediately called the President's best friend, Vernon Jordan. You will recall that Ms. Lewinsky testified that the President previously told her to call Betty Currie if she was subpoenaed. She called Mr. Jordan instead because Ms. Currie's brother recently died, and she did not want to bother her.

Mr. Jordan invited Lewinsky to his office, and she arrived shortly before 5 PM, still extremely distraught. Sometime around this time, Jordan called the President and told him Monica had been subpoenaed. During the meeting with Ms. Lewinsky, which Jordan characterized as "disturbing," she talked about her infatuation with the President. Mr. Jordan also decided that he would call a lawyer for her. That evening, Mr. Jordan met with the President and relayed his conversation with Ms. Lewinsky. The details are extremely important because the President, in his deposition, did not recall that meeting.

Mr. Jordan told the President again that Ms. Lewinsky had been subpoenaed, that he was concerned about her fascination with the President, and that Ms. Lewinsky had asked Mr. Jordan if he thought the President would leave the First Lady. He also asked the President if he had sexual relations with Lewinsky. Would not a reasonable person conclude that this is the type of conversation that would be locked in the President's memory? The President was asked:

> **Q.** Did anyone other than your attorneys ever tell you that Monica Lewinsky had been served with a subpoena in this case?
> **A.** I don't think so.
> **Q.** Did you ever talk with Monica Lewinsky about the possibility that she might be asked to testify in this case?
> **A.** Bruce Lindsey, I think—Bruce Lindsey told me that she was. I think maybe that's the first person [who] told me she was. I want to be as accurate as I can.

In the grand jury, the President first repeated his denial that Mr. Jordan told him Ms. Lewinsky had been subpoenaed. Then, when given more specific facts, he admitted that he "knows now" that he spoke with Jordan about the subpoena on the night of December 19, but his "memory is not clear." In an attempt to explain away his false deposition testimony, the President testified in the grand jury that he was trying to remember who told him first. But that was not the question. So his answer was again false and misleading. When one considers the nature of the conversation between the President and Mr. Jordan, the suggestion that it would be forgotten defies common sense.

December 28, 1997

December 28, 1997, is a crucial date, because the evidence shows that the President made false and misleading statements to the federal court, the federal grand jury, and the Congress of the United

States about the events on that date. It also is critical evidence that he obstructed justice.

The President testified that it was "possible" that he invited Ms. Lewinsky to the White House for this visit. He admitted that he "probably" gave Ms. Lewinsky the most gifts he had ever given her on that date, and that he had given her gifts on other occasions. Among the many gifts the President gave Ms. Lewinsky on December 28 was a bear that he said was a symbol of strength. Yet only two-and-a-half short weeks later, the President forgot that he had given any gifts to Monica.

Now, as an attorney, he knew that the law will not tolerate someone who says "I don't recall" when that answer is unreasonable under the circumstances. He also knew that, under those circumstances, his answer in the deposition could not be believed. When asked in the grand jury why he was unable to remember, though he had given Ms. Lewinsky so many gifts only two-and-a-half weeks before the deposition, the President put forth a lame and obviously contrived explanation: "I think what I meant there was I don't recall what they were, not that I don't recall whether I had given them."

The President adopted that same answer in Response No. 42 to the Committee's Request to Admit or Deny. He was not asked in the deposition to identify the gifts. He was simply asked, "Have you ever" given gifts to Ms. Lewinsky. The law does not allow a witness to insert "unstated premises" or mental reservations into the question to make his answer technically true, if factually false. The essence of lying is in deception, not in words.

The President's answer was false; he knew it then, and he knows it now. The evidence proves that his explanation to the grand jury and to this Committee is also false. The President would have us believe that he was able to analyze questions as they were being asked and to pick up such things as verb tense in an attempt to make his statements at least literally true. But when he is asked a simple, straightforward question, suddenly he wants us to believe that he did not understand it. Neither his answer in the deposition nor his attempted explanation is reasonable or true.

While we're on gifts, the President was asked in the deposition if Monica Lewinsky ever gave him gifts. He responded, "Once or twice."

This is also false testimony. He answered this question in his Response to the Committee by saying that he receives numerous gifts, and he did not focus on the precise number. The law again does not support the President's position. An answer that "baldly understates a numerical fact" in "response to a specific quantitative inquiry" can be deemed "technically true" but actually false. For example, a witness is testifying falsely if he says he went to the store five times when in fact he had gone fifty, even though technically he had gone five times also. So, too, when the President answered once or twice in the face of evidence that Ms. Lewinsky was always bringing gifts, he was lying.

On December 28, one of the most blatant efforts to obstruct justice and conceal evidence occurred. Ms. Lewinsky testified that she discussed with the President the fact that she had been subpoenaed and that the subpoena called for her to produce gifts. She recalled telling the President that the subpoena requested a hat pin, and that caused her concern. The President told her that it "bothered" him, too. Ms. Lewinsky then suggested that she take the gifts somewhere, or give them to someone, maybe to Betty. The President answered: "I don't know" or "Let me think about that." Later that day, Ms. Lewinsky got a call from Ms. Currie, who said: "I understand you have something to give me" or "the President said you have something to give me." Ms. Currie has an amazingly fuzzy memory about this incident, but says that "the best she can remember," Ms. Lewinsky called her. There is key evidence that Ms. Currie's fuzzy recollection is wrong. Monica said that she thought Betty called from her cell phone.

Well, look at this record. This is Betty's cell phone record. It corroborates Monica Lewinsky and proves conclusively that Ms. Currie called Monica from her cell phone several hours after she had left the White House. Why did Betty Currie pick up the gifts from Ms. Lewinsky? The facts strongly suggest the President directed her to do so.

That conclusion is buttressed by Ms. Currie's actions. If it were Ms. Lewinsky that called her, did Currie ask—like anyone would— why in the world Ms. Lewinsky was giving her a box of gifts from the President? Did she tell the President of this strange request? No. Ms. Currie's position was not to ask the reason why. She simply took the gifts and placed them under her bed without asking a single question.

Another note about this: The President stated in his Response to questions No. 24 and 25 from this Committee that he was not concerned about the gifts. In fact, he said that he recalled telling Monica that if the Jones lawyers request gifts, she should turn them over. The President testified that he is "not sure" if he knew the subpoena asked for gifts. Why in the world would Monica and the President discuss turning over gifts to the Jones lawyers if Ms. Lewinsky had not told him that the subpoena asked for gifts? On the other hand, if he knew the subpoena requested gifts, why would he give Monica more gifts on December 28? This seems odd. But Ms. Lewinsky's testimony reveals the answer. She said that she never questioned "that we were ever going to do anything but keep this private" and that meant to take "whatever appropriate steps needed to be taken" to keep it quiet. The only logical inference is that the gifts, including the bear symbolizing strength, were a tacit reminder to Ms. Lewinsky that they would deny the relationship— even in the face of a federal subpoena.

Furthermore, the President, at various times in his deposition, seriously misrepresented the nature of his meeting with Ms. Lewinsky. First, he was asked: "Did she tell you she had been served with a subpoena in this case?" The President answered flatly: "No. I don't know if she had been."

He was also asked if he "ever talked to Monica Lewinsky about the possibility of her testifying." "I'm not sure...," he said. He then added that he may have joked to her that the Jones lawyers might subpoena every woman he has ever spoken to, and that "I don't think we ever had more of a conversation than that about it...." Not only does Monica Lewinsky directly contradict this testimony, but the President also directly contradicted himself before the grand jury. Speaking of his December 28, 1997, meeting, he said that he "knew by then, of course, that she had gotten a subpoena" and that they had a "conversation about the possibility of her testify-ing." Remember, he had this conversation about her testimony only two-and-a-half weeks before his deposition. Again, his version is not reasonable.

January 5–9, 1998:
Monica Signs the Affidavit and Gets a Job

The President knew that Monica Lewinsky was going to make a false affidavit. He was so certain of the content that when Monica asked if he wanted to see it, he told her no, that he had seen fifteen of them. He got his information in part from his attorneys and from discussions with Ms. Lewinsky and Vernon Jordan generally about the content of the affidavit. Besides, he had suggested the affidavit himself, and he trusted Mr. Jordan to be certain the mission was accomplished.

On the afternoon of January 5, 1998, Ms. Lewinsky met with her lawyer, Mr. [Frank] Carter, to discuss the affidavit. The lawyer asked her some hard questions about how she got her job. After the meeting, she called Betty Currie and said that she wanted to speak to the President before she signed anything. Lewinsky and the President discussed the issue of how she would answer under oath if asked about how she got her job at the Pentagon. The President told her, "Well, you could always say that the people in Legislative Affairs got it for you or helped you get it." That, by the way, is another lie.

The President was also kept advised as to the contents of the affidavit by Vernon Jordan. On January 6, 1998, Ms. Lewinsky picked up a draft of the affidavit from Mr. Carter's office. She delivered a copy to Mr. Jordan's office because she wanted Mr. Jordan to look at the affidavit in the belief that if Vernon Jordan gave his imprimatur, the President would also approve. Ms.

Lewinsky and Mr. Jordan conferred about the contents and agreed to delete a paragraph inserted by Mr. Carter which might open a line of questions concerning whether she had been alone with the President. Contrast this to the testimony of Mr. Jordan, who said he had nothing to do with the details of the affidavit. He admits, though, that he spoke with the President after conferring with Ms. Lewinsky about the changes made to her affidavit. The next day, January 7, Monica Lewinsky signed the false affidavit. She showed the executed copy to Mr. Jordan the same day. Why? So that Mr. Jordan could report to the President that it had been signed and another mission had been accomplished.

On January 8, 1998, Ms. Lewinsky had an interview arranged by Mr. Jordan with MacAndrews & Forbes in New York. The interview went poorly, so Ms. Lewinsky called Mr. Jordan and informed him. Mr. Jordan, who had done nothing from early November to mid-December, then called MacAndrews & Forbes CEO Ron Perelman to "make things happen, if they could happen." Mr. Jordan called Monica back and told her not to worry. That evening, Ms. Lewinsky was called by MacAndrews & Forbes and told that she would be given more interviews the next morning.

The next morning, Monica received her reward for signing the false affidavit. After a series of interviews with MacAndrews & Forbes personnel, she was informally offered a job. When Monica called Mr. Jordan to tell him, he passed the good news on to Betty Currie: Tell the President, "Mission Accomplished." Later, Mr. Jordan called the President and told him personally.

After months of looking for a job—since July according to the President's lawyers—Vernon Jordan just so happens to make the call to a CEO the day after the false affidavit is signed. If you think it is mere coincidence, consider this. Mr. Perelman testified that Mr. Jordan had never called him before about a job recommendation. Mr. Jordan, on the other hand, said that he called Mr. Perelman to recommend for hiring: (1) former Mayor David Dinkins of New York; (2) a very talented attorney from Akin Gump; (3) a Harvard business school graduate; and (4) Monica Lewinsky. Even if Mr. Perelman's testimony is mistaken, Monica Lewinsky does not fit within the caliber of persons that would merit Mr. Jordan's direct recommendation to a CEO of a Fortune 500 company.

Mr. Jordan was well aware that people with whom Ms. Lewinsky worked at the White House did not like her and that she did not like her Pentagon job. Vernon Jordan was asked if at "any point during this process you wondered about her qualifications for employment." He answered, "No, because that was not my judgment to make." Yet when he called Mr. Perelman the day after she signed the affidavit, he referred to Monica as a bright young girl who is "terrific." Mr. Jordan said that she had been hounding him for a job and voicing unrealistic expectations concerning positions and salary. Moreover, she narrated a disturbing story about the President leaving the First Lady and how the President was not spending enough time with her. Yet none of that gave Mr. Jordan pause in making the recommendation. Do people like Vernon Jordan go to the wall for marginal employees? They do not, unless there is a compelling reason. The compelling reason was that the President told him this was a top priority, especially after Monica was subpoenaed.

The Filing of the False Affidavit

Just how important was Monica Lewinsky's false affidavit to the President's deposition? It enabled Mr. Clinton, through his attorneys, to assert at his January 17, 1998, deposition "there is absolutely no sex of any kind in any manner, shape, or form, with President Clinton." When questioned by his own attorney in the deposition, the President stated specifically that the infamous Paragraph 8 of Monica's affidavit was "absolutely true." The President later affirmed the truth of that statement when testifying before the grand jury.

Paragraph 8 of Ms. Lewinsky's affidavit states: "I have never had a sexual relationship with the President, he did not propose that we have a sexual relationship, he did not offer me employment or other benefits in exchange for a sexual relationship, he did not deny me employment or other benefits for rejecting a sexual relationship."

Recall that Monica Lewinsky reviewed the draft affidavit on January 6 and signed it on January 7 after deleting a reference to being alone with the President. She showed a copy of the signed affidavit to Vernon Jordan, who called the President and told him that she signed it.

Getting the affidavit signed was only half the battle. To have its full effect, it had to be filed with the court and provided to the President's attorneys in time for his deposition on the 17th. On January 14, the President's lawyers called Monica's lawyer and left a message, presumably to find out if he had filed the affidavit with the court. On January 15, the President's attorneys called her attorney twice. When they finally reached him, they requested a copy of the affidavit and asked him, "Are we still on time?" Ms. Lewinsky's lawyer faxed a copy on the 15th. The President's counsel was aware of its contents and, as we will see, used it powerfully in the deposition.

Monica's lawyer called the court in Arkansas twice on January 15 to ensure that the affidavit could be filed on Saturday, January 17. He finished the motion to quash Monica's deposition in the early morning hours of January 16 and mailed it to the court, with the false affidavit attached, for Saturday delivery. The President's lawyers called him again on January 16, telling him, "You'll know what about."

Obviously, the President needed that affidavit to be filed with the court to support his plans to mislead Ms. Jones's attorneys in the deposition.

On January 15, Michael Isikoff of *Newsweek* called Betty Currie and asked her about Monica sending gifts to her by courier. Ms. Currie then called Monica and told her about it. The President was out of town, so later, Betty Currie called Monica back and asked for a ride to Mr. Jordan's office. Mr. Jordan advised her to speak with Bruce Lindsey and Mike McCurry. Ms. Currie testified that she spoke immediately to Mr. Lindsey about Isikoff's call.

Clinton and Bennett at Deposition

The President also provided false and misleading testimony in the grand jury when he was asked about Mr. Bennett's representation to the Jones court that the President is "fully aware" that Lewinsky filed an affidavit saying that "there is absolutely no sex of any kind in any manner, shape, or form, with President Clinton...." Mr. Clinton was asked about this representation made by his lawyer in his presence and whether he felt obligated to inform the federal judge of the true facts. The President answered that he was "not even sure I paid much attention to what [Mr. Bennett] was saying." When pressed further, he said that he didn't believe he "even focused on what Mr. Bennett said in the exact words he did until I started reading this transcript carefully for this hearing. That moment, the whole argument just passed me by."

This last statement by the President is critical. First, had he planned his answer to the grand jurors? Of course he [had]. He spent literally days with his attorney going over that deposition with a fine-tooth comb and crafting answers in his own mind that would not be too obviously false. Second, he knew that he could only avoid an admission that he allowed a false affidavit to be filed by convincing the grand jury that he had not been paying attention. Take a look at this tape, and you decide (1) whether he was paying attention and (2) whether the President of the United States, a former Rhodes Scholar, could not follow his lawyer's argument.

[The committee reviews the tape of the Jones deposition; on the tape, Clinton appears to be listening intently as Bennett discusses the Lewinsky affidavit.]

Do you think for one moment, after watching that tape, that the President was not paying attention? They were talking about Monica Lewinsky, at the time the most dangerous person in the President's life. If the false affidavit worked and Ms. Jones's lawyers were not permitted to question him about her, he was home free. Can anyone rationally argue, then, that the President wasn't vitally interested in what Mr. Bennett was saying? Nonetheless, when he was asked in the grand jury whether Mr. Bennett's statement was false, he still was unable to tell the truth—even before a federal grand jury. He answered with the now famous sentence, "It depends on what the meaning of the word 'is' is."

That single declaration reveals more about the character of the President than perhaps anything else in this record. It points out his attitude and his conscious indifference and complete disregard for the concept of the truth. He picks out a single word and weaves from it a deceitful answer: "Is" does not mean "was" or "will be," so I can answer, no. He also invents convoluted definitions of words or phrases in his own crafty mind. Of course, he will never seek to clarify a question because that may trap him into a straight answer.

Can you imagine dealing with such a person in any important matter? You would never know his secret mental reservations or the unspoken redefinition of words. Even if you thought you had solved the enigma, it wouldn't matter—he would just change the meaning to suit his purpose. But the President reinforced Monica's lie. Mr. Bennett read to him the paragraph in Ms. Lewinsky's affidavit where she denied a sexual relationship with the President.

QUESTION: Is that a true and accurate statement as far as you know it?
PRESIDENT: That is absolutely true.

When asked about this in the grand jury and when questioned about it by this Committee, the President said that if Ms. Lewinsky believed it to be true, then it was a true statement.

Well let's see. First, Monica admitted to the grand jury that the paragraph was false. Second, the President was not asked about

Ms. Lewinsky's belief. He was asked quite clearly and directly by his own lawyer whether the statement was true. His answer was, unequivocally, yes. Even by the President's own tortured reading of the definition of sexual relations, that statement is false. To use the President's own definition, Lewinsky touched "one of the enumerated body parts." Therefore she had sexual relations with him even as he defined it.

Lastly, the President wants us to believe that, according to his reading of the deposition definition, he did not have sexual relations with Ms. Lewinsky. The definition was an afterthought conceived while preparing for his grand jury testimony. His explanation to the grand jury, then, was also false and misleading.

The President does not explain his denial of an affair or a sexual affair—he can't. Neither can he avoid his unequivocal denial in the answers to interrogatories in the Jones case. These interrogatories were answered before any narrow definition of sexual relations had been developed.

Deposition Aftermath

By the time the President concluded his deposition, he knew that someone was talking about his relationship with Ms. Lewinsky. He knew that the only person who could be talking was Ms. Lewinsky herself. The cover story that he and Ms. Lewinsky created, and that he used liberally himself during the deposition, was now in jeopardy. It became imperative that he not only contact Ms. Lewinsky, but that he obtain corroboration from his trusted secretary, Ms. Currie. At around 7 PM on the night of the deposition, the President called Ms. Currie and asked that she come in the following day,

Sunday. Ms. Currie could not recall the President ever before call-ing her that late at home on a Saturday night. Sometime in the early morning hours of January 18, 1998, the President learned of the *Drudge Report* about Ms. Lewinsky released earlier that day.

As the charts indicate, between 11:49 AM and 2:55 PM, there were three phone calls between Mr. Jordan and the President. At about 5 PM, Ms. Currie met with the President. The President said that he had just been deposed and that the attorneys asked several questions about Monica Lewinsky. This, incidentally, was a viola-tion of Judge Wright's gag order prohibiting any discussions about the deposition testimony. He then made a series of statements to Ms. Currie:

1) I was never really alone with Monica, right?
2) You were always there when Monica was there, right?
3) Monica came on to me, and I never touched her, right?
4) You could see and hear everything, right?
5) She wanted to have sex with me, and I cannot do that.

During Ms. Currie's grand jury testimony, she was asked whether she believed that the President wished her to agree with the statements:

Q. Would it be fair to say, then, based on the way he stated [these five points], and the demeanor that he was using at the time that he stated it to you, that he wished you to agree with that statement?
A. I can't speak for him, but—
Q. How did you take it? Because you told us at these [previous] meetings in the last several days that that is how you took it.

A. [Nodding]

Q. And you're nodding your head, "Yes." Is that correct?

A. That's correct.

Q. Okay, with regard to the statement that the President made to you, "You remember I was never really alone with Monica, right?" Was that also a statement that, as far as you took, that he wished you to agree with that?

A. Correct.

When the President testified in the August 17, 1998, grand jury, he was questioned about his intentions when he made those five statements to Ms. Currie in his office on that Sunday afternoon. The President stated:

> I thought we were going to be deluged by the press comments. And I was trying to refresh my memory about what the facts were. And what I wanted to establish was that Betty was there at all other times in the complex, and I wanted to know what Betty's memory was about what she heard, what she could hear. And what I did not know was—I did not know that. And I was trying to figure out... in a hurry because I knew something was up. So, I was not trying to get Betty Currie to say something that was untruthful. I was trying to get as much information as quickly as I could.

Though Ms. Currie would later intimate that she did not necessarily feel pressured by the President, she did state that she felt the President was seeking her agreement (or disagreement) with those statements.

Logic tells us that the President's plea that he was just trying to refresh his memory is contrived and false.

First consider the President's options after he left his deposition:

1) He could abide by Judge Wright's order to remain silent and not divulge any details of his deposition;

2) He could choose to defy Judge Wright's order, and call Betty on the phone and ask her open-ended questions (i.e., "What do you remember about...?"); or

3) He could call Ms. Currie and arrange a Sunday afternoon meeting, at a time when the fewest distractions exist and the White House staff is at a minimum.

The President chose the third option.

He made sure that this was a face-to-face meeting, not an impersonal telephone call. He made sure that no one else was present when he spoke to her. He made sure that he had the meeting in his office, an area where he was comfortable and could utilize its power and prestige to influence future testimony.

Once these controls were established, the President made short, clear, understandable, declarative statements *telling* Ms. Currie what his testimony was. He was not interested in what she knew. Why? Because he did not want to be contradicted by his personal secretary. The only way to ensure that was by telling her what to say, not asking her what she remembered. You do not refresh someone's memory by *telling* that person what he or she remembers. And you certainly do not make declarative statements to someone regarding factual scenarios of which the listener was unaware.

Betty Currie could not possibly have any personal knowledge of the facts that the President was asking [about]. How could she know if they were ever alone? If they were, Ms. Currie wasn't there.

So, too, how would she know that the President never touched Monica? No, this wasn't any attempt by the President to refresh his recollection. It was witness tampering, pure and simple.

The President essentially admitted to making these statements when he knew they were not true. Consequently, he had painted himself into a legal corner. Understanding the seriousness of the President "coaching" Ms. Currie, his attorneys have argued that those statements to her could not constitute obstruction because she had not been subpoenaed and the President did not know that she was a potential witness at the time. This argument is refuted by both the law and the facts.

The United States Court of Appeals rejected this argument, stating, "[A] person may be convicted of obstructing justice if he urges or persuades a prospective witness to give false testimony. Neither must the target be scheduled to testify at the time of the offense, nor must he or she actually give testimony at a later time."

As discussed, the President and Ms. Lewinsky, concocted a cover story that brought Ms. Currie into the fray as a corroborating witness. True to this scheme, the President, as previously noted, invoked Ms. Currie's name frequently as a witness who could corroborate his false and misleading testimony about the Lewinsky affair. For example, during his deposition, when asked whether he was alone with Ms. Lewinsky, the President said that he was not alone with her or that Betty Currie was there with Monica. When asked about the last time he saw Ms. Lewinsky, which was December 28, 1997, he falsely testified that he only recalled that she was there to see Betty. He also told the Jones lawyers to "ask Betty" whether Lewinsky was alone with him or with Betty in the White House between the hours of midnight and 6 AM. Asked whether Ms. Lewinsky sent packages to him, he stated that Betty handled packages for him. Asked whether he may have assisted in any way with Ms. Lewinsky's job search, he stated that he thought Betty suggested Vernon Jordan talk to Ms. Lewinsky and that Monica asked Betty to ask someone to talk to Ambassador [Bill] Richardson about a job at the [United Nations].

Of course, Ms. Currie was a prospective witness, and the President clearly wanted her to be deposed as a witness, as his "ask Betty" testimony demonstrates. The President claims that he called Ms. Currie into work on a Sunday night only to find out what she knew. But the President knew the truth about his relationship with Ms. Lewinsky, and if he had told the truth during his deposition the day before, then he would have no reason to worry about what Ms. Currie knew. More importantly, the President's demeanor, Ms. Currie's reaction to his demeanor, and the suggested lies clearly prove that the President was not merely interviewing Ms. Currie. Rather, he was looking for corroboration for his false cover-up, and that is why he coached her.

Very soon after his Sunday meeting with Ms. Currie, at 5:12 PM, the flurry of telephone calls began looking for Monica Lewinsky. Between 5:12 PM and 8:28 PM, Ms. Currie paged Monica four times. "Kay" is a reference to a code name Ms. Lewinsky and Ms. Currie created when contacting one another. At 11:02 PM, the President called Ms. Currie at home to ask if she ha[d] reached Lewinsky.

The following morning, January 19, Currie continued to work
diligently on behalf of the President. Between 7:02 AM and 8:41 AM,
she paged Ms. Lewinsky another five times. After the 8:41 page,
Betty called the President at 8:43 AM and said that she was unable to
reach Monica. One minute later, at 8:44 AM, she again paged
Monica. This time Ms. Currie's page stated, "Family Emergency,"
apparently in an attempt to alarm Monica into calling back. That
may have been the President's idea, since Betty had just spoken with
him. The President was obviously quite concerned because he called
Betty Currie only six minutes later, at 8:50 AM. Immediately thereafter, at 8:51 AM, Currie trie[d] a different tack, sending the message,
"Good news." Another one of the President's ideas? If bad news
does not get her to call, try good news. Ms. Currie said that she was
trying to encourage Ms. Lewinsky to call, but there was no sense of
"urgency." Ms. Currie's recollection of why she was calling was
again amazingly fuzzy. She said at one point that she believe[d] the
President asked her to call Ms. Lewinsky, and she thought she was
calling just to tell her that her name came up in the deposition.
Monica Lewinsky had been subpoenaed; of course her name came
up in the deposition. There was obviously another and more important reason the President needed to get in touch with her.

At 8:56 AM, the President telephoned Vernon Jordan, who then
joined in the activity. Over a course of twenty-four minutes, from
10:29 to 10:53 AM, Mr. Jordan called the White House three times,
paged Ms. Lewinsky, and called Ms. Lewinsky's attorney, Frank
Carter. Between 10:53 AM and 4:54 PM, there [were] continued calls
between Mr. Jordan, Ms. Lewinsky's attorney, and individuals at
the White House.

Later that afternoon, things really went downhill for the President. At 4:54 PM Mr. Jordan called Mr. Carter. Mr. Carter relayed that he had been told he no longer represented Ms. Lewinsky. Mr. Jordan then made feverish attempts to reach the President or someone at the White House to tell [him] the bad news, as represented by the six calls between 4:58 PM and 5:22 PM. Vernon Jordan said that he tried to relay this information to the White House because "he [the President] asked me to get Monica Lewinsky a job" and he thought it was "information that they ought to have." Mr. Jordan then called Mr. Carter back at 5:14 PM to go over what they had already talked about. Mr. Jordan finally reache[d] the President at 5:56 PM and [told] him that Mr. Carter had been fired.

Why all this activity? It shows how important it was for the President of the United States to find Monica Lewinsky to learn to whom she was talking. Betty Currie was in charge of contacting Monica. The President had just completed a deposition in which he provided false and misleading testimony about his relationship with Ms. Lewinsky. She was a coconspirator in hiding this relationship from the Jones attorneys, and he was losing control over her. The President never got complete control over her again, and that is why we are here today.

Grand Jury Testimony

On August 17, the last act of the tragedy took place. After six scorned invitations, the President of the United States appeared before a grand jury of his fellow citizens and took an oath to tell the truth. We all know what happened. Mr. Clinton equivocated and engaged in legalistic fencing, but he also lied. During the course of this presentation, I have discussed several of those lies specifically. Actually, the entire performance—and it was a performance—was calculated to mislead and deceive the grand jury and eventually the American people. The tone was set at the very beginning. Judge Starr testified that in a grand jury a witness can tell the truth, lie, or assert his privileges against self-incrimination. President Clinton was given a fourth choice. The President was permitted to read a statement.

That statement itself is false in many particulars. President Clinton claims that he engaged in wrong conduct with Ms. Lewinsky "on certain occasions in early 1996 and once in 1997." Notice he did not mention 1995. There was a reason. On the three "occasions" in 1995, Monica was a twenty-one-year-old intern. As for being alone on "certain occasions," the President was alone with Monica more than twenty times at least. The President also told the jurors that he "also had *occasional* telephone conversations with Ms. Lewinsky that included sexual banter." Occasional sounds like once every four months or so, doesn't it? Actually, the two had at least fifty-five phone conversations, many in the middle of the night, and in seventeen of these calls, Monica and the President of the United States engaged in phone sex. I am not going into any details, but if what happened on these phone calls is banter, then Buckingham Palace is a house.

Here we are again with the President carefully crafting his statements to give the appearance of being candid, when actually his intent was the opposite. In addition, throughout the testimony, whenever the President was asked a specific question that could not be answered directly without either admitting the truth or giving an easily provable false answer, he said, "I rely on my statement." Nineteen times he relied on this false and misleading statement; nineteen times, then, he repeated those lies.

You will recall when Judge Starr was testifying he made reference to six occasions on which, faced with a choice, the President chose deception. Make it seven.

In an effort to avoid unnecessary work and to bring this inquiry to an expeditious end, this Committee submitted to the President eighty-one requests to admit or deny specific facts relevant to this investigation. Although, for the most part, the questions could have been answered with a simple "admit" or "deny," the President elected to follow the pattern of selective memory, reference to other testimony, blatant untruths, artful distortions, outright lies, and half-truths—the blackest lie of all. When he did answer, he engaged in legalistic hair-splitting in an obvious attempt to skirt the whole truth and to deceive this Committee.

Thus, on at least twenty-three questions, the President professed a lack of memory; this from a man who is renowned for his remarkable memory, for his amazing ability to recall details.

In at least fifteen answers, the President merely referred to "White House records." He also referred to his own prior testimony and that of others. He answered several of the requests by merely restating the same deceptive answers that he gave to the grand jury. We have pointed out several false statements in this summation.

The answers are a gratuitous insult to your intelligence and common sense. The President, then, has lied under oath in a civil deposition and lied under oath in a criminal grand jury. He lied to the people, he lied to his cabinet, he lied to his top aides, and now he has lied under oath to the Congress of the United States. There is no one left to lie to.

In addition, the half-truths, legalistic parsings, evasive and misleading answers were obviously calculated to obstruct the efforts of this Committee. They have had the effect of seriously hampering this Committee's ability to inquire and to ascertain the truth. The President has, therefore, added obstruction of an inquiry and an investigation before the Legislative Branch to his obstructions of justice before the Judicial Branch of our constitutional system of government.

I would like to take a few moments to address some of the matters that have been put before you by the President's defenders.

Ever since this inquiry began, we have heard the complaint that no factual witnesses were being called by the Majority. Actually, there are many factual witnesses: Monica Lewinsky, Vernon Jordan, Betty Currie, Sidney Blumenthal, Erskine Bowles, John Podesta—all of whom have testified one or more times under oath either in a formal deposition or before a grand jury. With minimal exceptions, I have avoided reference to interviews and the like. Interviewees are not under oath, and usually the report does not reflect the exact words of the witness. I note, though, that the President did rely solely on unsworn interviews and produced no factual witnesses whatsoever.

Some Members have suggested that none of those witnesses has been subjected to cross-examination. The answer is twofold:

First, this is not a trial; it is in the nature of an inquest. Any witness whose testimony is referred to in this proceeding will be subjected to full cross-examination if a trial results in the Senate. That is the time to test credibility. As it stands, all of the factual witnesses are uncontradicted and amply corroborated.

Second, if any Member or the President's counsel had specific questions for any of these witnesses, he or she was free to bring the witness in to testify in this proceeding.

Although the President's lawyers admit that his actions in the Jones case and in the Lewinsky matter were immoral and, I think they said, maddening acts, they argue that they do not rise to the level of criminal activity and certainly not to the level of impeachable offenses. They produced another gaggle of witnesses to testify that this really is not so bad, it's only lying about sex, that only private conduct is involved, and really the Congress should just close up the book, slap the President on the hand, and, well, just get on with politics as usual. Some even suggested that prosecutors would not even consider an indictment based upon the evidence available here. That remains to be seen. I doubt if any of those experts has read all the evidence I have read. We know that prosecutors are in possession of this evidence and perhaps much more. Whether to indict is their decision. And whether the offenses of President Clinton are criminally chargeable is of no moment. This is not a criminal trial, nor is it a criminal inquiry. It is a fundamental precept that an impeachable offense need not be a criminal act.

Concerning the perjury issue:

It is noteworthy that the President's argument is focused on only one aspect of his testimony—that regarding whether he had sexual relations. He glosses over or ignores the perjury claims premised on his denial of being alone with Ms. Lewinsky, his denial of any involvement in obtaining a job for her in his January 17 deposition, his falsely minimizing the number of occasions on which he had encounters with Ms. Lewinsky, and his lies regarding gifts to and from Ms. Lewinsky.

They also argue that because the President "believed" that he was telling the truth and there is no proof that he did not so believe, then he is not guilty of perjury. They assert that under the law, the subjective belief of the defendant is what controls. In fact, however, the question of perjury is judged by an objective standard advanced by the President's counsel.

The President's subjective belief is not sufficient. He admits that he is an attorney and at the time of his deposition was represented by Mr. Bennett as well as Mr. Ruff. He had an independent duty to review the definition of sexual relations and to determine whether in fact his conduct fell within that definition. He cannot rely on his attorney, who was not in possession of all the facts, to divorce himself from a determination of the truth. He cannot rely on what his attorney "thinks" when he, the President, is the only person who knows the relevant facts and is able to determine whether his conduct fell within the definition. In other words, there must be a reasonable basis for the President's subjective belief to have any merit. There was no reasonable basis.

Similarly, the argument that there is "no proof" that the President did not believe he was telling the truth as to whether he engaged in "sexual relations" under the Jones definition ignores the record. The proof that the President's "subjective belief" is contradicted by the evidence is overwhelming and has been addressed in detail. For the President now to advance the assertion that he had a subjective belief that his conduct did not constitute "sexual relations" continues the subterfuge and obstruction begun in the Jones case, continued in the grand jury, and presented here in Congress.

Another argument propounded by those who oppose impeachment is that the President's lies were not material to the Jones case. That is, the Lewinsky information was private and irrelevant. That argument, though, was disposed of by Judge Susan Webber Wright in her order of December 11, 1997. She said:

> The Court finds, therefore, that the plaintiff is entitled to information regarding any individuals with whom the President had sexual relations or proposed or sought to have sexual relations and who were during the relevant time frame [five years prior to May 8, 1991, to the present] state or federal employees. Plaintiff is also entitled to information regarding every person whom the President asked, during the relevant time frame, to arrange a private meeting between himself and any female state or federal employee which was attended by no one else and was held at any location other than his office. The Court cannot say that such information is not reasonably calculated to lead to the discovery of admissible evidence.

More than a month before the President's deposition, and six days before the President suggested that Monica Lewinsky could sign an affidavit to avoid testifying, the Judge had clearly concluded that the subject matter was neither private nor irrelevant. So much for the materiality issue. If the President's testimony concerning Monica

Lewinsky was not material, the Judge who was physically present during the deposition would never have allowed it.

Judge Wright's order is not the only decision on the materiality questions. A recently unsealed opinion from the United States Court of Appeals for the District of Columbia Circuit conclusively decided the issue.

In the opinion, filed under seal on May 26, 1998, the court addressed Ms. Lewinsky's argument that she could not have committed perjury or obstruction of justice because her false affidavit did not involve facts material to the Jones case. In a 3-0 decision, the Court of Appeals rejected the argument. Citing Supreme Court precedent, the court examined "whether the misrepresentation or concealment was predictably capable of affecting, i.e., had a natural tendency to affect, the official decision." The judges unanimously concluded: "There can be no doubt that Lewinsky's statements in her affidavit were—in the words of *Kungys* v. *United States*— 'predictably capable of affecting' this decision. She executed and filed her affidavit for this very purpose."

Of course, if Ms. Lewinsky's relationship with President Clinton was a material issue when she signed the affidavit, it certainly was a material issue when the President testified at a deposition. And just as those lies could support perjury and obstruction of justice charges against Ms. Lewinsky, they support perjury and obstruction of justice charges against the President. Both Ms. Lewinsky and the President are subject to the same criminal code.

However, even if the three judges on the D.C. Court of Appeals were wrong and if for some hypothetical reason the President's relationship with Ms. Lewinsky was not material in the Jones case, there can be no doubt in the President's or anyone else's mind that the relationship was absolutely material when he lied to the grand jury and lied to this Committee in his written responses about that relationship.

Make no mistake, the conduct of the President is inextricably bound to the welfare of the people of the United States. Not only does it affect economic and national defense, but even more directly, it affects the moral and law-abiding fiber of the commonwealth, without which no nation can survive. When, as here, that conduct involves a pattern of abuses of power, of perjury, of deceit, of obstruction of justice and of the Congress, and of other illegal activities, the resulting damage to the honor and respect due to the United States is, of necessity, devastating.

Again: There is no such thing as nonserious lying under oath. A lie is a lie is a lie. Every time a witness lies, that witness chips a stone from the foundation of our entire legal system. Likewise, every act of obstruction of justice, of witness tampering, or of perjury adversely affects the Judicial Branch of government like a pebble tossed into a lake. You may not notice the effect at once, but you can be certain that the tranquility of that lake has been disturbed. And if enough pebbles are thrown into the water, the lake itself may disappear. So too with the truth-seeking process of the courts. Every unanswered and unpunished assault upon it has its lasting effect, and given enough of them, the system itself will implode.

That is why those two women who testified before you had been indicted, convicted, and punished severely for false statements under oath in civil cases. [The committee heard testimony from two witnesses who were convicted of perjury for making statement similar in nature to the President's.] And that is why only a few days ago a federal grand jury in Chicago indicted four former college football players because they gave false testimony under oath to a grand jury. Nobody suggested that they should not be charged because their motives may have been to protect their careers and family. And nobody has suggested that the perjury was nonserious because it involved only lies about betting on college football games.

Apart from all else, the President's illegal actions constitute an attack upon and utter disregard for the truth and for the rule of law. Much worse, they manifest an arrogant disdain not only for the rights of his fellow citizens, but also for the functions and the integrity of the other two coequal branches of our constitutional system. One of the witnesses that appeared earlier likened the government of the United States to a three-legged stool. The analysis is apt because the entire structure of our country rests upon three equal supports: the Legislative, the Judicial, and the Executive. Remove one of those supports, and the State will totter. Remove two and the structure will either collapse altogether or will rest upon a single branch of government. Another name for that is tyranny.

The President mounted a direct assault upon the truth-seeking process which is the very essence and foundation of the Judicial Branch. Not content with that, though, Mr. Clinton renewed his lies, half-truths, and obstruction to this Congress when he filed his answers to simple requests to admit or deny. In so doing, he also demonstrated his lack of respect for the constitutional functions of the Legislative Branch.

Actions do not lose their public character merely because they may not directly affect the domestic and foreign functioning of the Executive Branch. Their significance must be examined for their effect on the functioning of the entire system of government. Viewed in that manner, the President's actions were both public and extremely destructive.

The apples-and-oranges method employed to defend the President is well illustrated in the matter of President Nixon's tax returns. Thus, they argue from the fact that Mr. Nixon was not impeached for lying on a tax return that perjury is not an impeachable offense. But President Nixon avoided that charge only because there was not enough evidence to prove deliberate lying. That is like arguing that because Lizzie Borden was acquitted of killing her mother with an ax, it is not a crime to kill one's mother with an ax.

Today, our country is at a crossroads from which two paths branch off. One leads to the principles—at once familiar and immortal—contained in the Declaration of Independence and the Constitution. These are principles that for over two hundred years have so affected our actions as to earn the admiration of the world and to gain for the United States the moral leadership among nations. There was a time not so very long ago when a policy decision by the President of the United States was saluted as "the most unsordid act in the history of mankind."

The other path leads to expediency, temerity, self-interest, cynicism, and a disdain for the welfare of others and the common good. That road will inevitably end in iniquity, dishonor, and abandonment of the high principles that we, as a people, rely upon for our safety and happiness. There is no third road.

This is a defining moment both for the Presidency and especially for the Members of this Committee.... If you do not impeach as a consequence of the conduct that I have just portrayed, then no House of Representatives will ever be able to impeach again. The bar will be so high that only a convicted felon or a traitor will need to be concerned.

Remember, experts came up before you and pointed to the fact that the House refused to impeach President Nixon for lying on an income tax return. Can you imagine a future president faced with possible impeachment pointing to the perjuries, lies, obstructions, tamperings, and abuses of power by the current occupant of the office as not rising to the level of high crimes and misdemeanors? If this is not enough, what is? How far can the standard be lowered without completely compromising the credibility of the office for all time?

It is likewise a defining moment for you, the Members of the Judiciary Committee. The roster of this Committee over the years has contained the names of several great Americans: Peter Rodino, Emanuel Celler, Tom Railsback, Bill McCulloch, and Barbara Jordan. These very walls are infused with the honor and integrity that have always prevailed in this chamber. Now it is your turn to add to or subtract from that honor and integrity. You have heard the evidence, you have read the law, you have listened to the experts, and you have heard all the arguments.

What I say here will be forgotten in a few days, but what you do here will be incised in the history of the United States for all time to come. Unborn generations—assuming those generations are still free and are still permitted to read true history—will learn of these proceedings and will most certainly judge this Committee's actions.

What will be their verdict? Will it be that you rose above party and faction and reestablished justice, decency, honor, and truth as the standard by which even the highest office in the land must be evaluated? Or will it be that you announced that there is no abiding standard and that public officials are answerable only to politics, polls, and propaganda? God forbid that that will be your legacy.

The choice, though, is yours.

On Tuesday one of the witnesses referred to our country as the Ship of State. The allusion is to the poem "The Building of the Ship" by Longfellow. Permit me to quote the stanza:

> Sail on, O Ship of State!
> Sail on, O Union, strong and great!
> Humanity with all its fears,
> With all the hopes of future years,
> Is hanging breathless on thy fate!

How sublime, poignant, and uplifting; yet how profound and sobering are those words at this moment in history. You now are confronted with the monumental responsibility of deciding whether William Jefferson Clinton is fit to remain at the helm of that Ship.

Thank you, Mr. Chairman.

As soon as I finished, I walked out of the committee room and back into the lounge. The only person there was my wife, Jackie. She stood up and gave me a hug, and I said to her, "Do you realize what I have just done? I've spent two-

and-a-half hours attacking the most powerful man on the face of the earth."

Jackie shrugged her shoulders and said, "Dave, somebody had to do it."

CHAPTER 12

Impeached!

> "Just the place for a snark;
> I have said it twice.
> That alone should encourage the crew.
> Just the place for a snark, I have said it thrice.
> What I tell you three times is true."
>
> —LEWIS CARROLL, The Hunting of the Snark

L ewis Carroll captured the attitude of the Democrats who repeatedly chose to ignore evidence and who thought that if they shouted "partisanship" and "unfairness" three times each in the impeachment debate, they won the argument.

One Democrat I thought might be different was John Conyers, the ranking member on the committee. From our first meeting I liked him. Like me, he was from the inner city, and we hit it off immediately. I was convinced that, but for the politics of the situation, he would have voted to impeach. He had been a member of the committee that voted to impeach Nixon. He was a man of honor and common decency. When I finished my final argument, Conyers startled everyone in the room by congratulating me—on the record. I walked up to him and told him how grateful I was for his most gracious comments.

He smiled and said, "You deserved it."

I also credit his cooperation with Hyde for helping push the impeachment vote through as quickly as possible.

On December 11, Article One, the grand jury perjury, passed on a straight party-line vote.

Article Two, perjury in the Jones deposition, passed with all the Republicans voting "aye," except Lindsey Graham, and all the Democrats voting "nay."

Article Three, obstruction of justice, passed on a party-line vote.

The next day, December 12, the Gekas amendment to Article Four, abuse of power, passed with support from all of the Republicans.

For only the second time in the history of the United States, the Judiciary Committee of the House of Representatives had voted for the impeachment of an elected president.

The feeling of accomplishment was short-lived. Immediately the attacks began. They were expected from the Democrats and the President's supporters. We found, though, that even Republican members of the House were criticizing and distancing themselves from the action of the committee. We heard that there was no support for impeachment among the Republican leadership—and there wasn't. The spin was that Clinton-haters had forced the Republicans to be stampeded into an ill-advised move. They hadn't. It was said that "the people" were against impeachment, and the polls did, indeed, seem to support this. Even Republicans were saying there was no possibility of winning a vote on impeachment in the House. One Republican said he knew forty Republicans who would vote nay. The Republicans on the committee never expected unanimity, but they were both surprised and dismayed by the criticism from their own party.

The plan was to have the articles debated and voted on by the full House the week of December 14. The day before the scheduled debate, Hyde had a morning meeting of Republican committee members. The meeting was in progress when Steve Buyer, Republican from Indiana, entered the room. Buyer, who was also on the House Armed Services Committee, said, "We just learned that Clinton is bombing Iraq tonight."

There was stunned, unbelieving silence. Hyde blurted, "My God!—*Wag the Dog*," referring to the popular film in which the White House staged a phony war to distract the public's attention from a breaking scandal.

The new Speaker-designate, Bob Livingston, called a Republican caucus to discuss the impeachment schedule given this manufactured foreign crisis.

The immediate cry from the Democrats was, "How can you impeach the Commander in Chief when our armed services are engaged in foreign combat?"

A better question might have been, "How can you defend a president who's willing to put our servicemen and women at risk just to defend his own sorry neck?" You want abuse of power, you just got it in spades.

At the caucus, Livingston ordered everyone who was not a member—that included me—to leave the room. For the next two or more hours, I sat talking to other excluded staff. When the meeting broke up, I saw a smiling Lindsey Graham. He told me the debate was postponed, but only for a couple of days.

The next morning, Steve Buyer noted that every Republican who had seen the evidence in the secure room voted to impeach. Jim Rogan joined him in recommending that *all* House members be invited to examine the secure room evidence. Hyde agreed.

My staff was inundated by the response, guiding Congressmen through the secure room from 8 AM until after midnight. We showed videos, played tapes, and provided transcripts, statements, reports, and any other material we had. They asked questions, requested explanations, and often argued with my lawyers. Most of the time I remained in my office to answer phone inquiries and meet several members who didn't need to see the evidence but wanted to discuss some aspect of our case.

In all, some sixty-five members came in a four-day period. In reviewing the sign-in sheets, I found out later, to my amazement, that *all* our visitors were Republicans. *Not one Democrat saw fit to examine the evidence.*

I also discovered that most of our visitors were ambivalent or leaning against impeachment. Yet of those sixty-five who actually examined the evidence and asked us questions, *sixty-four* voted to impeach. President Clinton's bombing gambit had backfired. It had given us time to convince enough Republicans to ensure impeachment.

Two encounters from those four days stand out in my mind.

Republican Congressman Christopher Shays of Connecticut told me he had no problem with the facts, which convinced him that the President had engaged in serious misconduct and perhaps criminal acts. But he wasn't sure they qualified as "high crimes and misdemeanors" that justified removing him from office. We discussed the law for thirty minutes. I thought I had convinced him, but I was wrong. Shays not only voted against impeachment but even spoke against the articles, the only Republican to do so. I was on the floor during the debate and couldn't help but offer Shays my hand.

"Mr. Shays, I don't agree with your vote on the articles, but I want to tell you how much I admire your courage. You read and looked at the evidence and asked all the right questions. I know you must have agonized over this and voted your conscience. I am proud to know you, sir."

Shays smiled broadly, took my hand, and said, "Thank you, Dave, you made my day."

The second meeting that I will never forget was with a Republican Congresswoman, again in the private office of the secure room. At the time, I happened to be in the room with a couple of members who were questioning me. The

Congresswoman reviewed a video, read transcripts, and opened the file on Juanita Broaddrick. She put her head in her hands and cried, "My God, this is his M.O." Seeing our shocked faces, she told us a story:

A couple of years earlier, several women from her district attended a White House meeting for pro-choice women hosted by Hillary Clinton. There were about fifty to seventy-five women present. When the conference was nearly over, the President entered the room. Mrs. Clinton froze, scowled, and stalked out. Clinton worked the room, talking to all the women, even hugging a few.

Among the attendees were two beautiful young women with long blonde hair. The two were acquainted but seldom met apart from functions of mutual interest. Shortly after the conference, each of the women independently received a call from a man who identified himself as a Secret Service agent on the White House detail. The caller said that the President was quite interested in what they had discussed about women's rights and would like to explore the matter more thoroughly. He said that Mr. Clinton would like to schedule a personal meeting so as to discuss mutual concerns.

Both women said they would be delighted. The caller said he would get back to them with a date and time. Before the "agent" called back, the two women happened to meet and were astonished they'd received the same call. Why would Mr. Clinton invite two women to meet with him—separately and alone—to discuss the very same matter? When the invitation came, both politely but firmly declined.

On the morning of Saturday, December 19, 1998—
Impeachment Day—Jeff Pavletic and I were assigned a
place just outside the Republican cloakroom where we
could answer questions. Jim Rogan and Lindsey Graham
came up and asked which article I would rather present in
the Senate trial: Article Two, charging perjury in the deposition, or Article Three, charging obstruction of justice.
They explained that while discussing the case on the floor,
they had found many who would support Article Two but
were unsure about Three. By the same token, many who
were strongly in favor of Three were waffling on Two. I
told Jim and Lindsey that I would prefer to have both, especially since we all knew we couldn't win Article Four on
abuse of power. But in my opinion Article Three was
absolutely essential. If we had Article Two only, we would
be precluded from producing evidence of widespread
obstruction and tampering. If we had Article Three, all the
evidence, including the evidence of perjury, would be relevant and admissible in the trial. I said, "We need to have
Article One or Two, and we *must* have Article Three."

The afternoon wore on. The Democrats' speeches were
the same: attacking the process, not the facts.

Finally, the vote was called. Article One passed, with no
cheering, no smiles, no handshakes, no celebration. I turned
to Jeff and said, "My God, Jeff, we have just impeached the
President of the United States!" Article Two was voted
down. Article Three passed. Article Four was a loser, and
we all knew it early on. So we would be trying two articles
of impeachment in the Senate: perjury and false statements

under oath in a grand jury, and obstruction of justice. If the Senate gave us a fair trial and if the Senators voted their consciences, President Clinton would be convicted and removed from office.

Jeff and I left the chamber before the final vote on Article Four. Jeff drove me to the airport, and my wife and I flew back to Chicago for Christmas. All through the trip, I was making notes and thinking about our trial strategy.

CHAPTER 13

Weak Knees and Monica

B ut it was all downhill from there. It was made blatantly clear to us that the Republican senatorial leadership did not want a real impeachment trial. That went double for the Democrats. The leaderships were united, but for different reasons.

On the Democratic side, because they were well aware that their forty-five votes were sufficient to block conviction, they elected to present a solid front with the White House to save Mr. Clinton at all costs. To accomplish this, they had to employ party discipline to keep every member in line so that no one would be tempted to break ranks and vote to convict.

Several Democratic Senators had earlier demonstrated disgust at the President's actions, and some were quite vocal in condemning him. Consequently, the House Managers honestly believed that once all the evidence was presented, we would have the twelve Democratic votes necessary for conviction. The White House also knew, at least in general, the evidence that we had available. Thwarting our intent to produce that evidence publicly on the floor of the Senate became the highest priority. The White House reasoned that if all the evidence was available to the public, the President's approval ratings might drop and some Democratic Senators might, in conscience, change their votes. Hence the adamant refusal to allow live witnesses, or any evidence for that matter, that had not already been made public. The Democrats wanted the impeachment vote to be based solely on what was already known. If it hadn't hurt the President in the polls so far, it wouldn't do so now, they figured.

The Senate Republicans, on the other hand, had fifty-five votes—not enough to convict, but more than enough to control the procedure for the trial. Had the Republican leadership exerted the same control as the Democratic leadership, we would have been permitted to try our case as we hoped, with live testimony and other evidence. The Senate Republicans were far from unanimous in their condemnation of the President and certainly didn't present a strong or solid bloc of votes. Several were still unconvinced that the conduct of the President merited removal from office. Some others doubted that the information they possessed even rose to the level of high crimes and misdemeanors.

If we hoped to obtain all Republican votes, we would

need to produce a full and complete picture of the conspiracy to obstruct justice and the unlawful means used to further it. That could not be done based solely on the record that was already public. We absolutely required live witnesses so that the Senators could hear for themselves the testimony and judge the demeanor and credibility of those witnesses.

Under the Senate rules, a simple majority (fifty-one votes) is all that is needed to issue a subpoena for live witness testimony or for documentary evidence. The Republicans had fifty-five votes. Consequently, before we were told otherwise, the Managers were confident that, with the backing of the leadership, witnesses would be presented and a full impeachment trial would take place.

But we had no strong backing from our Republican "friends" in the Senate.

It was obvious from the onset that the Republican leadership was totally at the mercy of the polls. As long as the President's approval rating remained high, the Republican leaders were not about to rock the boat. They were more interested in preserving the self-proclaimed "dignity" of the Senate than in performing the constitutional duty imposed upon them by the electorate. As in the House of Representatives, the Senate leaders were so terrified of being called partisan or unfair that they gave in to every demand—no, suggestion—coming from the other side of the aisle. Each time one of the Managers pointed out to Trent Lott that he had sufficient votes virtually to dictate the procedure and certainly to ensure presentation of evidence, he would complain that he couldn't ensure fifty-one votes to allow any given witness to be called. "They may get so sick of it that they won't allow any witnesses at all," he argued. The Managers then invited the Senators over to the Ford Building to view the evidence and question my staff. That move had worked in the House, and the Managers hoped it would work in the Senate. But it turned out that, as the sign-in sheets reveal, not one single Senator took the time to review the evidence we were clamoring to present openly. To this day, I find that appalling.

Our difficulty was with the Senate leadership, not the Republican Senators individually. Throughout the process most Republicans gave the Managers personal messages of support. Republican Senator Phil Gramm of Texas stands out, in my estimation, as our most loyal and courageous supporter. He talked personally with the Managers a number of times, always giving encouragement and even advice on procedure. Had he been the Majority Leader, things might have been radically different. Compromise has its place in American politics, as has bipartisanship—but certainly not at the expense of truth and justice. In my opinion, the most disturbing revelation came from Senator Trent Lott after the acquittal of the President on February 12, 1999. Lott told the press, in referring to the final vote, "I knew, I could have told you, what this vote was going to be on January 7."

"You could have predicted the exact splits?" a reporter asked.

"Oh, yeah, every one of them!"

He knew the outcome before any Senator took the oath to do equal and impartial justice and before a single word of evidence had been produced. As Congressman Chris Cannon of Utah said, "The whole thing was a farce from the beginning." I might add that obviously the oath was merely for show; nobody meant it. What has happened to the Senate?

Even after the midterm elections, the Managers were confident that many Democratic Senators, once under oath to do equal and impartial justice, would rise above party loyalty to vote their consciences. The first step, though, was to acquaint these Senators with all the facts. Any hope that we had to find support on the Democratic side was crushed before the trial was even scheduled to begin.

At 1 PM on the afternoon of Thursday, January 14, 1999, the formal Senate trial began. Before actually proceeding into the well of the Senate, all the Managers and attorneys met privately with the Chief Justice for a short time. He was cordial to all but quite somber in the face of the awesome responsibility he was about to undertake.

Throughout the proceedings in the Senate, the House Managers used the "Marble Room" across the hall from the Senate chambers as a headquarters, nerve center, lunchroom, and just about anything else. The room was equipped with phones, faxes, computers, typewriters, several television sets, and other equipment. From time to time, one or more of the Managers would leave the floor and go into the Marble Room for a short respite. Though I had a seat assigned to me on the floor, I spent quite a bit of time in the Marble Room meeting with Managers and discussing the trial. I also arranged it so every member of my staff was able to spend some time on the floor of the Senate.

Thursday, Friday, and Saturday were taken up with opening statements by each of the thirteen Managers. By Saturday afternoon, we were certain that enough had been said to ensure that there would be no summary dismissal of the charges. We observed that even Democratic Senators were listening and apparently affected by the clear, cold logic of the case against Clinton.

On January 22, however, Democratic Senator Robert Byrd of West Virginia, one of the most honored and respected persons in the Senate on constitutional matters, not only refused to support our efforts, but actually moved to dismiss the entire case without even a trial of the facts. That move thoroughly shook the Managers. They now realized that party loyalty trumped everything. On January 27 Byrd's motion to dismiss was defeated, but we noted that Democratic Senator Russell Feingold of Wisconsin was the only Democrat to vote with the majority.

It became more and more apparent that, despite suggestions to the contrary, there would be no live testimony on the floor of the Senate. First, we were told that only three witnesses would be permitted, but the Managers could pick which three. That precipitated a meeting of the Managers in the Judiciary Committee lounge.

Various Managers suggested several possible witnesses,

but the list was quickly narrowed down to four. The Managers were unanimous that Monica Lewinsky and Sidney Blumenthal were necessary for the obstruction and the perjury counts. There was a general debate concerning whether the third witness would be Betty Currie or Vernon Jordan. My personal choice was Currie. I felt that under stern but gentle cross-examination she might be induced to recount truthfully the events surrounding her picking up the gifts from Lewinsky, as well as the two witness-coaching sessions she had had with the President. I felt that we had gone as far as we would ever go with Jordan. He is a smooth article and very difficult to fluster.

Some of the Managers, though, voiced two main concerns. First, Currie seemed to back off any testimony unfavorable to President Clinton each time she was questioned; and second, they didn't want it to seem that we were picking on a nice, middle-aged lady. Those concerns convinced the others, and it was finally decided that our three witnesses would be Monica Lewinsky, Vernon Jordan, and Sidney Blumenthal. I suggested that the depositions of Lewinsky and Blumenthal be confined strictly to having them adopt their prior statements and grand jury testimony. I argued that both witnesses were still quite friendly to the President and would probably go out of their way, if given the chance, to help the President's cause and take the sting out of their prior testimony. I offered to have my staff prepare all the questions for each witness to adopt, under oath, everything previously said. Nobody seemed interested in that idea. We all knew right from the start that the depositions would be our only evidence. Nobody had said anything to the Managers directly, but it was obvious that once the Senators viewed the videotaped depositions they would refuse to permit any live testimony. That is exactly what happened.

In short, a trial, in the normal sense of the word, never even took place in the Senate. We were left to present three relatively short and harmless depositions. Neither the Senators nor the public heard anything new in the videotaped testimony of Monica Lewinsky, Vernon Jordan, and Sidney Blumenthal. Actually, *less* was developed than was already available in the released material from the Starr referral. The entire body of evidence on which the Senators based their verdict consisted only of the public part of that referral, nothing more.

And to think that *not one Senator* took the time to review the evidence my staff had gathered. That is perhaps the greatest sellout of all. It didn't matter at all that we had ample evidence of the President's offenses. As I now know, William Jefferson Clinton's acquittal in the Senate was a foregone conclusion before the "trial" ever began.

Although Lewinsky had given several statements and interviews to the FBI, and although she had testified more than once in the grand jury under oath, prudence dictated that she be interviewed prior to her testimony. All of the Managers had been prosecutors, and they were well aware that no witness should be put on the stand unless she has been pretried. In addition, we had no idea of her current feelings for President Clinton or her attitude toward the whole impeachment process and toward the Managers.

At Hyde's request, I asked Jeff Pavletic to call Lewinsky's attorneys and try to arrange an interview. He called and informed Mr. Jacob Stein that the Managers intended to subpoena his client to testify before the Senate and that we would like to arrange a meeting for the Managers to interview her. Stein told Jeff that he would get back to him.

A few hours later, Jeff and I received a call from Plato Cacheris, another of Lewinsky's lawyers. I called Jeff into my office so both of us could talk to him. After some small talk, I repeated our request for an interview. Cacheris said: "Dave, you're an old trial lawyer. If you were me, would you allow your client to submit voluntarily to an interview?"

I looked at Jeff, and we both smiled. I said, "I could lie to you and say that I would. But now that you ask, no, I wouldn't."

Plato replied: "Well, I'm a good lawyer, too, and that is also my decision. Tell the Managers that Monica politely declines their offer."

I asked Jeff to go into the secure room and pull Lewinsky's immunity agreement to see how much testimony she was required to give and to whom. A few minutes later Jeff came back and said it appeared clear to him that the agreement required her to cooperate with Congress, and that meant submitting to an interview. We then called Bob Bittman of the Independent Counsel's Office and told him what happened.

He, too, said that the immunity agreement as he remembered it required cooperation whenever requested and that, if she refused, the Independent Counsel could pull her immunity. Bittman said he wanted to reread the agreement to make certain of its terms. That afternoon he called back, confirmed our understanding, and told us that his office was going before a federal judge for an order compelling Lewinsky to submit to questions by selected Managers before testifying.

I reported this to Hyde, Judiciary Committee Majority Counsel Tom Mooney, and the House Managers on Friday, January 22. I told them that the Independent Counsel was certain he would get the order, so we should decide when and where the interview would take place. Everyone agreed that the three trial Managers, Ed Bryant, Asa Hutchinson, and Bill McCollum, should conduct the interview because one of them would probably put Lewinsky on the stand in the Senate or at least take her deposition. The Managers asked me to come along, and I asked Diana Woznicki to accompany me.

Originally it had been suggested that the interview might take place in the Cannon or the Longworth Building. The Rayburn Building was out because the media had it under virtually twenty-four–hour surveillance. Lewinsky was staying at the Mayflower Hotel in downtown Washington, and the press knew it. No matter what precautions were taken to conceal the meeting site, the press would follow the witness, and we would find ourselves in a circus atmosphere. It was therefore agreed that we would go to the hotel and meet Lewinsky there if and when the court ordered her to submit to questioning.

In the late morning of Saturday, January 23, I received a fax from Bob Bittman. It was an order signed by Chief Judge Norma Holloway Johnson directing Monica Lewinsky to allow herself to be debriefed by the House Managers or forfeit her protection under her immunity agreement. With that order in place, Lewinsky could no longer refuse to cooperate with us. Calls were exchanged between the Managers and Lewinsky's lawyers. It was finally agreed that only the Managers would do the questioning, but Diana, one or two other staffers, and I would also be present during the interview. The meeting was scheduled to take place at the Mayflower Hotel on Sunday evening, January 24.

Hyde, Mooney, a few other members of the Judiciary Committee staff, and the three trial Managers met in Hyde's office in the Rayburn Building to plan the questioning strategy. I specifically asked Diana to watch Lewinsky throughout the meeting and to give us her reading on the witness, her candor, and her credibility. We left the Rayburn Building in several cars. Each car was driven by a plainclothes member of the Capitol Police, and another police officer accompanied the passengers. The three trial Managers were in the lead car, and Diana and I followed immediately behind.

On the way to the hotel, the driver told us what to do: "Stay inside the car until we tell you to exit. Then, when you step from the car, do not hesitate, move rapidly for the door to the hotel." When we pulled up to the front door, we saw that the entire area was lit up in the stark glare of television cameras. The street was crawling with scurrying cameramen and photographers; strident and intrusive reporters clogged the space between our car and the Managers' car. Diana and I remained in the backseat until the police and security guards hustled Bryant, Hutchinson, and Rogan into the hotel. Then our driver said, "Okay, let's go. Follow right behind me."

Our car was double-parked about fifty feet from the main entrance. As we stepped from the car, we became the new targets. From all sides the media descended upon us. The Capitol Police officers were magnificent. They pushed through the melee and got us to the main entrance. The local police and security guards had cordoned off the sidewalk from the curb to the front door. Behind that cordon and on both sides there were hundreds of citizens drawn by all the activity. As we entered the hotel, we could hear people hurling vile obscenities and curses at us. I thought, "My God, what have we done to make them hate us so?"

Finally, we went through the revolving doors into the lobby of the hotel expecting peace and quiet. We quickly realized that a wedding was being held here, and the lobby was crowded with wedding guests. So even though the general public was not allowed inside the hotel, it seemed just as crowded as the street outside. At least the people here were better behaved and didn't swear at us.

The hotel security and more Capitol Police met us at the

door and hustled us through the lobby and into an elevator. The security people kept everyone else out of the elevator, and up we went to the tenth floor, where Lewinsky's suite was located. When the elevator door opened, we were met by still more security. Both Diana and I were required to identify ourselves. Then we were ushered down a long hall and into a sumptuous suite.

The first thing I noticed was that Monica Lewinsky was nowhere in sight. We walked into a large sitting room. Facing the entrance on a couch were Lewinsky's lawyers. Directly across from them, on another couch, sat the three Managers for the trial. In an open room to our right was Mitch Glazier of Hyde's staff and a few people I did not know. To my left was another room in which snacks and beverages were laid out. On the left of the two sofas were two folding chairs for Diana and me, and behind the chairs stood Bob Bittman and his assistant. Near the door and at spaced intervals throughout the suite, security people were stationed. I thought to myself that this suite was as crowded as the lobby downstairs.

After some preliminary pleasantries, Bittman opened the discussion. He reiterated that Lewinsky was under a court order to submit to a debriefing by the House Managers only and to testify in the Senate if required. Cacheris, Lewinsky's attorney, acknowledged the order and said his client was prepared to cooperate. Then he asked Bittman if the immunity granted to Lewinsky for her grand jury testimony would extend to anything she said to the Managers.

Bittman answered that the matter had not been discussed, but he assumed that it would not. Cacheris said that unless his client had immunity, he would not allow her to testify.

I turned to Diana and whispered: "Here comes trouble. Plato would be crazy to let Monica testify without immunity, and Plato isn't crazy." I knew that immunity given for grand jury testimony does not extend to any other evidence given later. Many times in my career I had refused to let an immunized client testify at trial until an order was entered renewing the immunity, so I knew there was going to be a problem.

Bittman asked that he and the Managers meet privately to discuss what should be done, at which point we went into a private room in the suite and Bittman asked the Managers what they would prefer. Asa Hutchinson asked Bittman to let us discuss the situation before coming to a decision. After Bittman left, we began to discuss the pros and cons of immunity for this interview. At first it appeared that nobody wanted to extend the immunity. McCollum suggested that with renewed immunity, Monica could, if she chose, back off her prior testimony with impunity. The rest agreed. McCollum asked my opinion. I said that in my mind we should go along with the immunity. The woman had testified several times and had been interviewed by the FBI and the prosecutors up one side and down the other. Her account of the events had not changed. "I am convinced that she will tell the truth. Unless she gets immunity, we won't get to interview her at all. That means putting the most important of our three witnesses on the stand cold. And whenever she testifies, she will have immunity anyhow; so what do we have to lose? Why don't we ask Bob Bittman what he thinks?" Everyone agreed, so I asked Bittman to join us.

Ed Bryant said, "You've been working with Monica in and out of the grand jury, what do you think she'll do if you extend the immunity?"

Bob didn't hesitate: "No way will she lie. She knows that part of her agreement with us is that she will always tell the truth, and she knows that if she changes her story, we won't hesitate to withdraw the immunity." Then he added: "She won't lie, but be very careful in your questioning. We think she is still in love with Clinton. If you give her any opening where she thinks she can help him, she will do it in a heartbeat."

"How could Monica possibly have any feeling for the President after what he did to her and said about her?" Diana asked.

Bittman shrugged his shoulders. "I have no idea; just be careful."

When Bob left, the discussion continued for about ten or fifteen more minutes, after which it was unanimously agreed that we would ask for the immunity extension. We informed Bob, and he left to call the Independent Counsel for permission to grant the immunity. We stayed in the private room, talking about what questions should be asked. After a few minutes, I asked if I could make a suggestion, and McCollum said yes. I said: "Ms. Lewinsky has appeared twice before the grand jury and testified under oath. That evidence is locked in, so there is no need to go over it. The material contained in her many interviews was not under oath, so we would need to have her adopt it. I suggest that the questioning be extremely limited. We should forget about the grand jury and merely determine that she had read all the evidence she gave in interviews and was standing on what she said. Just don't forget Bittman's warning, because if you try to clarify or try to make her testimony more damaging, we may get hurt. She might spin us off our chairs."

At this point, I was thinking of the extent of Lewinsky's testimony, regardless of whether it was in a deposition or live in the Senate. Based on what Bittman said, Lewinsky's testimony should go no further than adopting everything she had told the FBI and the grand jury. Some time later, Bittman came back and said they were going to accede to Cacheris's demand. We had now been in that suite for about an hour-and-a-half and hadn't even seen Lewinsky.

We went back into the sitting room and waited while Bittman and Lewinsky's lawyers agreed on the ground rules. Then one of the lawyers left the room. After a few moments, he returned with Monica Lewinsky. We introduced ourselves, Cacheris again went over the ground rules, and Bittman assured her that she had the same immunity that she had been given originally. We all settled back, and the questioning began. Diana and I sat quietly on the sidelines, listening and watching.

All three Managers assured the witness that they were not interested in causing her any problem or embarrassment. They realized that she had been over the same scenario many, many times, and they were not going to go over it again. They merely wanted to clarify a few points. Actually, I knew that we were really there to meet Lewinsky so she would be comfortable testifying, to assess her demeanor and credibility, and to learn whether she was going to back off on any of her prior testimony.

Each of the Managers then asked specific questions focusing on the conversation with the President about their cover story, the false affidavit, and the gifts, both given to and received from the President. Right from the outset, it was clear to everyone in the room that Lewinsky was not going to give us any additional evidence if she thought it might hurt Clinton. At one point, McCollum asked Lewinsky to clarify her conversation with the President about the gifts: "Did he say or indicate that he would send Betty Currie to pick them up?"

For the first and only time during the questioning, Lewinsky bristled: "I don't want to wrinkle your shirt, Congressman, but that just didn't happen. What I told the grand jury is what happened." We were obviously going nowhere. The questioning continued for about another ten minutes. At the end, someone asked Lewinsky if she wanted to add anything. She told us how difficult it was to give evidence of any kind against President Clinton, but she was trying to tell the truth without coloring it.

Ed Bryant asked if she still felt any affection for the President, and she acknowledged that she still felt great affection and loyalty. Despite the agreement that only the Managers would question Lewinsky, I blurted out that I found it difficult to understand that she would have any good feelings after what Clinton had said about her. Lewinsky looked at me with a puzzled expression and asked what I meant.

"He said you were obsessed; he called you a stalker; he said that you threatened him." I then noticed that the book containing all the testimony, including Blumenthal's, was on the coffee table. "Look," I said, "it's right there in front of you."

Lewinsky's eyes began to tear up, and she was shaking her head. Turning to her lawyer, she asked, "What is he talking about?"

Her lawyers said, "I think that it is time we called an end to this interview."

The Capitol Police and security guards who were going to escort us out of the building came in and told us how we were going to get back to the Rayburn Building. They suggested that the Managers should leave last. The Independent Counsel staffers said they didn't need any escort because the real interest was in the Managers and the staff who may have conducted the interview. We had been in the hotel for well over two hours. The media had no idea that most of the time was spent arguing over the ground rules. They were anxious for information.

At the suggestion of the Capitol Police, Diana, Mitch Glazier, and I were the first to leave. We were escorted back the way we had entered. Down the long hall, into the waiting elevator, and to the lobby. Nobody said anything. I noticed that both the hall and the lobby were staffed with plainclothes police, all of whom wore radios and earpieces. As we approached the front door, we were met by the officer who was to ride with us. He told us that the mob outside had grown substantially and was beginning to get ugly because they had been waiting so long in the cold. The officer gave us the location of our waiting car. He again warned us to move quickly, to say nothing, and not to stop for anything. One of the officers who had escorted us from the suite said to me: "That is any ugly crowd out there. I don't think we can guarantee your safety. I am apologizing in advance, because if I see any problem I am going to be shoving you hard."

"You won't need to shove. Just say go, and I'll be off and running," I said.

The door opened and out we went. I have never seen anything like it. The press surrounded us. Reporters were calling out questions, pressing close, sticking microphones, television cameras, and flashbulbs in our face, and trying to impede our progress. Oh yes, the crowd had grown. It seemed as though the street and sidewalk were packed with people. And the crowd was ugly. We could hear threats and many obscenities. Such pleasantries as, "Why don't you assholes get off the President's back." And, "End the bull-shit." And the ever-instructive, "You all should be hung with Hyde."

The Capitol Police (God bless them) were again unbe-lievable. The ones in front opened a path, and the ones behind pushed us toward the car, protecting our rear. The whole thing probably took about thirty seconds, but believe me, it seemed a lot longer. The three of us piled into the car and the door slammed. The driver turned with a smile and said, "Welcome back. Quite a show!" Cameras were at every window. The driver began to make a U-turn, but there were people in the way. He sounded his siren and a path opened. He wheeled the car around the corners and left the area.

As we were driving back to the Rayburn Building, I was thinking of Lewinsky. I said to nobody in particular, "That poor kid—every time she goes anywhere in public, she has to go through that gauntlet." Later, I learned that the three Managers stopped outside the hotel and gave a news con-ference. Now that took guts, because many people in that crowd were not that far from violence. It must have been a nightmare for the police and security people.

We assembled in the Rayburn Building, where Hyde and the other Managers were waiting for us. They asked Diana her opinion. She thought that Lewinsky was trying to tell the truth but that she was obviously still in love with the President and would try to help him.

The discussion turned to which of the Managers should question Lewinsky in the formal trial. Everyone agreed that she clearly felt most comfortable with Bryant. He is a real southern gentleman, soft-spoken and always courteous. Hyde decided that Bryant would conduct the interrogation of Lewinsky.

The first thing Monday morning, January 25, my staff and I met so that Diana and I could report on the meeting with Monica. As soon as the meeting ended, we began to draft the limited questions to be asked of Monica Lewinsky, Sidney Blumenthal, and Vernon Jordan.

The depositions were scheduled for three consecutive days, February 1, 2, and 3. As planned, Ed Bryant questioned Monica Lewinsky on February 1, beginning at 9 AM. Bryant agreed to take the deposition in Room 1010 at the Mayflower Hotel, where we had met on January 24. I had no intention of subjecting myself to the insanity outside the hotel, so I asked Jeff Pavletic to attend in my place. When Jeff returned that afternoon, he was laughing.

As predicted, the streets were again crammed with reporters, cameras, and lights. What we hadn't anticipated was the scene in Room 1010. According to Jeff, the room was packed to the walls with Senators and Congressmen, all craning to get a look at Monica Lewinsky in person. "For a bunch of people who don't want to see Monica in the well of the Senate, they sure broke their necks to get a peek at her in that hotel room," Jeff said. He then told me that the questioning went just about as expected. Nothing new developed, but the witness didn't hurt us.

The next day, Asa Hutchinson deposed Vernon Jordan. The deposition took place on the Senate side of the Capitol, again with no startling results. On Wednesday, February 3, Jim Rogan questioned Sidney Blumenthal, in my opinion the most dangerous of the three. If he changed or added to his grand jury testimony concerning Clinton's remark about Lewinsky, it could vitally affect our case. Jim is a skilled trial lawyer, though, and he led Blumenthal through his testimony like a maestro leading an orchestra. Rogan was able to produce a bonus. In answering some of the questions, Blumenthal denied leaking material to the media. That testimony later caused some members of the House Judiciary Committee to call for a perjury investigation against Blumenthal.

On Thursday, February 4, at 1 PM, the Managers began the "evidence" phase of the impeachment trial of President William Jefferson Clinton. Nobody connected with the Managers was shocked or even surprised when the Senate opted for the deposition testimony in place of live testimony. The full deposition of Monica Lewinsky was not shown, just excerpts. That, of course, caused another outcry from the President's lawyers that we were being selective and unfair. Lewinsky's testimony was followed by the depositions of Vernon Jordan and Sidney Blumenthal. That was the extent of the "evidence" the Managers were permitted to present. With full knowledge that they were running in a rigged race, the President's lawyers neither cross-examined the prosecution witnesses nor produced any factual evidence in defense of the charges. Instead, they chose to play excerpts from the same depositions.

The "testimony" was followed, on Monday, February 8, by the final arguments. Then the Senators went into Executive Session to debate the articles. On Friday, February 12, 1999, Abraham Lincoln's birthday, the United States Senate, in a foreordained and actually anticlimactic vote, perfunctorily acquitted William Jefferson Clinton on both articles. We didn't even achieve a simple majority.

It was over; the Senate had voted. The constitutional system had failed in the Senate. It didn't fail because the President was acquitted. Every trial lawyer has had the experience of losing a jury verdict that he thought he should have won. If you believe in the jury system, as I do, you accept the verdict and move on to the next case. You believe that, most of the time, juries are right because the system itself is sound. In the case of the impeachment, however, the whole process was flawed because the prosecutors were not permitted to put on evidence to prove the charges.

We all left the Senate chamber and went into the Marble Room across the hall for the last time. Even though we had known for weeks that we were fighting a lost cause, everyone was still disappointed and dejected. Very little was said as we gathered up all our papers, charts, and other material. I personally felt that the American people not only didn't support us, but even despised us for what we had done to their President. When I mentioned this to Hyde, he said, "Dave, don't ever underestimate the American people."

We all left together, led by Hyde, to go back to the Rayburn Building. It was necessary for us to walk from the Senate side of the Capitol, through the great Rotunda, and out the doors on the House side. As we walked through the Senate corridor on the way to the Rotunda, we met several uniformed Capitol Police. Every one of them had a word of gratitude or encouragement: "God bless you guys," or "We're proud to know you," or just "Thank you." That helped raise our spirits, but what waited for us in the Rotunda was amazing.

The Rotunda was crowded with tourists and visitors who had wanted to be present during the impeachment vote. A roped-off passage through the center of the room had been erected for our passage. The first one to appear in the Rotunda was Henry Hyde, followed by the other Managers, some staffers, and me. As Hyde appeared, first one and then a few others began to clap. By the time we reached the center of the room, everyone in the Rotunda was applauding those thirteen beaten warriors. Some people reached over the barrier to shake Hyde's hand. Suddenly, every one of us began to walk a little faster and with a spring in our step. I looked at the Managers and saw that they were smiling, where a minute earlier they had been downcast. All along they knew that, come what may, they were honorably performing their constitutional duty. Now they realized that the great unpolled American people knew it, too. As usual, Chairman Henry Hyde was right: "Don't ever underestimate the American people."

As I write this, almost two years have passed since the President was impeached. My illustrious staff members have returned to their respective occupations, and I have returned to the practice of law in the Chicago Loop. President Clinton is still the President and is now boasting that it was he who upheld the Constitution and the rule of law. Several of the House Managers are facing the fight of their political lives just to get reelected.

At the same time, we are constantly being told by the ever-vigilant spinmeisters that the people of this country are sick to death of hearing about the scandals in the White House and disapprove of everything we attempted to accomplish in the impeachment proceedings. I don't believe that. I believe that the attitude of the citizens was evidenced more by the applause I heard in the Capitol Rotunda and by the hundreds of anonymous people who have approached me on the street, in church, on trains, and elsewhere to express gratitude for the courage of the House Managers.

Vice President Al Gore is the Democratic nominee for President, and Mrs. Clinton is a candidate for the United States Senate. Was the impeachment and the trial of William Jefferson Clinton the end of a shameful era in Washington? Only time will tell. But I am optimistic.

Make no mistake about it, the integrity of our public officers mirrors that of the citizens. I honestly believe that the American people will eventually realize the extent to which they were sold out and to which constitutional precepts were abandoned for political gain during the impeachment process. I hope this book will help them come to that realization. The American eagle may be slow to anger, but, once incensed, nothing can stand against it.

In the words of Thomas Jefferson, "Whenever the people are well-informed, they can be trusted with their own government; whenever things get so far wrong as to attract their notice, they may be relied upon to set them to rights."

The Evidence

I n making our case in the Senate trial, we were limited to the evidence from the Independent Counsel's referral that had already been made public. Unfortunately, a great deal of evidentiary material was received in Executive Session and will remain under seal for fifty years unless the House Judiciary Committee releases it.

Also excluded from the Senate trial was evidence my staff and I compiled in the course of independent investigations.

The documents that follow are just a small portion of the evidence that the American people would have seen. This paper trail shows that the White House pressured the Immigration and Naturalization Service (INS) to hurriedly naturalize immigrants who were likely Democratic voters. Moreover, the final document offers evidence that the President committed perjury.

U.S. DEPARTMENT OF HOUSING AND URBAN DEVELOPMENT
THE SECRETARY
WASHINGTON, D.C. 20410-0001

February 15, 1996

MEMORANDUM FOR: President William Clinton
Vice President Al Gore

FROM: Henry Cisneros

SUBJECT: Utilizing Volunteers to Reduce INS Naturalization Backlogs

You asked me the other day whether qualified volunteers could be generated to assist the INS in naturalization activities. The attached memo from the Industrial Areas Foundation in Los Angeles describes what is possible.

Attachment

Z000323

Based on this February 15, 1996, memo from Housing Secretary Henry Cisneros, the White House apparently decides to expedite the naturalization process for aliens. The attached proposal spells out the significance to Clinton and Gore: "INS inaction will deny 300,000 Latinos the right to vote in the 1996 presidential elections [sic] in California." (2 pages)

SOUTHERN CALIFORNIA I.A.F. NETWORK
ACTIVE CITIZENSHIP CAMPAIGN
^UNO ^SCOC ^EVO ^VOICE
770 S. ARROYO PARKWAY, SUITE 115
PASADENA, CALIF. 91105
TEL. 818-584-0774   FAX   818-584-0972

Background: On Jan. 30, 1996 IAF's Active Citizenship Campaign leaders from New York, San Francisco, Chicago and Los Angeles joined by Congress member Xavier Becerra, met with INS Commissioner Meissner. That day ACC leaders offered a specific proposal to address backlog, increase efficiency and reduce cost without compromising the quality of adjudication's.

INS inaction will deny 300,000 Latinos the right to vote in the 1996 presidential elections in California.

IAF's Active Citizenship Campaign will produce thousands of trained volunteers to identify, screen and process applications for Naturalization.

IAF's Active Citizenship Campaign is willing to work with INS to increase efficiency by testing and screening applicants.

IAF's Active Citizenship Campaign will submit a minimum of 1200 quality applications per month.

IAF's Active Citizenship Campaign is willing to produce 100's of volunteers to work with INS to facilitate administrative swearing in.

IAF's Active Citizenship Campaign will register 26,000 citizens to vote.

IAF's Active Citizenship Campaign will identify and turn out 52,000 occasional voters, conduct 5000 house meetings, encourage vote by mail and create voter interest around issues of Affirmative Action and Minimum Wage.

IAF's Active Citizenship Campaign will influence 300,000 voters in preparation for Nov. 1996.

IAF's Active Citizenship Campaign will target 960 under-represented precincts, produce 5000 precinct leaders and turn out 96,000 voters for the 1996 presidential election.

IAF's Active Citizenship Campaign is willing to fight along side the Clinton Administration in efforts to maximize INS efficiency and effectiveness and to decrease massive backlogs while increasing the number of New Americans.

Z000325

Memo for President Clinton

Subject: Improving Service for Citizenship Applicants

You asked us to expedite the naturalization of nearly a million legal aliens who have applied to become citizens. INS had begun last year gearing up to process the growing backlog of applicants but, largely because of bureaucratic delays, has not made much of a dent in it yet.

Members of my National Performance Review staff have been working to remove the bureaucratic roadblocks so that INS offices in Los Angeles, San Francisco, Chicago, New York, and Miami can quickly double or triple their production. Examples of the roadblocks include: hiring procedures that were taking months followed by employee background investigations that were taking more months (we have now speeded it all up some), prohibitions against using temp agencies, time-wasting procedures requiring paper records that duplicate computer records, cumbersome centralized control over computer systems, the list goes on. Hardly any of the roadblocks are statutory; we have the administrative authority to remove most them.

But, INS Commissioner Doris Meissner warns that if we are too aggressive at removing the roadblocks to success, we might be publicly criticized for running a pro-Democrat voter mill and even risk having Congress stop us. Indeed, many of the roadblocks originate with her own INS staff -- people who might well complain if we waive the regulations and procedures they have created and followed for years -- people whose complaints might seem credible to the public.

I see two options:

Option 1. To get anywhere near a million applicants naturalized before the summer is out, we are clearly going to have to force some serious "reinvention" on INS. I believe we can reduce -- but not eliminate -- the risk of controversy over our motives by appointing one of our proven NPR reinventors as Deputy INS Commissioner (the current deputy could be useful elsewhere in the administration -- with Barry McAffry, for example.) As part of the official INS management team, our reinventor would have

2000326

In this 1996 memo to President Clinton, Doug Farbrother of the National Performance Review notes INS Commissioner Doris Meissner's concern that "we might be publicly criticized for running a pro-Democrat voter mill" and suggests two options for proceeding. It seems the second option, to leave INS alone, is not seriously considered. (2 pages) more direct influence and the INS staff would be less likely to go public with complaints than they would over the interference of an outsider.

We should be putting proven reinventors into lots of agencies anyway. Having people who don't "get it" in top jobs has turned out to be ReGo's number one stumbling block.

Option 2. Our other option is to avoid any controversy over speeding up naturalization by letting the standard bureaucracy do the best it can. We will, of course, lend whatever help we can within the system. INS will be able to gear up production slowly, but a lot of people will still be waiting for their citizenship papers for a long time.

Z000327

doug farbrother at npr @ CCMAIL
09/19/96 09:35 AM

To: Deb Smith
cc:
Subject: Re(6): INS

New Forward Item:

-------------------------------- Forwarded --------------------------------
From: doug farbrother
Date: 3/21/96 8:28PM
•To: Elaine C. Kamarck at OVPNOTES
Subject: Re(6): INS

New Text Item: Re: Re(4): INS

I favor drastic measures. I am meeting with Jamie G and Chris S Friday at
1:30. If I don't get what we need, I will call for heavy artillery.

_____ Reply Separator _____
Subject: Re: Re(4): INS
Author: Elaine C. Kamarck at OVPNOTES
Date: 3/21/96 9:16 AM

THE PRESIDENT IS SICK OF THIS AND WANTS ACTION. IF NOTHING MOVES TODAY WE'LL
HAVE TO TAKE SOME PRETTY DRASTIC MEASURES.

Z000382

In this e-mail exchange from March 21, 1996, Elaine Kamarck of the Vice President's office indicates that President Clinton is closely monitoring the plan to expedite naturalization: "THE PRESIDENT IS SICK OF THIS AND WANTS ACTION." In response, Doug Farbrother indicates that he, too, favors "drastic measures" when it comes to the INS. (1 page)

Author: Doug Farbrother at NPR
Date: 3/22/96 3:46 PM
Priority: Normal
TO: Albert Gore at EOP_OVP
CC: Elaine C. Kamarck at EOP_OVP
CC: Bob Stone
CC: Laurie Lyons
Subject: INS
---------------------------------- Message Contents ----------------------------------

    I met with Jamie Gorelick, Chris Sales and various INS and Justice
staffers. I told them that, after visiting all five cities, I had
concluded that the only way to get the backlog processed in time is to
delegate broad authority to the managers in those cities, to waive
stupid rules, move money from one account to another as needed, and
recruit and hire people locally instead of through the slow
centralized process. Sales has been resisting such broad, bold
delegation and Jamie didn't push her far enough to suit me.

After the meeting Jamie told Elaine that they would:

    - delegate hiring authority
    - give each city manager a "project budget" to spend as needed
    - waive extensive background investigations on new employees
    - allow the cities "overhire authority."

Jamie said she would deliver by Tuesday.

I'll be in LA Tuesday waiting with the local INS manager for the
delivery. I'm skeptical on two counts: first that the promised relief
will arrive on time, and second that it will be all it's cracked up to
be.

I bet Elaine $10 that the LA manager won't get what he needs Tuesday.
Do you want in on the action?

*On March 22, 1996, Doug Farbrother e-mails Vice President Gore directly to give
a progress report on the INS and its backlog in naturalization applicants. Among
other things, he reports that he told the INS and the Justice Department to "waive
stupid rules" and to "delegate broad authority" to district directors. (1 page)*

FAX for Chris Sale

FROM; Doug Farbrother, *NPR*

When I met with Doris Friday, I told her that to get the results the Vice President wants, I need to get plenty of authority into the hands of your District Directors in the big cities. I simply don't have time to deal with the entire multi-layered organization. She deferred to you as the internal manager.

I need you or Doris to sign something like the attached. Please let me know soon.

13-000041 ᴊᴘ42

In this fax, Doug Farbrother instructs INS Deputy Commissioner Chris Sale to delegate broad authority to district directors in order to "get the results the Vice President wants." He has attached a memo to go to the INS directors in the five targeted cities. (2 pages)

Memorandum to:

Edward McElroy
District Director, New York

Brian Perryman
District Director, Chicago

Walter Cadman
District Director, Miami

Thomas Schiltgen
District Director, San Francisco

Richard Rogers
District Director, Los Angeles

Subject: Citizenship USA

We hereby delegate to you full authority to waive, suspend, or deviate from
DOJ and INS non-statutory policies, regulations, and procedures provided
you operate within the confines of the law. Please let us know which rules
you have waived.

We expect you to use this authority to strengthen security against
naturalization of aliens who do not meet statutory qualification standards
for American citizenship, and to enhance the speed and convenience of the
process for those who do. We hold you responsible for your judgment and
the results.

Jamie Gorelick   Chris Sale
Deputy Attorney General   Deputy Commissioner

ZU00251

JAT

doug farbrother at npr @ CCMAIL
09/19/96 09:43 AM

To: Deb Smith
cc:
Subject: Re: Re[2]: INS

New Forward Item:

-------------------------------------- Forwarded ---------------------------
From: Albert Gore at OVPNOTES
Date: 3/28/96 7:02PM
To: doug farbrother at NPR
Subject: Re: Re[2]: INS

New Text Item: Re: Re[2]: INS

We'll explore it. Thanks.

To: Albert Gore
cc: Elaine C. Kamarck, bob stone at npr @ CCMAIL, Laurie Lyons at
          npr @ CCMAIL
From: doug farbrother at npr @ CCMAIL
Date: 03/28/96 03:31:00 AM
Subject: Re[2]: INS

New Text Item: Re: INS

No sir, the bet was not just about Kelly Girls. I had bet Elaine that INS
headquarters would not give their managers in Los Angeles, San Francisco,
Chicago, New York, and Miami enough authority, in general, to make me
confident they could produce a million new citizens before election day.
Unfortunately, I was right.

What the five city managers need is complete authority to waive any INS
rule, provided they stay within the law. That's not at risky as it might
sound. The people in charge of the five cities are very experienced and
very conservative. I couldn't get them to take big chances if I used a
gun.

The kind of broad delegation I want has precedent; GSA and Commerce have
both given that authority to their Reinvention Labs -- and not a single
thing has gone wrong.

   Here's the sort of thing that could go right if INS would give its
front line managers that authority.

   - They could get workers on the job quickly; they could run a "help
wanted" ad in the local paper, interview and hire people on the spot,
start training them the next day, and simultaneously run a quick National
Agency Check on them to see if they have a record. That is precisely what
the National Archives's Federal

Z000384

*Doug Farbrother again e-mails the Vice President on March 28, 1996, this time
to warn Gore that if INS procedures aren't changed quickly, "we are going to
have way too many people still waiting for citizenship in November." He also asks
the Vice President to put pressure on INS Commissioner Doris Meissner. Gore
responds: "We'll explore it. Thanks." (2 pages)*

Records Center does -- and their employees handle the very same INS files in the very same building with the INS operation south of LA.

But INS headquarters is still insisting on a hiring and clearance process that will take well over a month to get people on board -- THEN they plan to do background investigations just like the Defense Department does for top secret clearance -- investigations that won't be finished until after the project is complete and the people are off the roles -- investigations that cost thousands of dollars each that could be spent processing citizens.

Speed in hiring and clearance is a VERY BIG deal because INS is experiencing high attrition in these temporary jobs.

- Local managers could choose to use temp services (here's the Kelly Girls). Contracts are already in place, and good, reliable people could be on the job in a few days. Even "inherently governmental functions," like citizenship determinations can be handled by contract workers under the proper supervision.

- The five city managers could stop wasting time and manpower following obsolete regulations. For example, INS regs require that every naturalization certificate be Xeroxed and a hard copy put in the archived file, even though a computer record exists. Here's another: clerks have to keep a handwritten ledger of every greencard that's collected at the swearing-in ceremonies, even though the cards are shredded and, again, there is a computer record. I've heard lots of examples like these from the field managers and dozens more would surface if they had authority to change things.

The way it is now, to get relief from obsolete rules, the field managers have to play "Mother may I?" with headquarters -- and the answer is so often "No, you may not." that they eventually give up.

- They could do some simple automation. For example, each naturalization certificate has a photo glued to it, embossed by hand (like a notary public seal), and stamped with Doris Meissner's signature. That all takes a lot of time, money, and manpower that could be devoted to interviewing applicants. But headquarters is slow to adopt digital photos (like you have on your driver's license) and they won't permit Doris's signature to be digitized so that it can be laser printed instead of stamped on the certificates. Lots of modern technology could be locally grafted to the centrally programmed system if headquarters would allow it.

I could go on. But the point is that, unless we blast INS headquarters loose from their grip on the frontline managers, we are going to have way too many people still waiting for citizenship in November.

I can't make Doris Meissner delegate broad authority to her field managers. Can you?

doug farbrother at npr @ CCMAIL
09/19/96 09:32 AM

To: Deb Smith
cc:
Subject: In case we don't connect by phone.

New Forward Item:

------------------------------- Forwarded -----------------------------------
From: doug farbrother at npr
Date: 3/29/96 12:37PM
*To: Elaine C. Kamarck at EOP_OVP
*To: bob stone at npr
Subject: In case we don't connect by phone.

New Text Item: Text_1

here are two ideas:

To blunt any charge that we are running a citizenship/Clinton voter mill.
I am working with the FBI to find a way to tighten up the ridiculously
loose fingerprint check system, i.e. INS doesn't know who's prints they
have, the prints are often too smudged for the FBI to read, and INS simply
assumes that everything is okay if they hear nothing from FBI (which is
90% of the time). A breakthrough here will look good to the anti-alien
lobby.

Rather that having me appear to be working against Doris, put me to work
for her. Move Chris Sales into another job (like Deputy Director for
Programs at the NPR) and make me the INS Deputy Commissioner.
From there, I could do more, faster. And I could solve the airport
problems too.

Z000388

In this March 29, 1996, e-mail, Doug Farbrother again betrays concern that it may appear "we are running a citizenship/Clinton voter mill." He offers two ideas to "blunt any charge" about the White House's motives. (1 page)

During the Paula Jones lawsuit, President Clinton submitted this handwritten account of a conversation with Dolly Kyle Browning. White House aide Marsha Scott's own notes on the conversation, which she claims to have overheard, begin near the bottom of the second page. In our investigation we uncovered evidence showing that Clinton's handwritten statement is perjurious. (3 pages) money to live on — & I think she said she was doing some public interest housing work — but that for years she had been writing, or wanting, to write. First she tried writing songs (I remember this because at her request I got a songwriter to listen to some of these several years ago) and then she started working on a novel. She told me there was a novel done and she was trying to find a publisher for it. She said it involved a woman having a love affair with a Southern governor, and of course "Like a good fiction" it was not autobiographical and she imagined & wouldn't want it published. She said people would figure out it was who she was writing about. When I pointed out that it wasn't true, she said "Well I'll say it's just fiction, just a story." She then rambled for awhile, reminiscing about how she had loved me for years since she was very young, and through her two marriages, and now. I had never really been there for her because it wasn't my friendship that she wanted. She said she would say it was a fantasy but she needed the money and she didn't care if it hurt me or the presidency, that others had made money and she felt abandoned. At the end of the conversation she suddenly calmed down and said maybe she wouldn't try together with her book, at least now. She talked to me about her son, of whom she was very proud, and said he wanted to go into politics and would like to visit the White House. & I told her that he'd be welcome and we could set it up through my personal office or direct through the White House. Before we stopped talking she said she really didn't want to hurt me, that maybe it wasn't my fault, that & never got involved with her and made her fantasy come true, but that she needed money. She must have talked for 30 minutes in an agitated state. When I left I wasn't sure what she would do but I was glad I'd had Nadine listen to the conversation.

I stood by the President the entire conversation and heard and watched her the entire time. The conversation lasted over 30 minutes — close to 45 and at times she was very animated and threatening acting. I had been concerned

WJC-0064

all courm and had been watching her carefully all evening.
It was a bizarre conversation because she repeatedly
said her story was not true but that she was angry
and needed money. She would throw out an accusation
and then say it was a lie. It was this erratic
behavior that made me stay so attentive to what she
was doing and saying

Spechie Sntt

The Voice of the People

During the impeachment hearings, I was inundated by mail. Some of it was hate mail to die for, with venom by the tanker load. My personal favorite: "Have a Horrible Christmas and a Nasty New Year. I hope you drop dead."

Of course, it wasn't all hate mail. To the contrary, the majority of the correspondence I received supported those Congressmen and Senators who backed impeachment. Regardless of their political beliefs, though, I wrote to many letter writers that I am, and always have been, of the firm belief that Congress must continue to do its duty even if 99 percent of the American people do not agree. Congressmen are not mere surrogates for their constituents; rather, they are Representatives under a republican form of government. They are expected—indeed required—to vote their consciences, regardless of the caprices of public opinion.

If individuals can decide when to ignore a solemn oath to tell the truth, then the only remaining test to ensure truth in judicial proceedings is torture, which has been abandoned by every civilized nation for hundreds of years.

Here are some of the most poignant, the most touching, and, in my opinion, the most representative of all the letters I've received. A fair warning to readers, however: I have left all letters as written, even those in which disapproving citizens resorted to obscenities to express their outrage.

In order to protect the privacy of the letter writers, I have withheld their names and instead just written their hometowns. In all cases, I sent handwritten responses, some of which are printed here, as well.

To those who wrote, thank you for taking the time to share your concerns and feelings. Thank you for your honesty, for your support, and, above all, for believing your voice counts over this moral and legal crisis that continues to face our nation.

Supportive Letters

October 11, 1998

As a layman, not schooled in the law, I was amazed as to the clarity of your presentation of potential articles of impeachment, and I agree with all fifteen items you set forth.

But, as much as I appreciated your presentation, I was profoundly moved by your closing remarks stating your belief as a citizen that those elected should remember that those who died throughout the world in defense of America would be "looking down" as they addressed the impeachment process.

For your memento file of your participation in this historic process, I enclose my only original photograph of the Sixth Marine Division Cemetery taken when I was on Okinawa. Maybe you will hang it on your office wall when this process is concluded. I wish you the best.

> Respectfully,
> An old Marine
> Stratford, New Jersey

Dear Mr. ——,

As a former Marine (if there is such thing as a former Marine), you are not a stranger to the enduring concepts of courage, honor, and sacrifice, concepts that are sorely lacking in today's world. As a veteran of World War II who obviously saw combat, you are one of the true, if unknown, heroes of our time. Unfortunately, I did not serve in the Corps, but I have a grandson, of whom I am infinitely proud, who is currently serving at Camp Pendleton in a Recon unit.

I have taken the liberty of making a copy of the picture that you so graciously sent to me. That copy is now on my wall next to my grandson's picture. It will serve to remind me of the real reason that we must continue this process regardless of the cost. The original of that picture belongs in the custody of the man whose comrades lie beneath those rows of crosses. I am therefore returning it to you.

> *Sincerely,*
> *David P. Schippers*

■ ■ ■

October 27, 1998

There are thousands, if not millions of citizens of this country who do not know men who are committed to efforts to protect our constitutional rights and put our country's needs ahead of their own.

Please, please, do all you can to remove from office anyone who is not worthy to represent the citizens of this United States of America.

> Mesa, Arizona

■ ■ ■

November 19, 1998

Happy Thanksgiving and Happy Holidays and May God Bless.

Thanks for your magnificent talk at the conclusion of the hearings today.

Outstanding.

> With respect and admiration,
> Captain and Mrs. ——
> USMC (ret) 22 years
> Mead, Oklahoma

■ ■ ■

We watched the entire impeachment proceedings. You did the best job of the day in telling the American people what the score is on the impeachment matters. If we had a few more like you, the President would soon be out of office.

I am a retired criminal investigator and followed your evidence all the way. You were right on target, and we do hope that millions of people will understand what you had to say and will act on it.

Keep up the good work!

Huntsville, Alabama

■ ■ ■

Thank you for your work today and in the past. We who love our country and who are *participant* citizens feel strongly impeachment is the *least* that should happen.

Coral Gables, Florida

■ ■ ■

November 20, 1998

I totally agree with your thoughts, and I too believe that Judge Starr really did an outstanding job on the thankless job assigned to him. You put the erroneous allegations in their proper perspective.

I should like to offer an apology for the comments and conduct of the less than "Gentle Lady" Representative from Texas, but I don't know where to begin.

Fredericksburg, Texas

■ ■ ■

To us, who have been watchful since this possible impeachment came about, it is unimaginable that learned men and women in positions of power cannot and/or will not admit that this President has been guilty of sexual harassment, tampered with witnesses, attempted to obstruct justice, abused his power as President, and committed perjury. They have, rather, attacked anyone and everyone who has tried to investigate and hold the President accountable for his actions.

Thank you for helping us to believe that our system of government can still work in these times of legalese and "spinmeisters." We are thankful that there are still men like you and Ken Starr who exemplify what our forefathers expected and required of all those in offices of the United States government.

Lakeland, Florida

■ ■ ■

I thought for several hours that there would be no heroes at this hearing except Kenneth Starr himself. However, you quickly disgorged that thought with your presentation. I thank you for it.

Let me confess that I am a lifelong Democrat. In my defense, I have not voted for a Democrat for President since Harry Truman, and I do not see any waiting in the wings that I would vote for. I have never been as ashamed of my party as I have in recent years.

Professor of Law Emeritus
Wake Forest University
Winston-Salem, North Carolina

■ ■ ■

I would like to congratulate you. It was nice to see the way you exposed the unfair tactics used by the Democrats along with their rude behavior. It was even better when you emphasized the facts against Clinton which seemed to be neglected by the Democrats.

Thanks for a job well done. Keep up the good work.

Port Henry, New York

■ ■ ■

Bravo! You nailed it with "Mission accomplished."

That was a great idea... let someone have any doubts after that. Kendall came out looking like a sophomore.

Bonita Springs, Florida

■ ■ ■

November 27, 1998

Thank you!! Your exchange with Judge Starr was the highlight of the entire event!! You and Judge Starr have renewed my hope that this felon is removed from office and reinforced my pride in serving 22 years in the Corps.

Marietta, Georgia

Letters That Offered Advice

October 19, 1998

I listened to your testimony before the House Judiciary Committee on television, and also I've read the report which was sent to the House of Representatives. There are a couple of points which I think may have been missing in these presentations and to which I would like to call your attention.

Firstly, the oath which President Clinton has violated is his oath of office which requires him to defend the Constitution of the United States. I believe that his actions, which are in violation of the Criminal Code of the U.S., are also violations of his duty under the oath of office. If he violated his oath of office, then it must follow that he should be removed from that office.

Secondly, the oath which he violated in the Paula Jones case is a sacred oath ending with the words "So Help Me God." His motive for violating that oath was to try to avoid civil liability of an undefined amount, but the result of that would be to sell his integrity for liability and damages in that case. Therefore, it was not just an oath to tell the truth but was a violation of the oath for money.

I will close this letter with the following quotation: "To worship gods that are not yours, that is toadyism. Not to act when justice demands, that is cowardice." *The Analects of Confucius*, 2.24.

Attorney
Winnetka, Illinois

■ ■ ■

November 21, 1998

There is a trail of corruption in current presidential circles, and you are right to focus on the new catchphrase "mission accomplished." It is my fervent hope that you are determined to dig deeper as long as the liberals are determined to fill the grave with anything to mask the truth.

> Sincerely yours,
> "Historical Consultant for a law firm"
> Cedarburg, Wisconsin

Funny Letters

November 19, 1998

Well, Sports Fans, I hafta tell ya, that was the Lions and Christians and the Christians ate 'em alive, to be polite. That was the moral and physical equivalent of three pro football games, playing both ways, one after another, no timeouts. I'm in pretty fair shape, but that wore me out. And the quarterback/safety was going strong when the final gun sounded and the fans rose and roared in respect and admiration. You can fault the plan but not the execution. Putting one guy in that position for 12 1/2 hours against a steady stream of fresh antagonizers must resemble the Hanoi Hilton more than anything anyone in that chamber knows about.

Out here, in "unwashedCitizenLand," the unenlightened can only ponder the comparison between the velvet glove treatment of the investigated and bare knuckle treatment of the investigator. Humpty Dumpty is alive and well. Pogo is in shock. The Peter Principle has been enshrined.

Here's to Ken Starr, who took the most that could be thrown at him (forget rational behavior, fairness, and equal treatment—you have to be kidding) and shoved it right where it belonged. Here's to Henry Hyde, whose planning and judgment I would quibble with but whose endurance, patience, tolerance, and fortitude are indisputable. And here's to Waters, Frank, Schumer, Lee, Conyers, et al. who tried to play over their heads—they played their roles.

Joe Six-Pack

Unpolled American Person

Las Vegas, Nevada

P.S. I know you only by reputation and tonight's performance, and I'm no lawyer, but that looked pretty good to me. If it could have been done better, I'd like to have someone tell me how. I'm glad you're on the side you're on.

Dear Joe,

I was raised in a Chicago family of "Joe Six-Packs." They struggled through the Depression, fought in Europe and the Pacific, raised their children, and drank cold beer. When my last uncle died last year, his obit described him as "an Irish Catholic, Democrat, White Sox fan." That's not bad after 86 years.

The motto of my family is fight a good fight and never give up your honor and integrity. We will continue gathering evidence and presenting it to the committee. Then it's up to them.

The next time you snuggle up with a six-pack, pop one for me; and say a prayer for your country.

Sincerely,

David P. Schippers

■ ■ ■

February 22, 1999

Greetings! Mr. Schippers, I had never even HEARD of you before this Impeachment Trial, but since I heard your speech and then saw your interview on television, I am certain that you are Cool Incarnate.

Artist

Houston, Texas

Letters from Americans Who Disagreed

The following was a handwritten petition I received:

October 25, 1998

To: Chief GOP Counsel

The President

Should Not Be Impeached

Should Not Be Censored

Nor Made To Resign.

Signed by 13 people

from Chicago, Illinois

P.S. Tripp and Starr should not have been allowed to use the tapes (w/o permission) nor the Internet.

Dear Ms. ——:

Thank you for taking the time to circulate a petition and send it to me. I have taken the liberty of forwarding the petition to Chairman Hyde. I am proud that we are both from Chicago.

Sincerely,

David P. Schippers

■ ■ ■

November 19, 1998

Here is what I'd like to know. Do you protect those on your side who lie, and only prosecute the "other guys"? If not true, are you willing to investigate Ronald Reagan and George Bush for supporting the CIA in running *cocaine* into America in support of funding the contras?

I demand an answer! Are you willing to stand for truth?

Richmond, California

■ ■ ■

December 10, 1998

David Schippers, Henry Hyde, and Ken Starr have proved to me to be the south end of a northbound horse. All with a vendetta to get the President, all because he beat you Republicans two times in a row. So you decided to get him at all costs.

A Private Citizen and Proud of It

Ballinger, Texas

P.S. As I sit here and listen to you talk, the bigger hypocrite you became (David). I am a Christian and am supposed to forgive you this, but I cannot do so. I hope you rot in Hell.

■ ■ ■

Schippers, I have been watching you on TV and listening to your poison, spilled from your mouth. You are worthy of [a] Communist [or] a Nazi. You say, "I have more incriminating evidence which I can't reveal now." You son of a bitch! Are you really an American? Do you and that moon-faced K. Starr consider yourselves professionals?

Of course you are the point man in the campaign to destroy Clinton. Are you also on the Mellar [*sic*] Scaife payroll? Are you backed and encouraged by the Rutherford Institute?

In short, you are a cock-sucking murderer.

Ann Arbor, Michigan

■ ■ ■

December 11, 1998

You are a conniving deceitful distortion artist who is an insult to the legal profession. You are evil, a partisan liar, and a consummate constitutional twister. You should resign, not Clinton.

Are millions of Americans—who have more common sense than any of the asshole Republicans on your committee—wrong about this?

Had the committee most ardently pursued the *facts* they would see that the *evidence* and the *law* and *historical precedent* do not support the sinister, dangerous, and disgusting conduct of you and the committee. Stop the bullshit—get a job in a law firm where you can earn bigger bucks and represent crooks and liars and connivers like yourself.

You are totally an ASSHOLE looking to screw America under the guise of civility and false constitutionality.

Incidentally, this is of course all my opinion. I am sure it is shared by millions of Americans. You people are SCUM!

An Anonymous Citizen
New York, New York

■ ■ ■

December 14, 1998

I would like to ask you not to impeach President Clinton. The bad guy here is Mr. Starr. This is not the first time inopportune sex has happened in the White House or to an elected president. If the others had been investigated as vigorously as President Clinton, we may not have had the great leadership we experienced from: Thomas Jefferson, Franklin Roosevelt, Dwight Eisenhower, John Kennedy, and possibly more I am not aware of.

A 73-year-old Republican
and retired dentist
Flint, Michigan

■ ■ ■

March 31, 1999

I had the displeasure to see you on TV. You have a lot of guts to show your face after what you and your adulterer and hypocrite Henry Hyde thought you could get away with!

The American public thinks both of you are despicable evildoers, and don't think you both will not go down in history [as] malicious assholes—which you both are.

If you are a Democrat then that other traitor Judas was a saint.

Gary, Indiana

Poignant Letters

October 10, 1998

Today, it seems like far too many lawyers have abandoned their professional calling to search for the truth, to hold fast to principled beliefs, and to fearlessly engage in critical reasoning. Your presentation to the Judiciary Committee and the American people this past Monday was a proud testament to your professionalism and the vocation to which you have dedicated your life.

On behalf of the Congress, I thank you for your professionalism and hard work.

Newt Gingrich

■ ■ ■

October 27, 1998

I'm writing to urge you to vigorously and tenaciously pursue the impeachment of President Clinton. It is long overdue, and his continued presence in office will only undermine American moral standards and, more importantly, convey the devastating message that the U.S. justice system doesn't apply to everyone equally, with the President being above the law.

If perjury is allowed to go unpunished, the American judicial system will become a farce. Without serious sanctions against lying under oath, there can be no confidence in the testimony of any witness.

From the start of his administration, he has abused the power of his office and turned the full force of the Executive Branch on dozens of innocent U.S. citizens.

Also, witness tampering in the Lewinsky case was disgraceful. The efforts of him and his associates is something more to be expected of mobsters than of our President.

Needless to say, all of the above is not only criminal, but is far worse, and more destructive of public morale when done by the chief law enforcement officer.

While it is true the President has repeatedly and aggressively broken many laws, his immoral behavior and contempt for American standards of decency may be even more corrosive of our traditional values.

In spite of several national opinion polls, I know that there are more than 100 million people who know that the President must be impeached. Please help restore my confidence in the American justice system. Thank you.

Binghamton, New York

■ ■ ■

November 20, 1998

Sir, I was so glad when you came on to question Mr. Starr. I am 72 years old, and this has saddened me very much. This goes to show me what crooked losers and people in government can do to honest people.

All my life, I have been a poor person, but I have always been honest. I raised four fine young sons and a daughter, and I taught them to be honest and never slander anyone. But I don't see any way out of this mess that Clinton and his crooked clan have gotten the country into. I am sure that as long as you are there, you will see to it that your party will stay behind this tragedy.

I am so ashamed of the Democrat Party, I will never vote for any one of their party. And, I will see to it that no one in my family will either. The Democrat Party doesn't seem to care about anyone else except themselves. I am so upset with them. I have lost all respect for their party.

Thank you for being who you are. Please let us older American citizens see you more. I am a housewife, disabled, and live alone, but I know today that I never have to stay awake at night for being dishonest and treating other people the way the Democrat Party has done.

Thank you sir,

Martinsville, Virginia

P.S. I also have a grandson in Korea in the United States Army. Such a fine grandson, 19 years old.

■ ■ ■

November 21, 1998

I come from a long line of Democrats and am a distant relative of Harry S. Truman. I am 53 years old and a great-great-great granddaughter of a Revolutionary War soldier who is buried in Independence, Missouri. As his relative, I was presented the revolutionary flag from a ceremony given for him by the Sons of the American Revolution at his gravesite. I am a member of the Daughters of the American Revolution.

I give you my background so you will know who I am. I want to say that of all that I watched of the hearing with Kenneth Starr, it was you who made the greatest and lasting impression. You may have been last, but certainly not least. My husband and I sat and listened to your every word. It was as though the truth and gist of this whole mess had finally been made clear.

I hope you know that your presentation was not in vain. I equate what you did as a battle for this country and for what America should be. While those of us who desire justice are not being heard, we are out here.

You did not, and will not, get any recognition from the press, but speaking for the real American People, and I feel that I can, you did shine. Thank you for representing us, Mr. Schippers.

Sincerely,

Independence, Missouri

■ ■ ■

November 22, 1998

I had to fight in Korea in 1952 to defend our Constitution and was wounded. Some of my buddies got killed.

Now, you are on the front lines and you *must* defend our Constitution. The battle is *within* now! Will you fight for truth and right, or will you be a traitor? The consequences are far-reaching and the time is NOW. The majority in this country is asleep in power and greed. Now, we need leadership as never before!

Are you man enough to get wounded or killed and defend our Constitution?

God save this country,
Purple Heart Veteran
Prescott, Arizona

The Wisdom of Youth

Sometimes, it's the children who possess the clearest vision. Unjaded by life, which has not yet double-crossed them, they can see and speak truth with a clarity that only youthful innocence allows.

I have saved for last two letters written by children. To me, they address in simple, human terms the utter debasement and devaluation of decency that is at the core of President Clinton's crimes and his Presidency.

I am a third grader at Chase Elementary School in Chicago. I am writing this letter because I have something to tell you. I have thought of a punishment for the President of the United States of America. The punishment should be that he should write a 100 word essay by hand. I have to write an essay when I lie. It is bad to lie because it just gets you in more trouble. I hate getting in trouble.

It is just like the boy who cried wolf, and the wolf ate the boy. It is important to tell the truth. I like to tell the truth because it gets you in less trouble. If you do not tell the truth, people do not believe you.

It is important to believe the President because he is an important person. If you cannot believe the President who can you believe? If you have no one to believe in then how do you run your life? I do not believe the President tells the truth any more right now. After he writes the essay and tells the truth, I will believe him again.

Third Grader

Chicago, Illinois

P.S. I made my son either write you a letter or an essay as a punishment for lying. Part of his defense of his lying was that the President lied. He is still having difficulty understanding why the President can lie and not be punished.

Father

Chicago, Illinois

■ ■ ■

I am writing to you because my friend Eddie saw you on T.V. and said you were moral and tough. My Dad is a lot like the President because he likes to have ladies sleep over when my mom's away. I don't like that. I was wondering if you could help impeach my Dad? Could you also send me a picture? My friend helped me find your address.

Los Angeles, California

Acknowledgments

While there were many special and hard-working individuals who participated in the formulation and writing of this book, some must be specifically thanked.

Above all, I owe special gratitude to my wife, Jackie, who, during the long months of compiling the manuscript, patiently suffered my often testy disposition, and herself worked long hours to assist me.

Then there is my daughter, Ann Winter. She spent hours—literally days—meticulously searching through boxes of material and closely editing draft after draft of each chapter. I doubt this book would ever have seen the light of day but for the generous and consistent support and encouragement that Jackie and Ann offered.

I must also thank my Washington staff members who contributed so many details and helped to refresh my memory concerning events. Jeff Pavletic, Peter Wacks, Al Tracy, Diana Woznicki, John Kocoras, Nancy Ruggero, Bob Hoover, and Tom Schippers all contributed information and support both during our exile in Washington and while this book was being written. In addition, members of the Judiciary Committee staff, especially Tom Mooney, Jon Dudas, Bob Jones, and Sam Stratman, were always willing to assist in researching specific details.

There were several others, such as Marsha Mitchell and Jennifer Adames, who were involved in typing, compiling materials, editing text, copying, and such. Without them, this work might have taken years instead of months. In addition, Camille Brûlette lent valuable editorial support.

One other individual is worthy of special thanks and honor. Congressman Henry Hyde will always stand out in my mind as the finest gentleman on the American political scene. He entrusted a historic task to an unknown Chicago Democrat; in so doing, he risked his political life. He has been an example and mentor to me. His encouragement and support caused this book to be written.

Index